Blockchain for Teens

With Case Studies and Examples of Blockchain Across Various Industries

Brian Wu
Bridget Wu

Apress®

Blockchain for Teens: With Case Studies and Examples of Blockchain Across Various Industries

Brian Wu
Livingston, NJ, USA

Bridget Wu
Livingston, NJ, USA

ISBN-13 (pbk): 978-1-4842-8807-8
https://doi.org/10.1007/978-1-4842-8808-5

ISBN-13 (electronic): 978-1-4842-8808-5

Managing Director, Apress Media LLC: Welmoed Spahr
Acquisitions Editor: Aditee Mirashi
Development Editor: James Markham
Coordinating Editor: Aditee Mirashi

Cover image designed by eStudioCalamar

Distributed to the book trade worldwide by Springer Science+Business Media New York, 1 New York Plaza, Suite 4600, New York, NY 10004-1562, USA. Phone 1-800-SPRINGER, fax (201) 348-4505, e-mail orders-ny@springer-sbm.com, or visit www.springeronline.com. Apress Media, LLC is a California LLC and the sole member (owner) is Springer Science + Business Media Finance Inc (SSBM Finance Inc). SSBM Finance Inc is a **Delaware** corporation.

For information on translations, please e-mail booktranslations@springernature.com; for reprint, paperback, or audio rights, please e-mail bookpermissions@springernature.com.

Apress titles may be purchased in bulk for academic, corporate, or promotional use. eBook versions and licenses are also available for most titles. For more information, reference our Print and eBook Bulk Sales web page at http://www.apress.com/bulk-sales.

Any source code or other supplementary material referenced by the author in this book is available to readers on GitHub via the book's product page, located at www.apress.com/. For more detailed information, please visit https://github.com/Apress/Blockchain-for-Teens.

Printed on acid-free paper

Table of Contents

About the Authors

Brian Wu holds a master's degree in computer science and is an author and senior blockchain architect. Brian has over 20 years of hands-on experience across various technologies, including blockchain, DeFi, big data, cloud, AI, system, and infrastructure. He has worked on more than 50 projects in his career.

He has written several books, published by O'Reilly and Packt, on popular fields within blockchain, including *Learn Ethereum* (first edition), *Hands-On Smart Contract Development with Hyperledger Fabric V2*, *Hyperledger Cookbook*, *Blockchain Quick Start Guide*, *Security Tokens and Stablecoins Quick Start Guide*, *Blockchain By Example*, and *Seven NoSQL Databases in a Week*.

Bridget Wu is a blockchain, AI, and Metaverse enthusiast. She has had a passion to explore NFTs and the Metaverse beginning in 2020 and is also a programmer and artist who enjoys developing projects in her free time. She has hands-on experience with HTML, CSS, JavaScript, Java, Python, and writing algorithms. Combined with over a decade of practice in drawing, painting, and digital art, her unique background in machine learning and graphic design makes her eager to pioneer the NFT, Metaverse.

About the Technical Reviewer

 **Imran Bashir** has an MSc in information security from Royal Holloway, University of London. He has a background in software development, solution architecture, infrastructure management, information security, and IT service management. His current focus is on the latest technologies, such as blockchain, IoT, and quantum computing. He is a member of the Institute of Electrical and Electronics Engineers (IEEE) and the British Computer Society (BCS). He loves to write. His book on blockchain technology, *Mastering Blockchain*, is a widely accepted standard text on the subject. He is also the author of *Blockchain Consensus*, the first formal book on the subject introducing classical, blockchain, and quantum consensus protocols. He has worked in various senior technical roles for different organizations around the world. Currently, he is living and working in London, UK.

Acknowledgments

We thank everyone who made this book possible, including family and friends who supported us, colleagues who encouraged us, and reviewers and editors who polished our work.

Introduction

Blockchain for Teens is a beginner-friendly guide for young people looking
to build a basic foundation in blockchain technologies. Similar to the
Internet in the 1990s, blockchain now promises to revolutionize the world
by reforming current business models. In this new era, economies will
become decentralized—a concept where every individual contributes
to and benefits from the network. Blockchain's wide appeal comes from
its ability to ensure transparent, secure, and tamper-proof transactions
without the need for a central authority. With clear explanations covering
essential topics, including blockchain, cryptocurrency, cryptography,
Dapps, smart contract, NFTs, decentralized finance (DeFi), and the
Metaverse, *Blockchain for Teens* will help the reader develop various skills
to get them started on their Blockchain journey.

Chapter 1, "Blockchain: A Groundbreaking Technology," will talk
about the basics of blockchain. First, we will discuss how the current
monetary system works and how blockchain technology impacts
money, business, and the modern world. Then we look into how a
blockchain works by going over each step in the transaction process and
the PoW and PoS consensus algorithms that form the backbone of the
blockchain. We continue with the evolution of monetary systems, from
barter to cryptocurrency. At the end of this chapter, we briefly introduce
cryptocurrency and some basic concepts of the crypto market.

Chapter 2, "Cryptography: The Backbone of Blockchain Security," gives
a more thorough understanding of cryptography. This chapter will help
enrich your knowledge of symmetric key cryptography and asymmetric
key cryptography. You will also learn how digital signatures work.

INTRODUCTION

The chapter covers the hash algorithm, and we walk through elliptic curve cryptography to understand how it works. At the end of this chapter, you will learn how to generate an Ethereum address.

The main purpose of Chapter 3, "Bitcoin: The Future of Money," is to present a basic concept of the Bitcoin network. The chapter starts with a discussion on the history of Bitcoin. Then we learn about the Bitcoin wallet and Bitcoin network. Next, we also cover Bitcoin transactions to familiarize you with the key concepts behind the Bitcoin blockchain. Lastly, we briefly introduce Lighting Network.

Ethereum, the second-largest cryptocurrency after Bitcoin, is considered a distributed Turing machine machine–you'll learn more about what this means in the book. In Chapter 4, "Ethereum: A Gateway to Cryptocurrency," you will learn about the history of Ethereum as well as the key components behind Ethereum. The chapter also goes over Ethereum nodes and Ethereum clients while providing examples. By delving into the Ethereum architecture, you will understand how the Ethereum Virtual Machine (EVM) works, how smart contract Opcode is executed within the EVM, and the structure of the block, state, and transactions in EVM.

The best way to understand how the Ethereum smart contract works is to practice writing a smart contract and Dapps. Chapter 5, "Smart Contracts and Dapps: From Theory to Practice," will familiarize you with smart contracts and Dapps through a hands-on learning experience. You will write your first smart contract and deploy it to the public Ethereum network. We also demonstrate the basics of Dapp and web3.js and how Dapp interacts with smart contracts by connecting with the Metamask wallet.

NFTs, or nonfungible tokens, represent the future of collectibles and the expanding digital resource economy. NFTs will change not only art but also business, finance, and culture as mainstream interest in NFTs continues to grow. Chapter 6, "NFT: Crypto As Collectibles," gives you a general introduction to what NFTs are. Along the way, you will learn the applications of NFTs, the difference between fungible and nonfungible items, and the selling points of NFTs. We also provide examples of NFTs and cover the current NFT marketplace. By the end of this chapter, you will create your own NFT in the OpenSea market.

Although the Metaverse is still in its early stages, it is rapidly gaining more attention in recent years. The Metaverse will be a 3D Internet that is based on new technologies including virtual reality (VR), mixed reality (MR), augmented reality (AR), blockchain, artificial intelligence (AI), and the Internet of Things (IoT). Chapter 7, "Metaverse: The World Reimagined," will help you understand the basics of the Metaverse. We will also discuss immersive technology. By exploring the different layers of the Metaverse, we will learn about different products or services in the Metaverse landscape, including NFTs and cryptos. By entering a virtual blockchain world, you will experience the current stage of virtual real estate in the Metaverse. At the end of this chapter, we provide an overview of the future of the Metaverse.

Decentralized finance (DeFi) represents an innovative way to reshape the global financial industry. Chapter 8, "Decentralized Finance (DeFi): Reinventing Financial Services," will introduce you to DeFi's core concepts and structure, as well as provide an in-depth look at specific products in DeFi. We will discuss the most popular decentralized stablecoin and deep dive into the Maker stablecoin to understand how it works. Later, we also explore the most popular DEX—Uniswap. Finally, we provide a complete walkthrough on how to deploy your own ERC-20 token in the public blockchain, create a liquidity pool, add liquidity, swap your custom token, and get a staking reward in the Uniswap platform. In the decentralized lending and borrowing platform, we demonstrate how to lend, withdraw, swap, borrow, and repay crypto assets in the Aave platform. We also discuss decentralized insurance.

INTRODUCTION

At the end of the book, Chapter 9, "The Future of Blockchain," we will review topics from previous chapters in a discussion on the future of blockchain. You will learn about the evolution of the Internet and conclude with an overview of real-life examples of blockchain across various industries.

It is assumed that you have little to no experience in a professional blockchain environment. This book provides a general introduction to critical aspects associated with blockchain. We will not provide too many technical details, such as writing an advanced smart contract and setting up a professional development environment. Instead, we will give you practical information on the most important and latest concepts within blockchain, which will give you a strong basis for entering the world of blockchain.

CHAPTER 1

Blockchain: A Groundbreaking Technology

In recent years, there has been a rising number of Americans who own cryptocurrency. Even among those who don't, most Americans have heard of cryptocurrencies—does "Bitcoin" sound familiar? If you have heard about blockchain, but you are unsure of how it works, then do not worry; you are not alone! Although blockchain may seem like an intimidating topic at first, we are here to help you become familiar with important concepts of blockchain.

This chapter will begin with the basics of blockchain. Then, we will discuss how the blockchain works and gain a solid understanding of consensus algorithms. Next, we will learn about the evolution of the monetary system and how blockchain technology impacts money, business, and the modern world. Finally, at the end of the chapter, we will provide an overview of cryptocurrency.

In this chapter, we cover the following specific topics on blockchain:

- What is blockchain?

- How the blockchain works

© Brian Wu and Bridget Wu 2023

B. Wu and B. Wu, *Blockchain for Teens*, https://doi.org/10.1007/978-1-4842-8808-5_1

- Consensus algorithms

- The evolution of monetary system

- Understanding cryptocurrency

What Is Blockchain?

At the heart of all cryptocurrencies, we can find the revolutionary and decentralized technology known as blockchain. It's important to be clear about what we mean by decentralization, as this concept is frequently used in blockchain. Let's start by looking at the opposite of decentralization: centralization is when authority is held by a specific individual, organization, or location.

Figure 1-1 shows an example of a centralized organization.

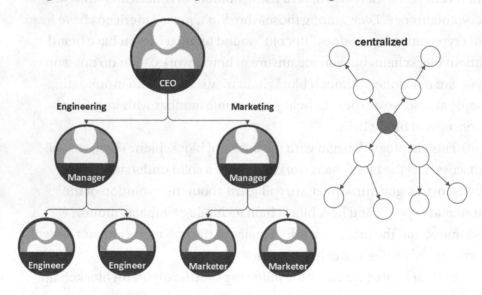

Figure 1-1. *Centralization example*

Think of a typical hierarchy within a company—the executives make all the critical decisions. Then, executives pass decisions down to managers, who are in charge of lower levels. They are expected to perform whatever tasks are assigned to them by the executives. Going one step further, the employees are expected to listen to their managers and complete assigned work. While a centralized company can make achieving objectives relatively quick and easy, employees often do not have visibility and communication with other departments and higher levels. Lack of such communication can cause issues and lead to failures, causing all levels to feel the consequences. Often, a flaw in any part of the company can compromise the goals, which is known as single point of failure.

Another example of centralization is online service providers, such as Meta (Facebook), Amazon, Apple, and Google. These Internet services follow a client-server architecture. The user uses a client machine (known as remote processors—think web browser or mobile) to send remote requests to a centralized server machine (known as a host system). The user receives results for their service request from this single course of complex service providers. On the bright side, billions of people use these superb digital services for everyday tasks, such as online shopping, posting photos, and calling family and friends, all without charge. But there is an overlooked cost to these "free" services: these companies collect and store large amounts of valuable data on user behavior in their centralized servers. With big data analysis and machine learning algorithms, this user data is converted into a product and sold to a third party. With this data, companies can target the users in ads and services, increasing opportunities to be exposed to security risks—this is all out of the user's control.

Now that we have looked at centralization, we can explore decentralization, which refers to the distribution of equal power from a top authority or location to every unit. Unlike the previous examples we looked at, decision making is not concentrated in a central authority or power in a decentralized organization. Rather than collectively relying on one authority, each member is independent and can decide on organizational activity. With decentralization, all members are involved and working with each other to reach a goal. Everyone can vote for decisions based on the organization's rules.

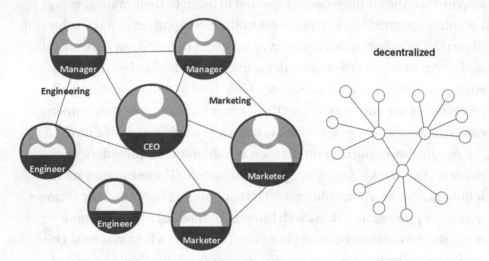

Figure 1-2. *Decentralization example*

In contrast to the centralized online service providers, the decentralized world offers users total control over their transactions and data. Every member has equal power when making their decisions. The system will receive the decisions sent from individual participants and utilizes cryptographic consensus methods (we will take a look at this later) to make a decision. There is no single authority to receive and respond to requests; the system still functions even if some individuals do not participate in decision making.

Table 1-1 provides a comparison of centralization and decentralization.

Table 1-1. *Comparing centralization and decentralization*

	Centralization	Decentralization	
Single point failure	Yes	No	The blockchain network is peer-to-peer, and each node possesses a complete copy of the blockchain data. Therefore, when a failure occurs, data will never be lost.
Who is in control?	Centralized authority	User	There is no centralized authority to control the blockchain network.

Now we understand the difference between centralization and decentralization. Still, what on earth is blockchain?

On an ancient island called Shell Island, people frequently traded with each other to get the resources they needed or wanted. In the beginning, the islanders trusted each other and only traded shells and food; this works well for some time. After a while, the islanders traded more elaborate goods, such as jewelry, clothes, and tools. As the trades became more frequent and complex, it became harder to trace them. For example, someone trades with 20 people every day, but trades different items with each person. To address this, the leaders of the island hired a trusted "middle man" to record all the transactions to keep things fair and auditable; this also works well for some time. However, the "middle man" started charging extra fees for his work and even began to accept bribes. With much unfair trade happening, corruption spread throughout the island, and no one trusts the "middle man" anymore. Business slowed down as a result of fewer trades. To help the people trade fairly again, the leaders of the island dismissed the "middle man" and agreed to replace him with a more efficient solution. In the center of the island is a giant rock, which could clearly be seen by everyone on the island. The leaders propose that the islanders can permanently mark every trade information sequentially on the rock after the traders complete and prove the trade, which makes the system verifiable. This rock is accessible to everyone, so anyone on the island can view and verify these transactions, which means the system is transparent. If any records are mismatched, the islanders can vote to verify the record, which gives everyone equal participating power. The islanders also do not need to trust each other for this system to work; they only need to visit the rock to look at the records instead of relying on the "middle man," which makes the system trustless. The islanders agree to follow these rules that the leaders proposed, and from then on, there was a happy ending for everyone, where fair trade was possible for all.

Similar to the Shell Island trading system, blockchain is a decentralized peer-to-peer network. In the blockchain network, participants can submit and confirm transactions without a need for centralized authority. Once the transaction data is saved in the network, it will be immutable, or unable to be altered. Members or network nodes can directly interact with one another on the network without a central authority or middleman to interfere with the transaction process.

Blockchain is also called distributed ledger technology (DLT). DLT allows all data to be shared across computer networks distributed across multiple entities or locations, referred to as nodes. Each node keeps a copy of the same data of the blockchain ledger.

Blockchain has the following key characteristics:

1. Decentralization

    As we learned, blockchain decentralization means distributing the central power to all participating users in the blockchain network, which eliminates the single point of failure. It generally exists in a peer-to-peer network.

2. Consensus protocol

    Distributed consensus is a crucial component of any
    blockchain network. All network participants must
    reach a common agreement to add a transaction
    record to the blockchain. This will enable a
    blockchain to present a single version of the
    transactions. There are many consensus protocols,
    including:

    - Proof of Work (PoW)

    - Proof of Stake (PoS)

    - Practical Byzantine Fault Tolerance (PBFT)

    - Delegated Proof of Stake (DPoS)

    - Proof of Elapsed Time (PoET)

    - Proof of Authority (PoA)

    - And more...

    We will discuss some of these consensus protocols
    in a later section.

3. Immutability

    Blockchain immutability means that once data has
    been recorded in the blockchain, it is impossible
    to manipulate, alter, or delete data. The blockchain
    data will stay there forever.

4. Transparency

    All blockchain transactions are publicly viewable by
    any party or individual, which creates transparency.

5. Security

    Since blockchain's immutability and
    decentralization features eliminate the single point
    of failure, the records in the blockchain cannot
    be tampered with. This makes blockchain data
    extremely secure. When users transfer funds from
    blockchain wallets, they are cryptographically
    signed by their wallet's private key. We will explain
    this in Chapter 2.

Figure 1-3 shows blockchain key characteristics.

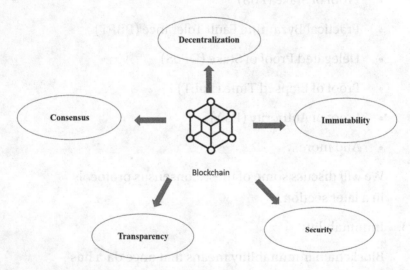

Figure 1-3. *Blockchain key characteristics*

Now that we have a fair understanding of the concept of blockchain,
we're going to take a look at how blockchain works.

How the Blockchain Works

A blockchain is made up of an ordered chain of blocks. When a new block is generated, it connects to the previous block through a hashing mechanism. This way, the most recent data can be always added at the top of the chain.

Imagine there is a daily wall calendar that covers a full year. The calendar initially starts on January 1. After the day is over, the owner of the calendar flips to the next page, which will be January 2. Because the numbers of the days follow a linear sequence, it is easy to tell if any page is missing or modified.

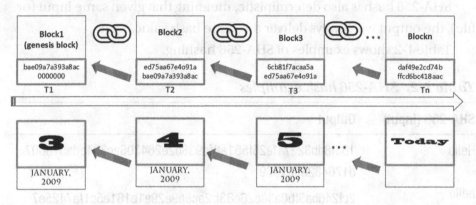

***Figure 1-4.** Block diagram of blockchain*

It is also important to know that a bit is a binary digit (either 0 or 1) and is the smallest unit of data that is stored on a computer. 8 bits make 1 byte.

A hash is a unique identifier that uses a mathematical function to generate a fixed-length character string from the input text or data records. (We will explain the hash and encryption functions in more detail in Chapter 2.) The cryptographic hash function is designed to protect data against any alterations.

9

The blockchain hashing algorithm SHA-256, or Secure Hashing Algorithm 256, generates a hash code of size 256 bits or 32 bytes. SHA-256 is a one-way hash function, meaning that it is easy to compute but impractical to reverse the hash to find what the initial input was. Even the slightest change to the input message typically makes the output hash completely different. To crack hash results, the best way is through a brute-force strategy, which means to test every possible combination one by one. The approach is to guess what was the original value being hashed by applying the same hash function to see if the result matches. We need to process 2^{256} variants of 256-bit string, which results in a total amount of $3.2 * 10^{79}$ possible combinations. The total calculation time would be more than a billion years.

SHA-256 hash is also deterministic, meaning that given same input (or file), the output will always deliver the same hash value.

Table 1-2 shows examples of SHA-256 hashing.

Table 1-2. *SHA-256 hash examples*

SHA-256 (Input)	Output
Hello	185f8db32271fe25f561a6fc938b2e264306ec304eda518007d1764826381969
hello	2cf24dba5fb0a30e26e83b2ac5b9e29e1b161e5c1fa7425e73043362938b9824
blockchain for teens	ae398c6f1d78e76d472c26e091869b9913f7624abea82901c00893a0015ccd50
Blockchain hash	f067428fdeb5984a6eeff5dbbe39a60cdb9dbffecdb80f18830eeb1e91d3dde5

You can see that the length of the input data does not affect output length—the output will always be 64-character text. Because of this, it is nearly impossible to guess the input from the output. Blockchain uses this SHA-256 hash function to hash transaction data and ensure transactions cannot easily be altered. If someone wanted to tamper with a transaction, they would need to rehash it, which would completely change the output. So, when we say a hash, we are referring to the 64-character text output of a hashing algorithm.

The structure of each block is separated into a block header and body, as shown in Figure 1-5.

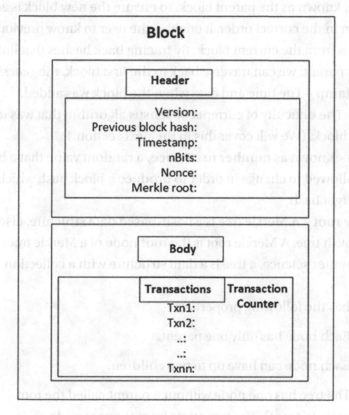

Figure 1-5. *Blockchain block structure*

Block Header

The Block Header is made up of a few components of block version, previous block hash, timestamp, nBits, nonce, and Merkle root:

Block version – The version number of the blockchain.

Previous block hash – The current block must refer to the previous block hash, known as the parent block, to ensure the new block is added to the chain in the correct order. It enables the user to know previous transactions from the current block. By tracing back hashes that link each block to its parent, we can traverse back to the first block, the *genesis block*.

Timestamp – The time and date when the block was added.

nBits – The difficulty of current consensus algorithm that was used to create this block. (We will cover this in the next section.)

Nonce – Known as **number used once**, a random value that a block creator is allowed to change in order to produce a block hash which is less than the target hash.

Merkle root – A Merkle tree is a hash-based data structure, also known as Binary hash tree. A Merkle root is the root node of a Merkle tree.

In computer science, a tree is a data structure with a collection of nodes.

A tree has the following properties:

- Each node has only one parent.

- Each node can have up to two children.

- The tree has one node without a parent called the root node (or root). The tree starts from the root node.

- Nodes are connected via an edge.

- Each node has a data element inside.

Figure 1-6 is an example of binary tree. A, B, C, D, E, F, G, and H are all nodes. A is the root node, and B and C are children of A; they are connected by edge. E and F are children of B. G and H are children of C.

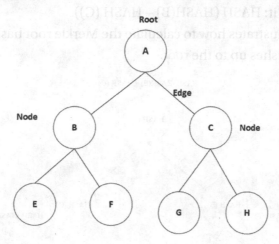

Figure 1-6. *Tree data structure*

Since a Merkle tree is classified as a binary hash tree, it will share the same tree structure. Each leaf node is a hash of a block of data. Each node contains blockchain transactions data, meaning that the children's hash is contained in the parent node.

In our previous tree example, the leaf nodes will be E, F, G, and H since these nodes don't have children. B, C, and A are parent nodes, A is the root node.

If we assume node E has a transaction value, the block data is hashed using hash function HASH (E), which will be similar for other leaf nodes: HASH (E), HASH (F), HASH (G), HASH (H). When we reach the parent node, each pair of child nodes is rehashed recursively (repeatedly, based on a rule) until we reach the root node.

Parent node B is the hash of their child nodes E, F – HASH (HASH (E) + HASH (F)).

Parent node C is the hash of their child nodes G, H – HASH (HASH (G) + HASH (H)).

And root node A is the Merkle root; it contains the hash of the tree nodes following it: HASH (HASH(B) + HASH (C)).

Figure 1-7 illustrates how to calculate the Merkle root hash value from the leaf-node hashes up to the root.

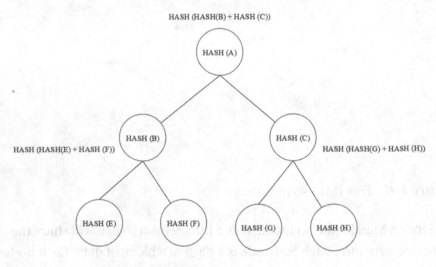

Figure 1-7. *Merkle tree hash calculation*

Why we do need Merkle root hash?

In the earlier example, H (B) = H (E) + H(F).

Assume E is 1, F is 2. We will use the SHA-256 hash function.

SHA-256(1) = 6b86b273ff34fce19d6b804eff5a3f5747ada4eaa22f1d4 9c01e52ddb7875b4b

SHA-256(2) = d4735e3a265e16eee03f59718b9b5d03019c07d8b6c5 1f90da3a666eec13ab35

For simplicity, let's concatenate(combine) both hash values together into a long string (H (1) + H(2)), so we get the following value:

33b675636da5dcc86ec847b38c08fa49ff1cace9749931e0a5d4dfdb dedd808a

But if we modify it by changing the order to concatenating $(H(2) + H(1))$, we get 9704a05c9afffc927899ad21907866ec72b166fd58250b57bca6a184e 462d554

You can see that even the slightest change will lead to completely different results. Considering that each block data needs to include transaction data, time stamps, and many other types of data, changing any of these values will cause the Merkle root hash to be completely different. In the earlier example, we can calculate the Merkle root hash as follows:

Merkle root hash = H (B) + H(C) = H (E) + H(F) + H (G) + H(H).

Root node hash represents the fingerprint for the entire node data. To verify the node data's integrity, you don't need to download the data of the entire block and transverse the entire Merkle tree; you just need to check whether the data is consistent with the Merkle root hash. If a copy of the block in the blockchain networks has the same hash value of Merkle root to another, then the transactions in that block are the same. Through this way, the transaction data can be proved very quickly.

In the blockchain, each block has a Merkle root stored in the block header. The Merkle tree allows every node on the network to verify individual transaction without having to download and validate the entire block. If a copy of the block in the blockchain networks has the same Merkle root as another, then the transactions in that block are the same. Even a bit of incorrect data would lead to vastly different Merkle roots because of the properties of the hash. Therefore, it is not necessary to verify the amount of required information.

All blocks are connected through their previous block hash as a pointer in the blockchain and form a block list. Since the block header contains the Merkle root hash, we can verify whether the block header and transactions data have been tampered with by executing the Hash operation. Any tiny modification of transaction data will cause an entire chain change of all the block hash pointers.

So now the blockchain is linked by a continuous sequence of blocks. It will look like Figure 1-8.

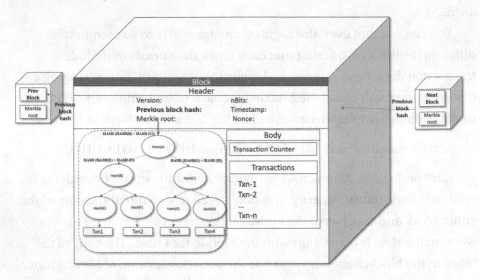

Figure 1-8. *The sequence of blocks with Merkle tree and previous block hash*

Block Body

The block body consists of a transaction counter and transactions.

Transaction Counter

A transaction number represents the number of transactions that is stored in the block. Transaction Counter is 1 to 9 bytes. It is typically used to measure blockchain daily transaction count or "tps"—transactions per second. The following diagram (from https://studio.glassnode.com/) shows daily transaction counts for Bitcoin:

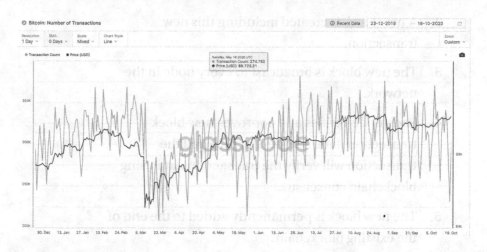

Transactions

A transaction refers to a single logical group of actions that need to be treated as a single action. The transaction request can be executed successfully or fail. The process will ensure data integrity in the system. In a blockchain, a transaction is a fundamental element to build block. Transaction data can include the asset, price, timestamp, and user account address.

Now that we have learned the components in a block structure, let's take a look at how blockchain process a transaction request submitted by a user. Alice wants to send Bob five Bitcoins (BTC) to the blockchain network; in order to join this network, Alice and Bob both need to have an account address. When Alice sends five BTC to Bob, the transaction request will be processed on a blockchain:

1. Alice sends five Bitcoin from her address to Bob's Bitcoin address. A transaction request was created and authenticated (signed by Alice wallet's private key).

2. A new block is created including this new transaction.

3. The new block is broadcast to every node in the network.

4. Each node verifies and approves new block transaction data. A node that received the transaction will verify the transaction data using blockchain consensus.

5. The new block is permanently added to the end of the existing blockchain.

6. All nodes update and include this new block.

7. The transaction is now complete.

Figure 1-9 depicts each step in the transaction process.

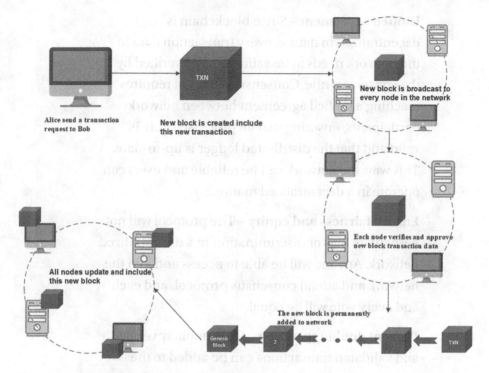

Figure 1-9. *Block transaction process*

Consensus Algorithms

Consensus algorithms form the backbone of blockchain by helping all the nodes in the network reach the necessary agreement on the global state in the chain. The consensus validates transactions or data, then broadcasts it across the network. All the other nodes will receive a copy of the data and add it to the new block by verifying using the same rule.

These are some important properties of the distributed consensus protocol:

>   **Fault tolerance** – Consensus protocol will ensure
>   that the network continues operating smoothly,
>   regardless of any failures.

Unified agreement – Since blockchain is decentralized in nature, every transaction data in the network needs to be validated and verified by the consensus rule. Consensus protocol requires reaching a unified agreement between network participants, ensuring that all processed data is valid and that the distributed ledger is up-to-date. This way, the network can be reliable and users can operate in a decentralized manner.

Ensure fairness and equity – The protocol will not perpetuate bias or discrimination in a decentralized network. Anyone will be able to access and join the network and attend consensus protocol, and each and every vote will be equal.

Prevent double spending – Only publicly verified and validated transactions can be added to the blockchain ledger. All nodes will agree on a single source of truth. This guarantees the different nodes have the same final result in the network.

Each consensus algorithm possesses different features and properties to achieve the desired outcome. With the basics of blockchain consensus properties we just covered, let's dive deeper into popular blockchain consensus algorithms in the current market.

Proof of Work (PoW)

Proof of work, also referred to as PoW, is one of the most common consensus algorithms used by blockchain and cryptocurrencies such as Bitcoin, Ethereum, Bitcoin Cash, ZCash, Litecoin, and others.

The concept was first published by Cynthia Dwork and Moni Naor in 1993. The term "Proof of Work" or POW was used by Markus Jakobsson and Ari Juels in a 1999 paper. The first cryptocurrency, Bitcoin, was created by Satoshi Nakamoto in 2008. It was the first time that proof of work protocols were used as consensus in the blockchain.

Proof of work describes a mechanism where computers in the network, called miners, race each other to be the first to solve complex math puzzles. When miners solve this "puzzle," they are allowed to add a new block to the blockchain and receive rewards.

In "How the Blockchain Works" section, we discussed that all blocks are connected through a previous block hash to form a block list. The miner needs to solve exceptionally difficult math problems to add a new block. To find a solution, miners have to guess a random number (aka nonce) using the brute-force approach till they find the solution. The nonce is a 32-bit (4-byte) field. Each block hash value was generated by SHA-256 (previous block hash), Merkel root, timestamp, nonce and the predefined value of the difficulty target. The difficulty target is shown by the leading zeros before the hash. More leading zeros before the hash value will make the whole process take more time and resources to compute. With computers' power growing, miners can solve these puzzles faster, and so the difficulty target of the blockchain will increase accordingly. Figure 1-10 describes how to calculate a block hash in the proof of work.

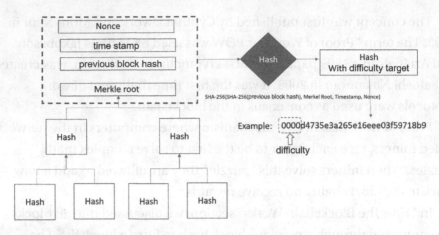

Figure 1-10. *Hash in proof of work*

Here is an example of recent Bitcoin difficulty (there are 19 leading 0s):
00000000000000000000469f80aeb7bac1b440652a9ef729658c1010d2
3962a1cdi

It will take a powerful mining machine around ten minutes to mine
each Bitcoin block. A solo miner will be rewarded around 1 BTC after
successful mining.

As we learned before, SHA-256 hash function is a one-way function,
which means there is no way to revert to the original value. The fastest
solution that we know is brute force. Miners need to try different
nonce numbers to calculate hashes as fast as possible until they find a
matching hash.

Here is the process of proof of work:

1. New transactions are broadcasted to all nodes.

2. Each node collects the transactions into a
    candidate block.

3. Miner verifies the transactions and proposes a
    new block.

4. Miner competes to solve a difficult puzzle to find a solution of proof of work for its block.

5. When a miner finds a solution, the PoW is solved and broadcast across the block to all nodes.

6. Nodes verify that the transactions in the new block are valid and accept adding the new block.

7. Miner gets the reward.

Figure 1-11 visualizes the process of proof of work:

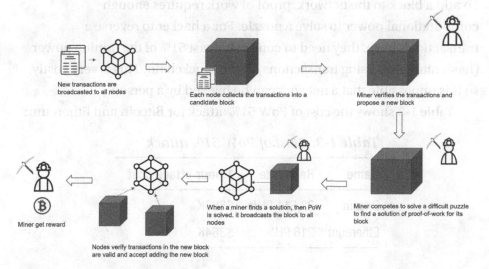

Figure 1-11. *The process of proof of work*

Energy Consumption

In 2008, you could easily mine one Bitcoin using your personal machine. Today, you'd need around 149.2PH/s to mine a Bitcoin. PH is one peta hash:

1 PH/s = 1,000,000,000,000,000 (one quadrillion) hashes per second

The process typically needs a room full of mining machines, which usually cost thousands of dollars, specially designed to improve hash rate ratings and optimize power consumption. A large amount of electricity is required to operate these mining nodes continuously. In 2022, global Bitcoin mining accounted for 0.12% (188 TW/h, Terawatt/hour) of the world's energy production—which exceeds the energy consumption of Norway.

The 51% Problem

To add a block to the network, proof of work requires enough computational power to solve a puzzle. For a hacker to reverse a transaction's hash, they need to control at least 51% of the mining power (hash rate) processing transactions on the blockchain. This is very costly, so it is impossible that a network can be hacked by a person.

Table 1-3 shows the cost of PoW 51% attack for Bitcoin and Ethereum:

Table 1-3. *Cost of PoW 51% attack*

Name	Hash rate	1 hour attack cost
Bitcoin	33,511 PH/s	$583K
Ethereum	216 PH/s	$364K

However, if a group of powerful miners collaborate with each other and control this majority, they then ultimately can control the entire network and decide which transactions can be added to network. This is known as a 51% attack.

Due to these disadvantages, many other new consensus mechanisms have been proposed and implemented over these years. The most popular one of these is proof of stake (PoS).

Proof of Stake (PoS)

Proof of work is a *validation competition* approach where miners verify transactions and get rewards by solving cryptographic puzzles. The process consumes lots of energy on proof-of-work computations. Miners exchange energy for profit. Think of it like "one cpu, one vote."

The proof-of-stake (PoS) mechanism seeks to reduce the scalability and environmental sustainability concerns by substituting staking for computational power. Scalability here refers to blockchain network which is able to handle the increased requests in terms of more users and applications. Staking is similar to the mining function in proof of work. The miner stakes their cryptocurrency as collateral for the chance to validate blocks. These miners become "validators." The PoS algorithm selects validators to validate new transactions and add them to the blockchain, and validators reward some crypto in exchange. The more cryptocurrency miners stake, the better chance there is for the node to be chosen to participate in network validation.

In order to solve the block transaction validation, the calculation only depends on the staked amount of cryptocurrency owned by the node. We may simplify it as "one coin, one vote."

The network will randomly select some validators and ask them to provide the "correct" transactions.

An unverified transaction in the validator node as the input satisfies the following conditions:

$$\text{Hash}(s, c) \leq \text{Ncoin} * \text{Tcoin}$$

Ncoin is current staked coins amount in the nodes

Tcoin is the time accumulation for the coin

Ncoin* Tcoin represents the coin age of the node, and a larger coin age means more chance to satisfy the conditions at the same difficulty level.

PoS was first mentioned back on July 11, 2011, when QuantumMechanic presented the concept on the BitcoinTalk online forum. Sunny King and Scott Nadal published a paper on this for the first time in 2012.

Here is the process of proof of stake:

1. Miner as "validators" lock up set amounts of cryptocurrency or crypto tokens.

2. The network runs protocol formula $f(x)$ to select a validator.

3. Selected miner verifies the transactions and proposes a new block.

4. Miner broadcasts the new block to all nodes.

5. Nodes attest the new block:

    a. If block is valid, the new block is added to network. Miner gets reward.

    b. If block is invalid, nodes vote again the new block. Miner loses staked coins.

Figure 1-12 visualizes the process of proof of stake.

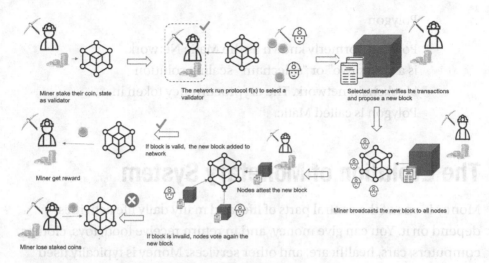

Figure 1-12. *The process of proof of stake*

As one of the most common consensus mechanisms, PoS is adopted by many cryptocurrencies. Here is a list of popular cryptocurrencies that supported proof-of-stake coins.

1. ETH 2.0

    Ethereum 2.0 switched the current PoW-based Ethereum blockchain 1.0 to PoS. In addition, the Beacon Chain bring PoS to Ethereum 2.0.

2. Cardano

    Cardano, created in 2017, runs on the proof-of-stake Ouroboros consensus protocol. The cryptocurrency token in Cardano is called ADA.

3. Avalanche

    Avalanche is one of the fastest smart contracts platform based on PoS.

    Avalanche is a blockchain platform with the native token AVAX.

4. Polygon

    Polygon, formerly known as the Matic Network,
    is a "layer two" or "sidechain" scaling solution
    blockchain network. The cryptocurrency token in
    Polygon is called Matic.

The Evolution of Monetary System

Money is one of the central parts of life, and many daily life activities
depend on it. You can give money, and in return receive food, toys, clothes,
computers, cars, healthcare, and other services. Money is typically used
for purchasing goods and services on markets, but occasionally, people
may directly trade goods for goods without using money. For example, in
August 1984, Saudi Arabia pumped out $1 billion dollars in oil in exchange
for 10 Boeing 747 jumbo jets for their national airline. This kind of trade is
called direct exchange or barter.

A Barter System

A barter system is an ancient method of exchange. The system can be traced
back to 6000 BC, even before the invention of money. The Mesopotamians
introduced the system, and the Phoenicians adopted it. Later on, the
Babylonians also improved their bartering system, by paying Roman
soldiers salt as their salaries, since salt was so precious. Many things can be
used for trade, including food, tea, weapons, spices, and tools.

The barter system supported early economies for millennia, but it can
be inefficient and does not always work well.

- Time

    For example, if a person has wheat and wants to
    exchange it for cloth, then the person not only has to

find someone who owns cloth, but have both sides agree wheat for cloth is a fair trade. If this doesn't work, the person would have to wait or find other people until someone agrees to the terms. These arrangements take time.

- Goods that cannot be divided

  Many goods cannot be divided without losing value. Let's say the price of cloth is equal to five eggs. If a person only has four eggs, the cloth needs to be divided or cut into pieces to complete the transaction. But the cloth will lose some of its value.

- Lack of standard units

  There is a lack of a common unit of measurement in the barter system, so every deal needs to be a bargain. This is very time-consuming and inefficient. For instance, how many eggs are needed to trade for a cloth? How about the size of the eggs? Is the cloth new? All these factors may not be seen equally by both sides.

- Difficulty of deferred payment (payment in future)

  Some goods are time-sensitive. For instance, a fisherman wants to sell fresh seafood for wheat, but the farmer can only provide wheat a few weeks later. As time passes, the value of fish will decrease, so it is not possible to make this exchange in the future.

- Difficulty of transportation of value
  It is risky to transport large amounts of delicate or valuable items and animals to distant markets for exchange.

- Difficulty of storage of large or very costly goods

  In the barter system, some goods require additional purchases to store, like cows, pigs, sheep, etc.

Commodity Money

Salt gradually became a popular form of payment and was accepted by society. Because trust in salt payment developed over the years, an owner could use salt to trade for many other useful goods anytime. The word "salary" comes from the Latin word "salarium," meaning "salt money."

When one type of commodity becomes a popular medium of exchange for trading goods and services, it is trusted and has intrinsic value. The commodity becomes a form of Money called "commodity money." Various items have been used as commodities money over history, such as salt, tobacco, cattle, cowry shells, precious stones, and grain.

The Yap Islands, located in the Caroline group of the central pacific, has a very peculiar giant stone money known as "Rai." The Yapese made a stone in the shape of a disk with holes in the middle to help transport them. The price of stones was determined by their scarcity and the cost of bringing new stones to the island. Sometimes the stone doesn't need to move after the bargain; people just need to transfer the ownership of the stone. It was used as currency for daily trade until the 1960s.

Here are few other examples of commodity money:

Tobacco leaves:

Throughout the seventeenth century, Virginia, Maryland, and North Carolina used tobacco as the official currency for taxes and trade all other transactions.

Cattle:

From around 9,000 to 6,000 BC, the oldest form of money included cows, camels, sheep, and other livestock. Cattle could be transported relatively easily transported in ancient times as a commodity currency.

Although commodity money greatly helped the movement of goods and services in ancient times, people soon encountered difficulties in this money form:

- Goods that cannot be divided:

  Some commodity money is difficult to divide or split into smaller units per one's needs. For example, cattle and cowry shells cannot be divided into smaller pieces for daily purchases.

- Perishability:

  It is challenging to keep the commodity's value in the case of perishable commodities.

  When people use livestock as commodity money, these animals may be got sick, injured, and even die during transportation. Commodity food items lose their value after being stored for a long time.

- Lack of portability:

  Some commodities, like the Yap stones, were difficult to transfer from one location to another

- No universal acceptably:

  The commodities were not standardized across regions. This makes pricing difficult when trading with different commodities.

But like barter, to overcome these difficulties, people shifted to metallic coin as another type of money.

Metallic Coin

The Kingdom of Lydia (now part of modern-day Turkey) minted the first gold and silver coins around 700 BC. The coin weight is close to a US nickel. A soldier's salary was about three coins per month. The Lydia coin was the first time the coinage concept was issued by a central authority. Lydian coins were typically made from gold, silver, or electrum (a mixture form of gold and silver) and engraved with pictures of gods and emperors.

Since the coins had a standard weight and size, they became easier to carry and exchange. In addition, compared to commodity money, metal coins are much more durable. Metal is divisible and fungible if you recollect and melt it to build tools, weapons, and new coins. A coin can have the same value for a very long time and also be difficult to counterfeit.

Metallic money has become the main form of money throughout recorded human money history. Each coin has its own designed value and size. It is easy to use when dealing with a small number of transactions. However, the exchange became problematic once people needed to travel a long distance or carry out large transactions. It is not safe nor convenient to carry a large number of coins.

And because of the scarcity of the metals, the supply of coins was limited. It took a large amount of work to periodically gain more metal to satisfy the fast-growing economy.

In Ancient Greece and the Roman Empire, most of the coins were made from gold, silver, and electrum, but a small amount of coins were made using copper, bronze, and alloys. These small coins were typically used for small transactions where coin value has less intrinsic value than its face value. This initiated the principle of token money.

Mohammad Bin Tughlaq ruled over the northern parts of the Indian subcontinent and the Deccan from 1324 to 1351 AD. During this time, there was a shortage of gold and silver. But Muhammad Bin Tughlaq understood the nature of the token currency well and issued a copper currency named Tanka, the world's first token money. Tanka's value was equal to a silver coin.

For centuries, most countries minted their coins using gold, silver, and other cheaper copper, zinc, and nickel. The coin value gradually became independent of its metal and more represented by its marked value. This evolution led to the invention of paper, marking a crucial stage in the development of money.

Paper Money

The main problem with metallic money was that it was incredibly inconvenient when dealing with large transactions with vendors or need long-distance travel. To overcome this problem, the Chinese began using the first paper banknotes—"flying money"—in exchange for goods and services in 118 BC. People could use banknotes as letters of credit and transfer them over large distances. The success of paper banknotes led to the beginning of paper currency.

The Song dynasty issued the first true paper money in 1023, once Emperor Chen Tsung established the Bureau of Exchange. The bureau printed and issued universal bills, which circulated with merchants.

The paper bill can be used as a receipt for goods, services, or labor, and be redeemed after the service is completed.

Paper banknotes are issued and backed by the government to be legal tender, not from a traditional commodity such as gold or silver. This is the world's first Fiat money (from Latin: fiat, "let it be done").

As the first country to adopt banknotes in Europe, Stockholms Banco, Sweden's first bank, issued the Swedish banknote in 1661. The banknotes worked as bank deposit certificates. Because paper money was easier to create, lighter, and more convenient to carry than metallic coins, banknotes quickly became popular. By the 1600s, governments and banks all over the world had started to issue paper money to their society.

Making metallic coins required the raw material, refining, melting, casting, and many other processes until they could be stamped and distributed. Compared to metallic money, paper money could be printed much faster by the Bureau, and the total supply would not be limited by the amount of metal.

In today's world, paper money is used everywhere in our daily life. It has undeniable benefits; but, like the other types of money, cash has some disadvantages.

One of the disadvantages of using cash is that you need to always carry cash. When you purchase expensive goods, you need to bring a large amount of paper currency from one place to another place.

The second disadvantage is you could lose cash when you lose your wallet—or it is stolen. There is no way to guarantee that the cash can be returned. And you hand cash over after the transaction is done, so if the exchanged goods have an issue, there is no guarantee that the money can be returned.

These drawbacks of paper currency led to bank inventing plastic money like credit cards, which is becoming much more popular in today's payment.

Plastic Money

With the development of the Internet and computer technology, transactions can happen not only offline but also online, and are much quicker and easier. Today, credit card companies like Mastercard, Visa, American Express, and Discover are the most widely accepted payment type worldwide.

John Biggins, a Brooklyn banker who worked for the Flatbush National Bank, invented the first credit card in 1946. The bank card was called the "Charg-It" card.

The Charge-It card was only valid at local merchants within a two-block radius of his bank. The cardholder would have accounts in Flatbush National Bank. Instead of letting the cardholder pay the merchant directly, the bank will pay first after reviewing the bill of the cardholder's purchase. The goal is to bring more loyal customers to the bank. This concept enables a customer to purchase products before payment because it is built on the trust that payment will be made in the future.

In 1950, Diners Club created the first multipurpose charge card, allowing consumers to use it at various merchants.

In 1958, American Express launched its first charge card—the American Express Purple Card, in the United States and Canada. It is the first plastic credit card that we know of today.

In that same year, Bank of America launched its first nationally licensed credit card program and labeled it the BankAmericard. The credit card was sent out by Bank of America through the mail and was "dropped" into the mailboxes, which still occurs in this day.

In 1960, IBM invented a magnetic stripe used on the back of the credit card. The magnetic stripe contains embedded cardholder information, including the cardholder name, card expiration date, and account number.

In 1966, several banks in California decided to join together to form a new association of banks—the Interbank Card Association (ICA) and launch Mastercard.

In 1976, BankAmericard expanded around the globe and eventually became known as VISA.

In 1986, Sears launched its own credit card program for the first time, offering a "cash back" rewards program while selling more than products inside their stores. The credit card was called the Discover Card.

Figure 1-13 shows plastic money history.

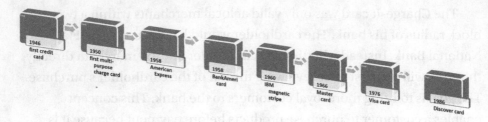

Figure 1-13. *Plastic money history*

Credit cards have slowly but surely changed how we use and think about our "credit" and money.

People deposit cash in their bank account and use the credit card (credit money or bank money) for daily purchases. It performs the same function as paper money. Plastic money largely reduced the need for carrying cash and brought an easier way to involve more and more complex modern payment systems.

Mobile Payments

On August 6, 1991, Berners-Lee launched the world's first website from a lab in the Swiss Alps. Today, more than two decades after its creation. there are nearly 1.9 billion websites that exist. Since then, eCommerce has evolved rapidly over the last few decades.

On August 11, 1994, the world's first online purchase occurred with an order for a pepperoni and mushroom pizza from Pizza Hut. Visa processed the first-ever online payment.

In 1995, Amazon launched its online bookstore as one of the first eCommerce sites.

In 1998, Paypal launched the first money transfer tool, which is considered the first digital wallet, that allowed a customer to make a secure online payment.

In 1999, Ericsson and Telenor Mobil launched the first mobile wallet to purchase movie tickets using a phone.

In 2003, 95 million mobile users worldwide made a purchase via their phone.

In 2007, the iPhone and the android mobile operating systems were released.

In 2022, around 7.26 billion people own smartphones, making up 91.54% of the world's population. 79% of smartphone users have made their mobile payment in the last six months.

Figure 1-14 describes mobile payment history.

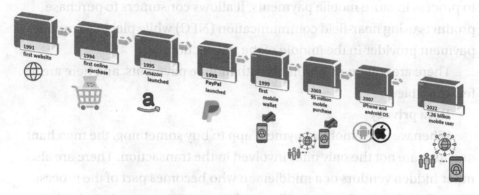

Figure 1-14. *Mobile payment history*

Some notable mobile wallets include Apple Pay, Amazon Pay, Google Pay, Venmo, PayPal, WeChat Pay, Zelle, and Square.

Mobile Payment Types

There are many mobile payment types available in the market, including the following.

NFC, or near-field communication, is the technology that allows mobile devices to securely connect together through a private channel. It typically requires the devices to be within a short distance (4cm or less) of each other to initiate a connection.

Mobile devices connect to merchants who are using NFC via NFC tags. Customers need to activate NFC to start one-on-one interactions.

QR code payments

Quick response codes, or QR codes, are a type of two-dimensional barcode. It encodes information so the product can be purchased on the spot. The information can be read by a digital device, such as a cell phone.

Many mobile wallet supports QR code payments such as PayPal, Zelle, Square, and Venmo.

Cloud-based mobile payments

Google, Amazon, GlobalPay, and GoPago use a cloud-based approach to process in-store mobile payments. It allows consumers to purchase products using near-field communication (NFC) while placing a mobile payment provider in the middle of the transaction.

There are still many problems with mobile payments, and here are a few examples:

Data privacy

When we use a mobile payment app to buy something, the merchant and user are not the only ones involved in the transaction. There are also other hidden vendors or a middleman who becomes part of the process. Each of the involved parties will record the transaction in their database for business. The vendors could use the collected data to study user behavior and target them with ads.

Hidden fee

Most of the mobile payment options are tied to credit and debit cards. Visa's digital wallet charges the same fee as those credit card payments. But PayPal, Venmo, and many other payment vendors charge more than the average big bank fee. Here are examples of common hidden fees: Balance Transfer Fee, Foreign Transaction Fee, Inactivity Fees, Late Fees, etc.

Wallet control

Even if you have your own payment account, you don't have full control. In certain circumstances, the payment issuer could temporarily suspend the user account and limit borrowing ability.

Using mobile payments has lots of advantages, but money continues to evolve. Figure 1-15 illustrates the evolution of monetary system.

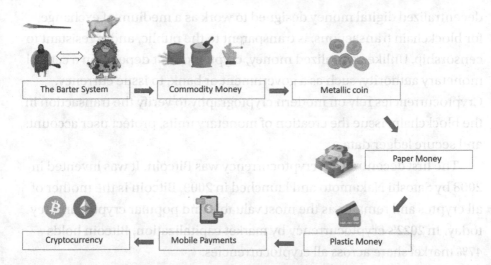

Figure 1-15. *The evolution of monetary system*

In mobile payments, all of the money is electronically stored on electronic systems or digital databases. Therefore, we typically broadly refer to it as Electronic Money, e-money. E-money can be used for electronic payment transactions with or without bank accounts.

Electronic Money has two types of systems: a centralized system and a decentralized system. The main difference between these two systems is decentralized digital money, also referred to as Cryptocurrency, is a native currency in a decentralized system. There is not a centralized authority to issue this currency, and Cryptocurrency is defined and generated by computer protocol in the blockchain network. We will discuss more in the next section.

Understanding Cryptocurrency

In a centralized money system, digital money is backed up by some central bank. People feel their currencies have value because they trust a government to issue this money. A cryptocurrency (or "crypto") is decentralized digital money designed to work as a medium of exchange for blockchain transactions, is transparent to the public, and is resistant to censorship. Unlike centralized money, crypto doesn't depend on a central monetary authority, such as a government or bank, to issue currency. Cryptocurrencies rely on modern cryptography to verify the transaction in the blockchain, issue the creation of monetary units, protect user accounts, and secure ledger data.

The first decentralized cryptocurrency was Bitcoin. It was invented in 2008 by Satoshi Nakamoto and launched in 2009. Bitcoin is the mother of all cryptos and remains as the most valuable and popular cryptocurrency today. In 2022's cryptocurrency by market capitalization, Bitcoin holds 47% market share across all cryptocurrencies.

Cryptocurrency Market

Since Bitcoin was introduced in 2008, cryptocurrencies have revolutionized the entire financial world. The total number of cryptocurrencies has proliferated quickly. To date, there are around 20,000 cryptos, with a total market value of nearly $1.2 trillion. Every 24 h, nearly $68b worth of cryptos are traded. More than 500 cryptocurrency exchanges are around the world.

The daily transaction volume for Bitcoin is around 270K/day at the time of writing, according to blockchain.com.

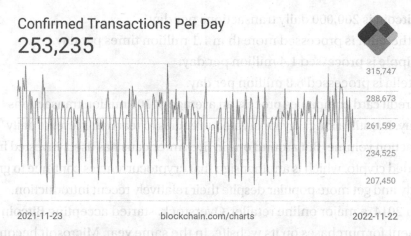

Figure 1-16. *Number of confirmed Bitcoin transactions per day (blockchain.com)*

statista.com shows the number of daily transactions on the blockchain in Bitcoin, Ethereum, and 13 other cryptocurrencies from January 2009 to November 7, 2021, displayed in Figure 1-17.

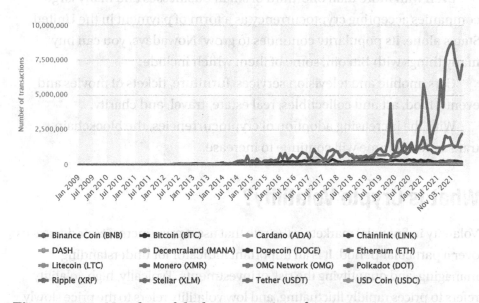

Figure 1-17. *Number of daily transactions for cryptocurrencies (statista.com)*

41

Bitcoin is 260,000 daily transactions per day.

Ethereum is processed more than 1.1 million times per day.

Ripple is processed 1.4 million per day.

Stella is processed 8.8 million per day.

Credit card companies process an average of 100 million transactions per day. It is still a long way for cryptocurrencies to reach this level of daily transaction volume. But around one in five Americans has used, invested in, or traded crypto, which is another sign that cryptocurrencies continue to grow quickly and get more popular despite their relatively recent introduction.

In 2014, a major online retailer, Overstock, started accepting Bitcoin as payment for purchases on its website. In the same year, Microsoft becomes one of the first big tech companies to adopt cryptocurrency as payment for games, apps, and other products.

Major mobile carrier AT&T accept online cryptocurrency payments through BitPay for customers. Tesla accepts Bitcoin and Dogecoin for some merchandise on its website.

Even with more than one-third of small businesses and many large companies accepting cryptocurrency as a form of payment in the United States alone, its popularity continues to grow. Nowadays, you can buy many things with Bitcoin, some of them which include:

Cars, mobile and television services, furniture, tickets of movies and events, food, art and collectibles, real estate, travel, and charity.

With the increasing adoption of cryptocurrencies, the blockchain transaction volume will continue to increase.

What Is Crypto Volatility?

Volatility in financial markets is the rate that asset price increases or decreases over a particular period. It is an important indicator for understanding, managing, and quantifying the risk of investments. Typically, high volatility refers to prices rapidly fluctuating, and low volatility refers to the price slowly changing within a small range, meaning the price is relatively stable.

High volatility often implies higher risks but higher returns. While low volatility usually means less risks and less returns, it is not always the case. An example of low volatility is government bonds, which are fully backed by the credit of the government and are typically considered low risk by the market. Gold is another example, since it has had a stable price for long period of time. Figure 1-18 illustrates high and low volatility.

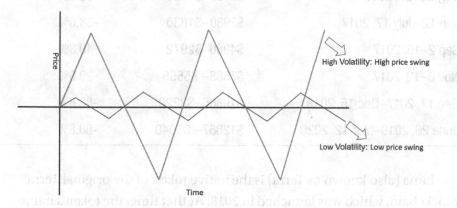

Figure 1-18. *High and low volatility*

Many people have heard of the cryptocurrency market's high volatility. Some crypto prices can lose 90% of its value in a very short time. Let's look at a few examples.

A market correction is generally referred to be a 10% to 20% drop from a recent peak value. Table 1-4 lists the history of Bitcoin correction from Nov 2013 to Mar 2020. For crypto newcomers, a crypto market crash is probably pretty scary. However, this market correction is nothing new to those who know Bitcoin's history. While these drops made people feel quite frustrated about Bitcoin's unstable price, the price started from $0.0008 in 2010 and over time, increased to $25K in June 2022.

Table 1-4. *History of Bitcoin correction*

Date	Price	Decline
Nov 30, 2013–Jan 14, 2016	$1163 - $152	-86.9%
Mar 10–25, 2017	$1350–$891	-34.0%
May 25–27, 2017	$2760–$1850	-33.0%
Jun 12–July 17, 2017	$2980–$1830	-38.6%
Sep 2–15, 2017	$4980–$2972	-40.3%
Nov 8–12, 2017	$7888– $5555	-29.6%
Dec 17, 2017–Dec 15, 2018	$19666–$3220	-83.6%
June 26, 2019–Mar 12, 2020	$12867– $5040	-60.8%

Luna (also known as Terra) is the native token of the original Terra blockchain, which was launched in 2018. At that time, the token's name was LUNA. Luna is a blockchain developed by the Korean firm Terraform Labs in 2018. The blockchain aims to transform modern financial systems.

In 2020, Luna started selling stablecoin called TerraUSD. Luna was a major crypto coin of top-ten market capitalization. But on May 11, 2022, LUNA dropped to 2% of its original price in 24 hours, according to the data from CoinMarketCap. LUNA price fell from $32.71 to $0.08384 in one day.

Figure 1-19. *Volatility in cryptocurrency market—Luna*

StepN is a move-to-earn fitness app, which introduces a new Web3 lifestyle app. Users must buy NFT sneakers to play the game. STEPN uses GST (Green Satoshi Token), which is a Solana blockchain-based token. The user can earn GST by walking or running outdoors through mobile GPS services tracing user movement or by "renting" out their NFT sneakers to other users. Some of the sneakers are worth thousands of dollars in the NFT market. StepN was launched in December 2021 by FindSatoshi Lab. The creative solution enabled STEPN to quickly disrupt the fitness industry and gain lots of attention from the market.

The Crypto market started to list GMT(STEPN) on March 9, 2022. The price at the beginning was $0.01. On April 28, price surged to $4.03—a 40200% increase in just 51 days (data from coinmarketcap). But after the entire crypto market dropped, the price sank to $0.6317 in June 2022. Figure 1-20 shows the volatility of the cryptocurrency market—STEPN. The diagram is from CoinGecko.

Figure 1-20. *Volatility in cryptocurrency market—Stepn (from CoinGecko)*

What Could Cause a High Volatility in the Crypto Market?

There are multiple factors that could contribute to the highly volatile and unstable environment. Let's explore some of these factors.

Emerging Market

Compared to the history of the Internet, cryptocurrency is still in the very early stages—it has only been a decade since crypto was introduced. The crypto market grew exponentially in this period.

The global crypto market cap reached around $1.25 trillion US dollars, while the global stock market cap in 2021 was 121 trillion US dollars. The Crypto market is still relatively small compared to the global stock market, and volatility comes with any emerging market. Even in the early days of Internet stocks, there was also high volatility, like the crypto market today.

Cryptocurrency still needs a long time for large-scale adoption. Unlike stocks, fiat currency, and other traditional finance products, the industry is still researching, understanding, and developing a reliable model to determine the fundamental value of cryptocurrency. This means that there is no reliable product to predict Crypto price in the current market.

New Technology

In the earlier LUNA example, LUNA invented TerraUSD (UST) concept. A stablecoin coin is controlled by Terra algorithms to serve as a fiat coin function, like the US dollar. It aims to peg the US dollar at a *1:1* ratio, but different from other major stablecoins, UST is not fully collateralized backed. LUNA also allows holders voting power over the protocol. The protocol worked as intended until there was a scalability problem. If users return UST when the market is down, LUNA protocol needs to bring UST back to $1 by issuing more UST tokens to the user. This led to the total token supply of LUNA jumping from about 725 million on May 5 to about 7 trillion on May 13. Stablecoin's 1:1 ratio is no longer maintainable. It drops from $1 to$ 0.009.

Decentralization

Crypto, like Bitcoin, is native to the blockchain network. Compared to gold, a physical asset in the real physical world, crypto is more like a "store of value." It is not backed by any physical commodity or central currency and only exists only virtually, so it does not have intrinsic value. The price is determined by supply and demand of the market, but many factors can cause the price to fluctuate.

Sentimental

Market sentiment, also known as investor attention, is the overall feeling of investors in regard to the price prediction of a particular asset. Many things could impact cryptocurrency's investor attention, which can trigger a period of significant volatility. Here is the list of few:

Governance, Regulations, Supply and demand, Security breaches, Competition, etc.

It may feel frustrating that crypto prices are volatile and hard to predict, so it is all the more important to manage risk, diversify your crypto across a range of different crypto assets, do research and technical analysis, invest what you can afford, and be in it for the long term, etc.

Difference Between Coin and Token

There is a common misunderstanding that a token and coin are the same thing.

In the evolution of the monetary system section, we know Metal coins were made of gold or silver to represent their intrinsic value. Mohammad Bin Tughlaq invented token money—Tanka, which used copper currency to represent the same value equal to a silver coin.

In the blockchain, coins and tokens both represent a store of value and can be used for processing payments. But there's some difference: crypto coins are the native asset of a blockchain. It is generated by blockchain consensus protocol. For example, Bitcoin in the Bitcoin network and Ether in the Ethereum network are coins.

Crypto tokens are built on top of the blockchain network, created by a smart contract (a self-executing program run on the network). The number of token creations can be defined by a smart contract when creating tokens.

Table 1-5 shows the difference between coin and token.

Table 1-5. *Comparing coin and token*

Coin	Token
Coin is an independent digital asset and native token to its own blockchain, valid by network consensus. Coin is similar to fiat currency.	Token creation requires a smart contract to define the token-basic properties, then build and operate.
Number of coin is defined by blockchain consensus.	Number of token is defined by Smart contract. Smart contract can define much more custom token attribute such as token name, total supply, some token transfer rule, etc.
The use of coin is mostly to build up the blockchain network by executing consensus protocol. Coins can be distributed through mining or transfer coin ownership	The use of token could be diverse, as their function is defined as Dapps (decentralized application) per business required.
Example: Bitcoin, Ether, Solana, Cardano, Doge, LTC, BnB, Ripple, etc.	Example: Security tokens, utility tokens, equity tokens, ERC-20 token, NFT token, etc.

Summary

In this chapter, we learned about the main features of blockchain and explored decentralization. Then we went over how the blockchain works by going over each step in the transaction process. Consensus algorithms, such as PoW, PoS, form the backbone of the blockchain. We then continued on to the evolution of monetary systems, from the barter system to cryptocurrency. At last, we briefly introduced cryptocurrency and understood some basic concepts of the crypto market.

In the next chapter, we will continue our learning journey and start to learn cryptography—The Backbone of Blockchain Security.

CHAPTER 2

Cryptography: The Backbone of Blockchain Security

Blockchains are built based on a range of different cryptographic concepts. From safeguarding wallets and securing transactions to protecting consensus protocols and encrypting private data for anonymous accounts, almost everything needs cryptography to ensure proper functioning. Cryptography is the backbone of blockchain security.

This chapter will dive into everything you need to know about cryptography in blockchains, starting with the basics. Then, you will be introduced to the classical symmetric key cryptography, asymmetric cryptography, and more. As you advance, you will become well versed in how digital signatures work.

This chapter will also cover how to utilize hash functions to hash data, and at the end of the chapter, you will get an in-depth look at elliptic curve cryptography (ECC), a key type of encryption cryptography that is used in blockchain.

In this chapter, the following topics related to cryptography will be discussed:

- The basics of cryptography
- Symmetric key cryptography

© Brian Wu and Bridget Wu 2023
B. Wu and B. Wu, *Blockchain for Teens*, https://doi.org/10.1007/978-1-4842-8808-5_2

- Asymmetric key cryptography

- Digital signatures

- Hash algorithms

- ECC

- Derived Ethereum addresses

The Basics of Cryptography

In Chapter 1, we have briefly discussed SHA-256 hashing cryptography which is used to hash block data.

Let's use an example to illustrate how secure messages can be sent to the public. Suppose Alice sends a personal message to Bob. Alice wants this message to be private. Only Bob can understand the message, and the message cannot be altered during transmission. The message sent over the Internet could secretly be intercepted and recorded by an intruder (see Figure 2-1). How can Alice and Bob stop this from happening? This is where cryptography comes in.

Figure 2-1. *A message sent through a network*

The word "crypto" comes from the Greek word "kryptós," meaning "hidden or secret."

"Cryptography" means "secret writing" and allows for the exchange of secure messages between willing parties.

The message is converted into a secret code equivalent called "ciphertext" via an encryption algorithm to prevent unauthorized access. The ciphertext is then sent over a public network, it is decrypted at the receiving end, and the recipient can view its contents.

In the preceding example, Alice uses a key to encrypt her message, converting it to ciphertext, and she sends it to Bob over the Internet. She does not need to worry about a hacker having access to her private message. To read ciphertext, a hacker must use a decryption key. When Bob receives this ciphertext message, he can use a key to recover the original plaintext via decryption.

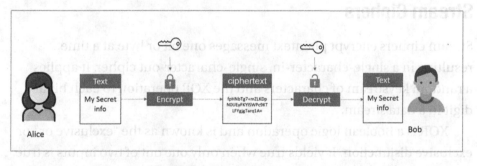

Figure 2-2. *Encrypting and message over the Internet*

Cryptography is mainly divided into three categories: symmetric key cryptography, asymmetric key cryptography, and keyless primitives such as hash function.

Symmetric Key Cryptography

Symmetric key cryptography is a cryptographic algorithm that uses a shared secret key between a sender and a receiver to encrypt and decrypt data. This secret key is called a symmetric key.

In the preceding example, Alice and Bob share the same secret key. Alice uses the secret key to encrypt the message, and the secret key is used in the decryption process when Bob reads the message. This shows how symmetric encryption works.

Symmetric encryption is typically more efficient than asymmetric encryption. Therefore, it is often used with large amounts of data encryption, personal data encryption, and decryption.

While there are several symmetric algorithms, the first US standard was DES.

Symmetric key cryptography can use either stream ciphers or block ciphers to encrypt data. Using stream ciphers is the preferred way to encrypt data in most cases.

Stream Ciphers

Stream ciphers encrypt plaintext messages one bit or byte at a time, resulting in a single-character-in, single-character-out cipher. It applies a random keystream of characters and the XOR operation to each binary digit in a data stream.

XOR is a Boolean logic operation and is known as the "exclusive or" or exclusive disjunction. It yields true when only one out of two inputs is true. If both or no inputs are true, the XOR operation output is false.

The truth table of an XOR logic is shown in Table 2-1 where 0 means FALSE, and 1 means TRUE.

Table 2-1. *Truth table for XOR*

Input		Output
A	B	A XOR B
0	0	0
0	1	1
1	0	1
1	1	0

So, if Bit A is 11000101, and Bit B is 10100110, the following shows what the output looks like when the XOR operation is applied for these two binary bits:

$$10101$$

XOR   00110

Output   10011

Keystream characters can be random combinations of any letters or numbers. Assume that we have a stream of plaintext bytes (p_1, p_2, p_3, ..., p_i), and the keystream generator outputs a stream of bytes (k_1, k_2, k_3, ..., k_i). To encrypt the stream of ciphertext bytes, the operand XOR needs to be applied to each plaintext and key to generate and encrypt the stream of ciphertext bytes (c_1, c_2, ..., c_i). This can be expressed through the following:

$c_1 = p_1$ XOR k_1, ..., $c_i = p_i$ XOR k_i

Figure 2-3 illustrates stream cipher encryption. P1 is 00110101, and K1 is 11100011. With XOR operation, the ciphertext encrypt result is 11010110.

00110101 (plaintext)

XOR   11100011 (key)

Output   11010110 (plaintext)

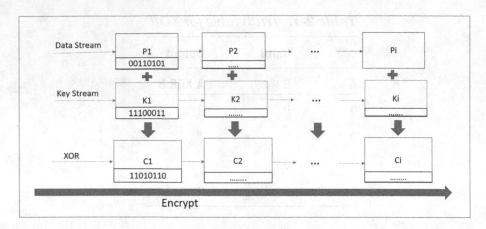

Figure 2-3. *Stream cipher encryption*

To decrypt the plaintext bytes, we apply the XOR operation with the ciphertext and key. The output will get the original plaintext bytes. This operation can be expressed by pi = ci XOR ki:

$$11010110 \text{ (ciphertext)}$$

$$\text{XOR} \quad 11100011 \text{ (key)}$$

$$\text{Output} \quad 00110101 \text{ (plaintext)}$$

Block Ciphers

The main difference between a block cipher and a stream cipher is that a block cipher takes a fixed-size block of plaintext bytes as a single unit and encrypts block data as a ciphertext byte. Generally, the block size is the same as the key size.

Assume we have a block of plaintext bytes **p** and key bytes **k**. To encrypt the block of ciphertext byte **c**, we need to encrypt the plaintext with **key c = encrypt (p, k)** and recover the plaintext by decrypting the ciphertext with **key p = decrypt (c, k).**

Each block is of equal size. Let's say the input is larger than the number of blocks, where the input size is 38 bits, and the block size is

6 bits. After 6 blocks, there will be 2 bits left (38 – 6 * 6 = 2). In this case, we typically add padding (two 0) and append it to the end of the block.

Figure 2-4 shows an example of block cipher encryption. The plaintext is divided by n block (p_n), and each block uses the same key to encrypt a ciphertext. The encryption process will start from the first block and end on the last block, and eventually, all block data will be encrypted.

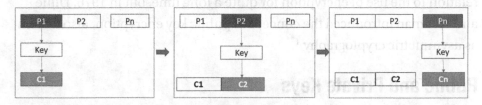

Figure 2-4. *Block cipher encryption*

The most commonly used types of block ciphers include advanced encryption standard (AES), data encryption standard (DES), and triple DES (3DES or TDEA).

Asymmetric Key Cryptography

Symmetric cryptography is relatively simpler and faster than asymmetric cryptography, only needing one key. It is typically used for big data encryption/decryption and confidentiality of bank transactions. Symmetric cryptography must share the same secret key before data encryption. In the previous example, the case becomes complex when Alice needs to send a private message to many people. If Alice uses a symmetric key (K) to encrypt all these messages and shares this key with Bob and others, there is a great risk that someone can secretly give a copy of K to others without Alice's knowledge. In this case, the entire communication channel has been compromised, and many unintended people can read and modify the messages and send them to any other members. To avoid this security risk, Alice must consider creating a large number of keys for each person that the message is sent to, but Alice will then have to remember all the secret keys. Alice needs to call her friends or be involved in face-to-face meetings over a trusted channel to distribute the secret keys. As a result, symmetric cryptography could quickly become less practical for many participants. This problem affected the industry in relation to the use of encryption for quite a long time, but in 1976, Diffie and Hellman introduced the concept of public key encryption, also known as asymmetric cryptography.[1]

Public and Private Keys

Whitfield Diffie and Martin Hellman described how public key encryption works when two communicating parties exchange information across an insecure channel using a key pair consisting of a public key and a private key.

A private key is known only to the owner, and a public key is considered public information that is available to anyone. Each key has been designed for a specific purpose.

The public key is used to encrypt a message and convert it into ciphertext. The private key is used to decrypt a message that has been encrypted with the public key.

How the Diffie-Hellman Algorithm Works

The Diffie-Hellman algorithm is based on a mathematic principle and uses the following formula:

$g^a \pmod p$

Modulo is the remainder of a division operation. For example, 5 mod 3 = 2 because 2 would be left over. Mod can also be expressed as %.

---

[1] Diffie, Whitfield (June 8, 1976), "Multi-user cryptographic techniques," *AFIPS Proceedings 4* **5**: 109–112

With p, g as a prime number, g is a primitive root modulo p. The g and p numbers are public and can be seen and used by anyone.

In math, a g number is a primitive root modulo n if every integer relatively prime to n is congruent to a power of g modulo n.

For example, 2 is a primitive root mod 5, all the numbers relatively prime to 5 are 1, 2, 3, and 4; and each of these (mod 5) is itself, meaning that 2 (mod 5) = 2:

$$2^0 = 1, 1 \ (mod \ 5) = 1, so \ 2^0 \equiv 1$$

$$2^1 = 2, 2 \ (mod \ 5) = 2, so \ 2^1 \equiv 2$$

$$2^3 = 8, 8 \ (mod \ 5) = 3, so \ 2^3 \equiv 3$$

$$2^2 = 4, 4 \ (mod \ 5) = 4, so \ 2^2 \equiv 4$$

Now, we will look at how the Diffie-Hellman algorithm works. Let's use a simple example to understand the algorithms of key exchange. Imagine Alice and Bob want to exchange information. Now, assume a hacker named Eve is trying to intercept the message.

Step 1 – Alice and Bob agree that all messages need to be calculated by the formula g^a (mod p) using a modulus p = 13 and base g = 6. Alice and Bob both select a secret number that is known only to them. However, the formula and numbers g and p are public to everyone.

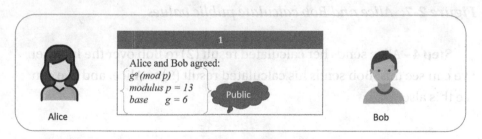

Figure 2-5. *Alice and Bob agree on public value*

Step 2 – Alice chooses a secret random number (a = 5) as her private key, and Bob chooses his private key (b = 4).

Figure 2-6. *Alice's and Bob's secret keys*

Step 3 – Alice and Bob will then use the formula to calculate public values using the p and g parameters and their private values.

Alice will calculate using the following:

6^5 (mod 13) = 7776 mod 13 = 2

Bob will calculate using the following:

6^4 (mod 13) = 1296 mod 13 = 9

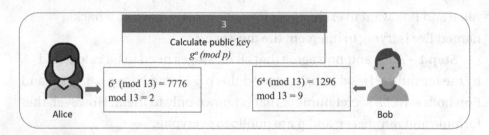

Figure 2-7. *Alice and Bob calculate public values*

Step 4 – Alice sends her calculated result (2) to Bob over the Internet. Eve can see this. Bob sends his calculated result (9) to Alice, and Eve can see this also.

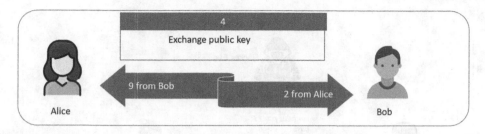

Figure 2-8. *Alice and Bob send their results to each other*

Step 5 – Alice and Bob both received the other side's public message, and they calculated the shared secret through the formula $g^a \pmod p$.

In this step, g is a public message sent from the other side.

Alice will calculate using the following equation:

$9^5 \pmod{13} = 59049 \bmod 13 = 3$

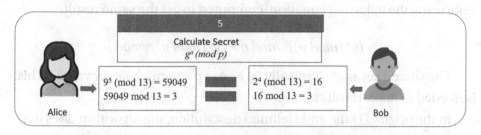

Figure 2-9. *Alice and Bob receiving the same values*

Bob will calculate using the following equation:

$2^4 \pmod{13} = 16 \bmod 13 = 3$

Both Alice and Bob have gotten the same values.

Eve is a hacker. She intercepts the message sent between Alice and Bob. Eve can see the public value ($g^a \pmod p$), g is, she can see what p is, and she knows the computed results from Alice and Bob. However, Eve does not know the secret numbers chosen by Alice and Bob, and she will not be able to find them easily.

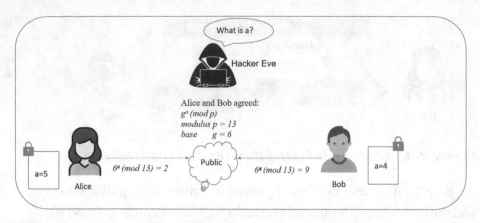

Figure 2-10. *Hacker Eve does not know Alice's and Bob's secret values*

From the Diffie and Hellman example, we can see that both Alice and Bob, using the following equation, computed to get the same result:

$$(g^a \ (mod \ p))^b \ mod \ p = (g^b \ (mod \ p))^a \ mod \ p$$

The shared key is g^{ab}. Typically, a, b, and p are much larger values. This is needed to make results secure.

In the original Diffie and Hellman description, the algorithm does not provide identity verification for communicating parties. This led to the algorithm being vulnerable to man-in-the-middle attacks.

Look at the following example:

Eve intercepts the message between Alice and Bob and blocks communication between them.

Eve intercepts Alice's public value (g^a(mod p)) and sends Alice her own public value (g^c(mod p)).

Eve intercepts Bob's public value (g^b(mod p)) and sends Bob his public value (g^d(mod p)).

Neither Alice nor Bob can detect any problem, and each may assume that the other side received their message, but in reality, Eve can decrypt, read, modify, and re-encrypt all of their messages.

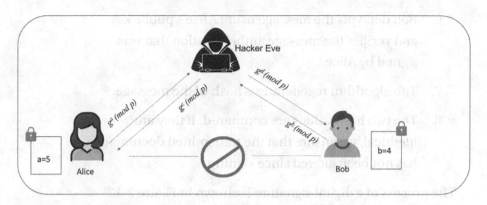

Figure 2-11. *A man-in-the-middle attack*

Diffie and Hellman is the first asymmetric cryptography protocol and provided the basis for many authenticated protocols, such as the elliptic curve Diffie-Hellman asymmetric algorithm and RSA, that are widely used today. Crypto, secure shell (SSH), secure sockets layer (SSL), email, and VPN security are all based on these asymmetric algorithms.

How Digital Signatures Work

If Alice wants to send a signed message to Bob over the Internet, the following steps should be followed:

1. We begin with the message on Alice's (the sender's) side.

2. The algorithm generates a one-way hash of the message based on the document checksum.

3. The hash is signed or encrypted using Alice's private key.

4. The message is sent to Bob.

5. Bob receives the message.

6. Bob decrypts the message using Alice's public key and verifies the message authentication that was signed by Alice.

7. The algorithm regenerates a hash of the message.

8. The two hash values are compared. If they are identical, we ensure that the transmitted document has not been altered since signing.

The process of a digital signature is shown in Figure 2-12.

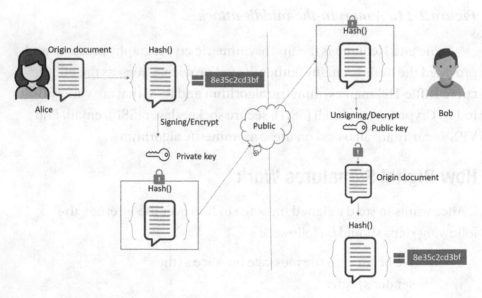

Figure 2-12. *The process of digital signatures*

Digital Signatures

A digital signature is an asymmetric public key cryptography technique that verifies digital messages or document owner authenticity.

We often use the public key for message encryption and the private key for message decryption in public key encryption. However, in the case of a digital signature, the message is encrypted with a sender's private key, or in other words, the message is signed.

As the signer's public key is known, anybody can verify a message's digital signature.

A digital signature includes the following characteristics:

- Authentication (verification of who signed the origin of the document)

- Nonrepudiation (the identity of the signer and document that they have digitally signed should be undeniable)

- Integrity (proof that the document has not been altered since signing)

Hash Algorithms

In Chapter 1, "How Blockchain Works" section, the hash concept was introduced, and the way that blockchain uses the SHA-256 hash function to hash transaction data was discussed. In the previous section, the process of digital signatures was discussed. The process indicated that the process needed to apply a hash function.

Hash algorithm is a mathematical function that divides original data input into smaller blocks of equal size and then executes the hash function to two fixed-size data blocks to generate a hash code. The algorithm starts from the first block of message data with a seed value that passes into the hash function, outputting the first hash code.

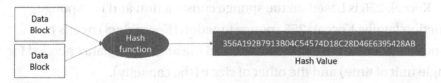

Figure 2-13. *Two fixed-size data blocks used to generate a hash code*

The process is similar to block cipher, discussed in the previous section. The hash process will start from the first block and end at the last block. This process can be repeated for as many rounds as are required by the algorithm. Eventually, all block data will be chained together and hashed.

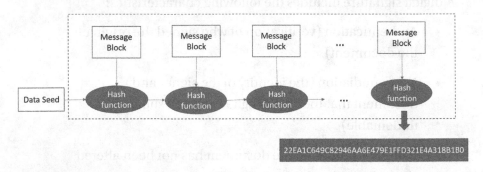

Figure 2-14. *The hash algorithm*

The Keccak-256 Algorithm

The Keccak-256 algorithm is a hash function that is widely used in an Ethereum blockchain. A few examples include Ethereum addresses, some smart contract functions, and the Ethereum consensus engine known as Ethash that plays an important role in producing blocks and other security actions.

The Keccak-256 is a family of SHA-3 hash functions. The function input can be a variable-length string or number, and generated output will always be a fixed-length, 64-character (letters and numbers) output. The output can be converted to hexadecimal numbers. Like all other hash functions, it is a one-way cryptographic hash function.

Keccak-256 is based on the sponge construction and is a sponge function family. Keccak-256 sponge function (Keccak[r,c]) needs two parameters: one of size r (the bitrate and the amount of data encoded for a single unit of time) and the other of size c (the capacity).

Padding

A padding function will append enough bits to the input data (M), and the length of the padded input can be split into multiple r-bit blocks.

Initialization

The padded input is broken into r-bit blocks, assuming the blocks' names are called M0, M1, M2, and so on.

The Absorbing Phase

The r-bit block is XORed with small chunks of the input data M0. The result is then passed to a compression function f. The output of function f XORed next message M1. The process is repeated until each of the message blocks Mn is processed. In each step, a small chunk of the input data (the bit length of r) is "absorbed" into the buffer.

The Squeezing Phase

The same process is repeated. The r-bit block of the buffer consists of the next r bits of output (Z0, Z1, Z2, and so on). The function f is used to extract r bits of data as the next r bits of the output. The process is repeated until the results are produced.

Figure 2-15 illustrates the Keccak-256 hash algorithm.

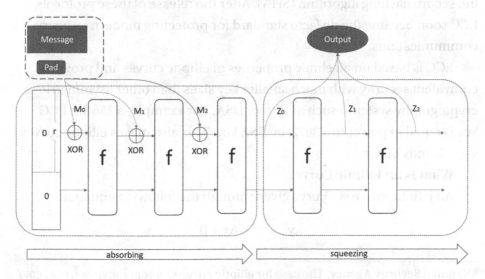

Figure 2-15. *The Keccak-256 hash algorithm*

Elliptic Curve Cryptography (ECC)

ECC was discovered in 1985 by Victor Miller (IBM) and Neil Koblitz (University of Washington) independently and is currently one of the most robust and widely used types of encryption cryptography. Blockchain networks, such as Bitcoin and Ethereum, use ECC.

In 2005, the US National Security Agency (NSA) announced a set of unpublished algorithms known as Suite B protocols and posted a paper titled "The Case for Elliptic Curve Cryptography" in which they recommended that the US government use ECC to secure sensitive and unclassified communications. [2]

The NSA commented that analysts should "take advantage of the past 30 years of public key research and analysis and move from first generation public key algorithms and on to elliptic curves."

Suite B's protocols included both elliptic curve Diffie-Hellman (ECDH) and elliptic curve Menezes-Qu-Vanstone (ECMQV) for key exchange, the elliptic curve digital signature algorithm (ECDSA) for digital signatures, the advanced encryption standard (AES) for symmetric encryption, and the secure hashing algorithm (SHA). After the release of these protocols, ECC soon became the de facto standard for protecting modern industry communications.

ECC is based on algebraic properties of elliptic curves and provides equivalent security with much smaller key sizes than other asymmetric cryptography systems, such as RSA or DSA. For example, a 256-bit ECC key is equal in power to a 3072-bit RSA key. This also makes elliptic curves significantly faster.

What Is an Elliptic Curve?

An elliptic curve is a curve given through the following equation:

$$y^2 = x^3 + Ax + B$$

---

[2] National Security Agency, The case for elliptic curve cryptography, www.nsa.gov/ia/industry/cryptoellipticcurve.cfm

The curve, as required, is nonsingular and needs to have no repeated roots or self-intersections. To ensure that the curve is nonsingular, the condition can be expressed through the following equation:

$$4A^3 + 27B^2 \neq 0$$

An example of the elliptic curve when A = -1 and B = 1 can be seen in Figure 2-16:

$$y^2 = x^3 - x + 1$$

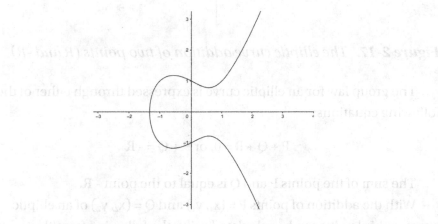

Figure 2-16. *Elliptic curve $y^2 = x^3 - x + 1$*

In an elliptic curve, there is a useful property to create an addition on the curve, turning it into an abelian group. Take two points, P and Q, on the curve, and draw a line through them. The line will intersect the curve at one more point (R). Take P + Q as R, and from R, another line can be drawn either straight up (if R is below the x-axis) or straight down (if R is above the x-axis) to the other side of the curve, opposite to the point -R (see Figure 2-17).

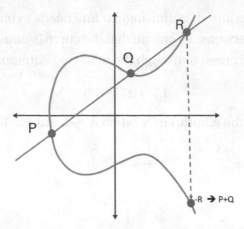

Figure 2-17. *The elliptic curve addition of two points (R and -R)*

The group law for an elliptic curve is expressed through either of the following equations:

$$P + Q + R = 0, \text{ or } P + Q = -R$$

The sum of the points P and Q is equal to the point - R.

With the addition of points $P = (x_1, y_1)$ and $Q = (x_2, y_2)$ of an elliptic curve, a third point can be calculated using the following formulas:

$P + Q = R = (x_3, y_3)$ where

$$x_3 = \lambda - x_1 - x_2$$
$$y_3 = \lambda(x_1 - x_3) - y_1$$
$$\lambda = \begin{cases} \dfrac{(y_2 - y_1)}{(x_2 - x_1)} & \text{If } P \neq Q \\ \dfrac{(3x_1^2 + A)}{2y_1} & \text{If } P = Q \end{cases}$$

Elliptic curve E over Z_p is defined by the following equations, and Z_p is field modulo p, meaning that $\{0, 1, 2, ..., n - 1\}$:

$$y^2 = x^3 + Ax + B \pmod{p}$$

$$A, B \in Z_p, \; 4A^3 + 27B^2 \not\equiv 0 \pmod{p}$$

By applying this formula, the elliptic curve E over Z_p - $E(Z_p)$ has a list of points (x, y). In the following example, elliptic curve $y^2 = x^3 + Ax + B = x^3 + 2x + 3 \rightarrow y^2 \pmod 5$, where A = 2, B = 3, and P = 5. This can be seen through the following:

$X = 0 \rightarrow y^2 = 3 \rightarrow$ no solution (mod 5)

$X = 1 \rightarrow y^2 = 6 \rightarrow 6 \pmod 5 = 1$

$\rightarrow y = 1, 4$ because $1^2 \pmod 5 = 1$, and 4^2
$\pmod 5 = 1$

$X = 2 \rightarrow y^2 = 15 \rightarrow 15 \pmod 5 = 0$

$\rightarrow y = 0$ because $0^2 \pmod 5 = 0$

$X = 3 \rightarrow y^2 = 36 \rightarrow 36 \pmod 5 = 1$

$\rightarrow y = 1, 4$ because $1^2 \pmod 5 = 1$, and 4^2
$\pmod 5 = 1$

$X = 4 \rightarrow y^2 = 75 \rightarrow 75 \pmod 5 = 0$

$\rightarrow y = 0$ because $0^2 \pmod 5 = 0$

Then, the elliptic curve has the following seven points:
(1, 1), (1, 4), (2, 0), (3, 1), (3, 4), (4, 0), ∞.
Now, rearranging the modulus operator P = 263 leaves the following equation:

$$(x^3 + 2x + 3) \pmod{263}$$

Scalar multiplication over the elliptic curve $y^2 = x^3 + 2x + 3$ in mod 263. The curve has 270 points, including the point at infinity.

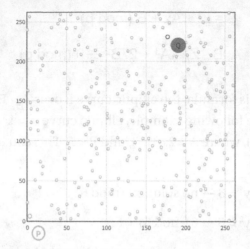

Figure 2-18. *Elliptic curve $y^2 = x^3 + 2x + 3 \pmod{263}$*

In the elliptic curve, when if P is $(x, y) \in E(Z_p)$, then $(x, y) + (x, -y) = \infty$ (the point at infinity).

So, if adding ∞ to any point P in $E(Z_p)$, we can always get P back. This can be expressed through the following equation:

$$P + \infty = \infty + P = P \text{ for all} \in E(Z_p)$$

In Alice's and Bob's message communication, P is a (x,y) point on the curve that both Bob and Alice will agree to. Bob's private key is represented by n, and K is his public key. We multiply P and n together to produce K, as shown as follows:

$$K = n P$$

If we multiply K with P, it will get the point on the elliptic curve.

Deriving an Ethereum Address

We have learned about cryptography so far. Now it is time to do some practice and apply our knowledge to generate an Ethereum address. We will utilize multiple online tools to do this exercise. Of course, you can choose a different tool if you find a better one, or you can even write code to implement the same result:

1. Create a random private key and derive the public key from this private key using EC curve (secp256k1).

    The private key is 64 hexadecimal characters long (32 bytes).

    Here we use an online tool (`https://kjur.github.io/jsrsasign/sample/sample-ecdsa.html`) to get a public and private key pair. The generated public and private key pair can be seen in Figure 2-19.

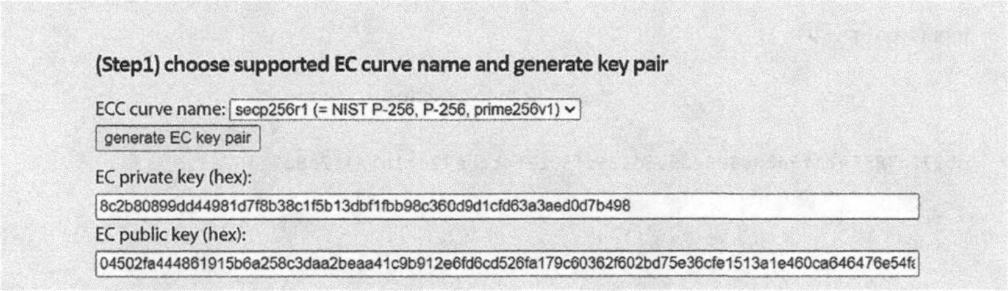

(Step1) choose supported EC curve name and generate key pair

ECC curve name: secp256r1 (= NIST P-256, P-256, prime256v1) ▾
generate EC key pair

EC private key (hex):
8c2b80899dd44981d7f8b38c1f5b13dbf1fbb98c360d9d1cfd63a3aed0d7b498

EC public key (hex):
04502fa444861915b6a258c3daa2beaa41c9b912e6fd6cd526fa179c60362f602bd75e36cfe1513a1e460ca646476e54f

Figure 2-19. *The elliptic curve generating public and private keys*

Private key: 8c2b80899dd44981d7f8b38c1f5b13db f1fbb98c360d9d1cfd63a3aed0d7b498

Public key: 04502fa444861915b6a258c3daa2beaa41c9b9 12e6fd6cd526fa179c60362f602bd75e36cfe15 13a1e460ca646476e54fab08aa42730068326 ab0a8a2e57d2829b

2.   Derive the address from the following public key:

Start with the public key (128 characters) and apply the Keccak-256 hash of the public key. It will generate a string that is 64 characters long (32 bytes). Let's use the Keccak-256 online tool (https:// emn178.github.io/online-tools/keccak_256.html) to see the hash result (see Figure 2-20).

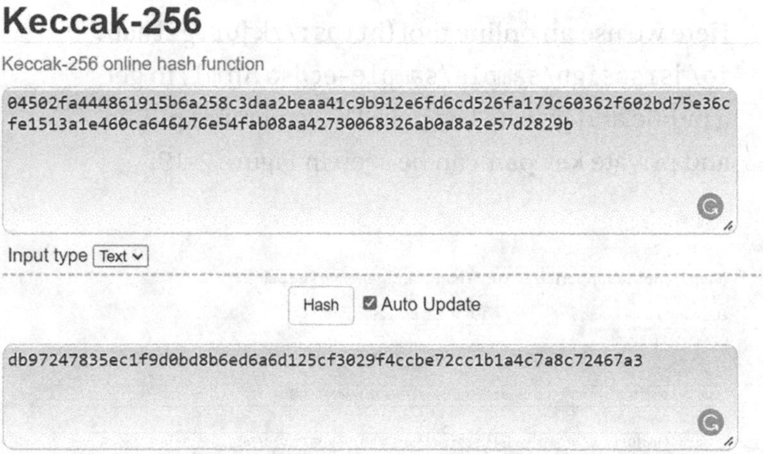

Keccak-256

Keccak-256 online hash function

```
04502fa444861915b6a258c3daa2beaa41c9b912e6fd6cd526fa179c60362f602bd75e36c
fe1513a1e460ca646476e54fab08aa42730068326ab0a8a2e57d2829b
```

Input type [Text ∨]

Hash   ☑ Auto Update

```
db97247835ec1f9d0bd8b6ed6a6d125cf3029f4ccbe72cc1b1a4c7a8c72467a3
```

Figure 2-20. *Keccak-256 hash public key example*

The result is db97247835ec1f9d0bd8b6ed**6a6 d125cf3029f4ccbe72cc1b1a4c7a8c72467a3**

3.   Get the Ethereum address

Take the last 20 bytes (40 characters) of the generated hash to get the Ethereum address with prefix 0x. 0x lets the people know the address in hexadecimal format. When prefixed with 0x, it becomes 42 characters long. So, in our example, the Ethereum address is

0x6a6d125cf3029f4ccbe72cc1b1a4c7a8c72467a3

4. Verify the Ethereum address

   We use one of the online Ethereum address validator tools (`www.rfctools.com/ethereum-address-validator/`) to verify our new Ethereum address.

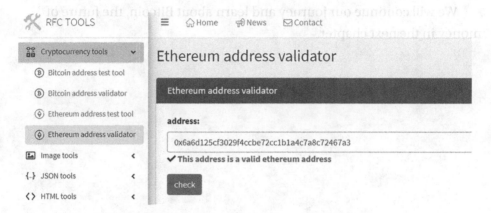

Figure 2-21. *Validating the generated Ethereum address*

Congratulations! We just generated a valid Ethereum address using our cryptography knowledge. At this level, you should get a good sense of how blockchain cryptography works.

Summary

Cryptography is an essential mechanism for securing blockchain technology. It is used to secure the blockchain consensus mechanism, protect blockchain data, keep user accounts safe, and more. The main purpose of this chapter was to give a more thorough understanding of cryptography by giving a quick overview of how it works.

Although it only scratches the surface of cryptography technologies, this chapter will help you to enrich your knowledge of symmetric key cryptography and asymmetric key cryptography. More importantly, we now know how digital signatures work. We covered the hash algorithm, and we walked-through elliptic curve cryptography to understand how it works. Lastly, we learned how to generate an Ethereum address.

We will continue our journey and learn about Bitcoin, the future of money in the next chapter.

CHAPTER 3

Bitcoin: The Future of Money

From the ancient Lydians, who invented coins as a payment type, to the first paper money in China, money and payments have been evolving for centuries. In 2008, an anonymous person or group using Satoshi Nakamoto published a white paper titled, *Bitcoin: A Peer-to-Peer Electronic Cash System*. Since then, Bitcoin (BTC) has ushered in a new era of decentralized digital currencies and blockchain technology. As a result, digital currencies have exploded in popularity in recent years. There are around 20,000 cryptos, with a total market value of nearly $1.2 trillion. As the original and most valuable cryptocurrency, Bitcoin holds about 45% of the whole cryptocurrency market. The second-largest cryptocurrency is Ethereum, which holds a 16% market value. The price of Bitcoin has fluctuated over the years, but it has generally increased in the long term. In November 2021, Bitcoin reached its highest-ever price of $68,789.63.

As a new payment technology invention, Bitcoin is a scarce resource because there are only 21 million Bitcoins that can be mined in the blockchain. This scarcity among other factors like supply and demand gives Bitcoin its value, and Bitcoin will continue to be digital gold in all cryptocurrencies.

The previous chapters were an excellent starting point for introducing blockchain fundamentals, where we covered many basic concepts such as cryptography, PoW consensus algorithms, and how blockchain works.

© Brian Wu and Bridget Wu 2023
B. Wu and B. Wu, *Blockchain for Teens*, https://doi.org/10.1007/978-1-4842-8808-5_3

In this chapter, we'll continue to explore Bitcoin. We will cover the following specific topics:

- Bitcoin history
- Getting to know Bitcoin
- Transactions
- Lighting Network

Bitcoin History

There are more than 106 million Bitcoin owners with 199,000 confirmed, active daily Bitcoin transactions as of July 2022. Around 34 million US adults and 10% of the global population own cryptocurrencies. Cryptocurrency popularity has skyrocketed in recent years. However, if there's one cryptocurrency you should first know about, it's Bitcoin, which most people generally refer to when they talk about digital currency. As the world's first cryptocurrency, Bitcoin is not the first project that has attempted to create a new digital money financial system. Before its creation, many projects tried to build digital money and/or electronic payment systems. Two of those projects, DigiCash and HashCash, mostly inspired Bitcoin.

Early Attempts

David Chaum published a paper called *Blind Signatures for Untraceable Payments* in CRYPTO 1982. Blind signature described how to protect digital cash users' privacy using a new type of digital signature.

To illustrate this blind signature process, David uses an electronic voting system as an example to show that an election voting center should verify all ballots.

The voter's selection privacy message must be protected during the verification process. No one except the voter knows his/her choice. The blind signature process is described as follows:

1. The voter fills a completed anonymous blinded ballot into a carbon paper-lined envelope with the voter's identification preprinted on the outside.

2. Officials verify the documents' credentials.

3. Officials sign the blinded ballot without knowing the message's content.

4. Once the ballot is signed, the envelope is returned to the voter.

5. The voter places the signed ballot into a new, unmarked, plain envelope.

6. This way, the voter's anonymity and privacy can be preserved.

The process flow is presented in Figure 3-1.

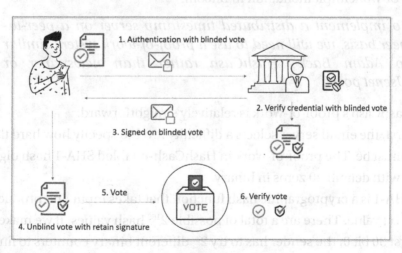

Figure 3-1. Blind signature example

Seven years later, David Chaum launched a company, DigiCash, in Amsterdam. Digital cash, also called DigiCash, eCash, or EMoney, is the first digital, anonymous currency. In 1994, DigiCash proved that small payments could be sent across the Internet. Unfortunately, David Chaum and his company had many problems that led to the company filing for bankruptcy in 1998 and the end of their revolutionary *eCash*.

As the Internet became more popular in the 1990s, many companies quickly recognized it as an excellent advertising tool. Even in later 1997, email spam was already becoming a serious concern to anyone with an email account. Anyone can send tens of millions of emails at almost no cost, and ad companies can use bulk email software to send a large number of emails every day. Email bombs, a denial-of-service attack (DoS) against an email server, started in the late 1990s and often cause network downtime.

Adam Back created HashCash in 1997 and used proof-of-work (PoW) algorithms to prevent email spam and DoS attacks. It has a crucial influence on Bitcoin and is used in Bitcoin for transactions. In the Bitcoin white paper, Satoshi cited the HashCash system as a reference for the proof-of-work implementation in Bitcoin:

> *To implement a distributed timestamp server on a peer-to-peer basis, we will need to use a proof-of-work system similar to Adam Back's HashCash rather than newspaper or Usenet posts.*

HashCash's proof-of-work is relatively straightforward.

First, the email server selects a difficulty level to specify how hard the PoW must be. The proof-of-work in HashCash-enabled SHA-1 hash digest starts with default 20 zeros in binary.

SHA-1 is a cryptographic hash function that takes input and produces a 160-bit value. There are a total of possible 2^{160} hash values. If we make the first 30 bit 0, the sender has to try 2^{30} different binary counters to find a hash with 30 leading zero bits. The more leading zero bit, the more difficult it is to find valid hash doubles, and it will take more time to solve.

A single leading zero in hexadecimal is the same as four 0s in binary. We can use the online SHA-1 tool and a brute force approach to generate a single leading zero with "Hashcash!". We start once from 0. Here is the result by trying different inputs.

Table 3-1. *Generate a single leading zero in hexadecimal*

Hexadecimal Value	Input Text
64a0565c8ef97e847d444c6961086c2ccdad9052	Hashcash!00
6e7072540d426f7bdc3d589dfd73aeac0e3050a9	Hashcash!01
0e4895d7a9ef022e313d72a1c5636e51a2f8dca	Hashcash!02
cf4d1b9d11cef8f1067e6e43b5593439fb412df9	Hashcash!03
e2185e4362440d1a9f41f58f50032097f195aeb1	Hashcash!04
05e82b6afcf3f6a4a81ba01cf9c6e44c2e16e244	Hashcash!05

As we can see, we need to try six times to guess just one single leading zero. Imagining default at 20 and leading 0 at 5 (2^5) require much more work.

To solve this PoW, the sender needs to keep trying different inputs until they figure out the HashCash header with correct leading 0s. The sender can then send an email to a recipient.

When a recipient receives an email, it first checks its valid HashCash header containing the required number of leading zero bits. The recipient only needs to compute the hash once and then save it to the database. When a new email is received, it just needs to compare the database's previous header version. So, it takes much less time to verify a stamp than to find a valid one. If email verification fails, it will move to the spam folder.

The Financial Crisis of 2008

During the late 1990s and early 2000s, the American economy had strong and steady economic growth, a low unemployment rate, and a surging stock market. It was fueled by rapid technological changes and low central bank federal interest rates from 6.5 to 1.75.

The significant decrease in federal interest rates enabled banks and lending institutions to offer consumer credit at a lower price. Many creative lending products like subprime mortgages increased during this time. Banks and lending institutions offer low-interest rate mortgages to many homeowners with poor credit history, few assets, uncertain income, or other factors that negate them from receiving a traditional mortgage.

With these high-risk (subprime) loans flooding in, lenders could then easily obtain the mortgages with all the risk, jeopardizing the entire banking system and global economy. With housing prices continuing to soar, subprime mortgages grew to an overwhelming degree, a large percentage of mortgages moved into default, and many banks and lending institutions began to face financial difficulties. In August 2007, investment banking giant Lehman brothers's stock fell sharply with the failure of two Bear Stearns hedge funds. In March 2008, Bear Stearns was broke, and six months later, Lehman filed for bankruptcy. The crisis led to the Great Recession, where housing prices dropped more than 30%, millions of people lost their jobs, and approximately 2.5 million businesses were closed. American households suffered worse, with an estimated $16 trillion in net worth loss.

The financial crisis shook people's faith and trust in the financial system, where people stored money with a central authority bank system. A central government authority could print more money, so there was no limit to the amount of money that the government could print. This will reduce the value of money already in circulation in the system. A central bank prints money based on the principles of modern monetary theory (MMT). The easy-money policies could sometimes lead to unpredictability and uncertainty regarding the decrease in the value of people's money.

People are starting to think about a new finance system to overcome regular currency shortcomings. The new system can demand a currency without depending on the trust of third parties, such as a central bank authority.

The Birth of Bitcoin

In August 2008, Bitcoin.org was registered by the Bitcoin project's first two developers, Satoshi Nakamoto and Martti Malmi. On October 31, 2008, an entity, under the name Satoshi Nakamoto, posted a white paper on Bitcoin.org titled *Bitcoin: A Peer-to-Peer Electronic Cash System*. Satoshi Nakamoto proposed a solution to prevent double-spending *using* a peer-to-peer network. The system introduced a proof-of-work consensus algorithm that eliminated the need for a centralized bank or government treasury.

In a traditional centralized finance system, it is impossible to physically copy gold or reproduce one ounce of gold into two ounces. That is why gold is a store of value and can be used as commodity money in exchange for goods.

Government-issued paper money is not easily duplicated. For example, one would need special equipment, the right currency paper, and many other materials like security threads and watermarks to replicate a dollar bill. Making paper money a legitimate fiat currency requires a very tedious, secure, and complex process.

When using physical currencies, you hand over the gold or paper money as proof of payment to someone when you buy something. Since the money is given physically, both sides can instantly verify the trade. The money was transferred from your side to the other, and you can't spend the same money twice.

Double-spending is a problem within digital currency transactions, whereby digital money or assets is a set of software codes that can be copied and sent to multiple recipients. A centralized approach typically involves one auditor (such as a bank) who oversees and controls the issuance, distribution, and verification of money. Therefore, it generally requires a lot of work to guarantee no double-spending by a centralized authority, resulting in commission costs on digital currency transactions.

On January 3, 2009, the first-ever Bitcoin genesis block, Block 0, was mined by Satoshi himself, representing the cryptocurrency's birthday. Here is the link for the Bitcoin genesis block detail from blockchain.com www.blockchain.com/btc/block/0.

This block contains a message from Satoshi. Let's have some fun finding out what it is and how you can verify this information for yourself.

By opening the above genesis block link, you will find the Transactions section. Click the hash link; it will navigate to the transaction page. Under the inputs section, you should find Sigscript data with a long hex vault starting from 5468652054696, as shown in Figure 3-2.

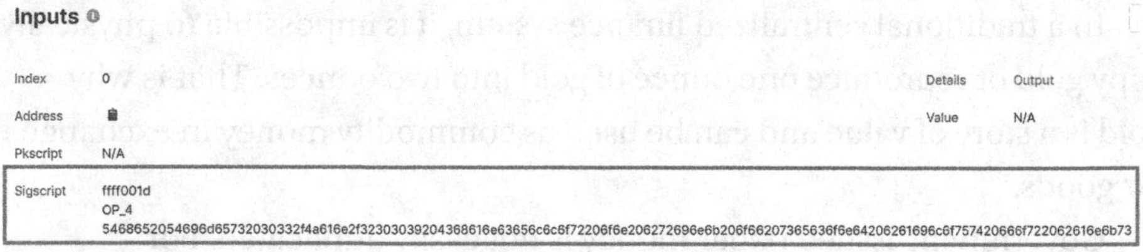

Figure 3-2. *Bitcoin genesis block transaction input from Satoshi*

Copy this encoded hex string. Now, go to the online hex decoder page: https://cryptii.com/pipes/hex-decoder. Decode this message from Satoshi.

If you did it correctly, your screen should look like in Figure 3-3.

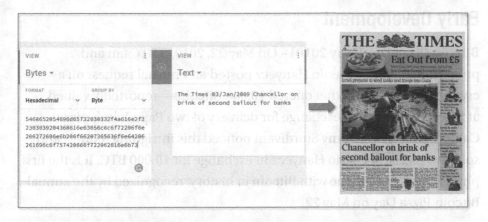

Figure 3-3. *Message from Satoshi for the first transaction*

We have revealed the hidden message from Satoshi Nakamoto. It reads: "The Times 03/Jan/2009 Chancellor on the brink of second bailout for banks." The same text appeared in a comment on line 1616 of Bitcoin's original code:

https://sourceforge.net/p/bitcoin/code/133/tree/trunk/main. cpp#l1613

The message may prove that the block time was mined on the same day by referring to a UK newspaper: *The Times'* story about big government spending. Or, it might indicate that big centralized banks were a problem for Satoshi.

The Genesis Block contained the first 50 Bitcoins ever created, and the reward went to Satoshi's address: 1A1zP1eP5QGefi2DMPTfTL5SLmv7DivfNa.

On January 12, 2009, Satoshi sent ten Bitcoins to Hal Finney as the first official Bitcoin transaction for mining block-70.

Early Development

Bitcoin Pizza Day (May 2010) – On May 22, 2010, a BTC fan and programmer named Laszlo Hanyecz posted an unusual request on a cryptocurrency forum that offered 10,000 Bitcoins—reportedly valued at $40 at that time—in exchange for delivery of two Papa John's pizzas. California student Jeremy Sturdivant noticed this intriguing request and sold two pizzas to Laszlo Hanyecz in exchange for 10,000 BTC. It is the first physical purchase made with Bitcoin in history, recognized by the annual Bitcoin Pizza Day on May 22.

Figure 3-4. *Two Papa John's pizzas worth 10,000 Bitcoins*

First Bitcoin exchange (July 2010) – In July 2010, Mt. Gox launched a Tokyo-based first cryptocurrency exchange, once the world's biggest Bitcoin exchange. Mt. Gox is an acronym for "Magic: The Gathering Online Exchange," sometimes referred to as MtGox or Mt Gox. Mt. Gox accounted for more than 70% of Bitcoin transactions at its peak.

First Bitcoin mining pool (September 2010) – In the earlier days of Bitcoin, mining was straightforward. You could easily generate 50 BTC using your personal computer. When more participants joined the network and some started mining with GPUs, the blocks were generated faster than desired. The Bitcoin network automatically adjusted the difficulty level of mining. To make mining more profitable and efficient, in September 2010, Marek Palatinus—also known as "slush" to many people—launched the world's first Bitcoin mining pool: Slush Pool, formerly known as Bitcoin. cz. On December 16, the pool mined three blocks in its first 24 hours of operation.

First Bitcoin online store (February 2011) – In February 2011, Silk Road launched the first online store to accept Bitcoin as payment. Silk Road is also the first modern darknet market. Darknet markets are dark web black markets that offer illicit goods such as drugs, stolen information, weapons, and services and often use cryptocurrencies as a payment method.

Silk Road was founded by Ross William Ulbricht, who was arrested in 2013 and is currently serving two life sentences in prison for his role in Silk Road. The FBI eventually shut down Silk Road in 2013.

US dollar parity (February 2011) – February 9, 2011 was a historic date that Bitcoin believers had long awaited. BTC reached one US dollar. This was the prediction by Bitcoin forum member "jimbobway" on January 11, 2011. He said, "When one Bitcoin reaches $1, we need to celebrate...I call it 'The Parity Party.' What will you do for your party?"

Litecoin (October 2011) – In October 2011, a former Google engineer named Charlie Lee created Litecoin (LTC), a cryptocurrency forked from the Bitcoin blockchain. Litecoin was initially designed to create fast payments with fewer block times and higher transaction throughput. As opposed to 10 minutes on Bitcoin, Litecoin takes roughly 2.5 minutes per block. Bitcoin uses SHA-256 encryption algorithm, and Litecoin uses Scrypt—a memory-intensive algorithm designed to make it more difficult and costly to perform large-scale hardware attacks by requiring large amounts of memory.

Bitcoin Foundation (September 2012) – In September 2012, Bitcoin Foundation was established. The original members included Gavin Andresen, Charlie Shrem, Mark Karpeles, Peter Vessenes, Roger Ver, and

Patrick Murck. The Foundation's mission is "aim to standardize, protect and promote the use of Bitcoin cryptographic money for the benefit of users worldwide."

First Bitcoin bubble (November 2013) – Just short of four years after Bitcoin's birth, on November 28, 2013, Bitcoin's price soared to the all-time high of $1,217, surpassing $1,000 for the first time. The total market value of Bitcoins in circulation was around $4 billion. This is the first Bitcoin bubble. After that, the price gradually declined, dropping to US$172.15 in January 2015.

Moving Mainstream

Overstock Bitcoin payment (January 2014) – Overstock (NASDAQ: OSTK) launched an international payment system to accept Bitcoin in January 2014 and became the first major online shopping store to accept cryptocurrency.

Mt. Gox hacked (Feb 2014) – At the beginning of 2014, Mt. Gox was the world's biggest Bitcoin exchange, handling over 70% of all Bitcoin transactions worldwide.

On February 7, 2014, Mt. Gox suddenly stopped all Bitcoin withdrawals, claiming it was merely "unusual activity" on its Bitcoin wallets, and they "performed investigations during the past weeks." Then, on February 24, 2014, the exchange suspended all trading and shut down the website.

On February 28, Mt. Gox filed for bankruptcy protection. During the Mt. Gox problems, Bitcoin's value declined by 40%, trigging a two-year bear market for Bitcoin. As the victim of a massive hack, Mt. Gox lost about 744,408 Bitcoins (6% of all Bitcoins in existence at the time) and an additional 100,000 Bitcoins as company liabilities. Although 200,000 Bitcoins were later found, the remaining 650,000 have never been recovered.

Bitcoin taxable (March 2014) – Since Bitcoin started its first public trade in 2009, Bitcoin holders have been nervous about the legalities of Bitcoin payment until the rule was announced by Internal Revenue Service (IRS). With the Bitcoin market's explosive growth in 2013, in March 2014, the IRS issued Notice 2014-21, 2014-16 I.R.B. 938PDF, explaining cryptocurrency holdings to be "property" for tax purposes and not a legitimate, state-backed currency. Therefore, any new Bitcoins mined will be treated as property for federal income tax purposes, in the same way as any other assets you own, like stocks, various real estate, or gold.

Microsoft Bitcoin payment (December 2014) – In December 2014, Microsoft (NASDAQ: MSFT) became one of the first big tech companies to support Bitcoin. It announced its acceptance of the digital currency as a payment option to buy digital content from its stores like Windows, Windows Phone, Xbox Games, and Xbox Music. Microsoft's payment system processes Bitcoin transactions when integrated with BitPay, which is a Bitcoin payment service provider founded in 2011.

NY BitLicense (June 2015) – In June 2015, the New York State Department of Financial Services (DFS) issued its BitLicense regulation. The regulation requires that companies in the state engaged in a wide range of virtual currency transactions—including transmitting, mining, and buying and selling virtual currency—apply to DFS for a BitLicense. In September 2015, Boston-based Circle Internet Financial (a global crypto finance company) was granted the first BitLicense. After that, many firms received the license to run crypto businesses in New York, like PayPal, Coinbase, Ripple Labs, BitPay, Square, Robinhood, and NYDIG.

CFTC labels Bitcoin a commodity (September 2015) – In September 2015, the United States Commodities Futures Trading Commission (CFTC) classified Bitcoin and other virtual currencies as commodities under the U.S. Commodity Exchange Act (the CEA). The CFTC is an independent U.S. federal agency established to regulate the U.S. derivatives markets, including the sale of commodity and financial futures and options. As a result, Bitcoin trading is the same as other commodities, like gold and oil, which must be regulated and supervised by the CFTC in the United States. Therefore, the new rule started restricting unregistered firms that trade cryptocurrency products.

In January 2018, the CFTC filed a complaint against defendants Patrick McDonnell and his company, CabbageTech, Corp., for operating a deceptive and fraudulent virtual currency scheme to induce customers. A New York federal judge assessed and adopted the CFTC's position that virtual currencies are commodities within the meaning of the Commodity Exchange Act. It is the first case testing the CFTC's ability to curb alleged fraud in the cryptocurrency business.

EU classifies Bitcoin as a currency (October 2015) – In October 2015, Europe's top Court of Justice decided Bitcoin was considered a currency, the same as other currencies. As a result, Bitcoins are not exempt from Value Added Tax (VAT). VAT is a consumption tax on all goods and services in the EU.

The Block Size War

In the Bitcoin network, miners use proof-of-work consensus to create a block every ten minutes. A block in Bitcoin is limited to one megabyte. As Bitcoin adoption became widespread, transaction volume dramatically increased, and more transactions needed to be processed in the network within a one-megabyte size limitation. It slowed down transaction processing speeds, and high amount transaction fees could cost a user $58-60 per transaction. However, Satoshi added a maximum block size limit of 1 MB in July 2010 without any comment or explanation (https://sourceforge.net/p/bitcoin/code/103/).

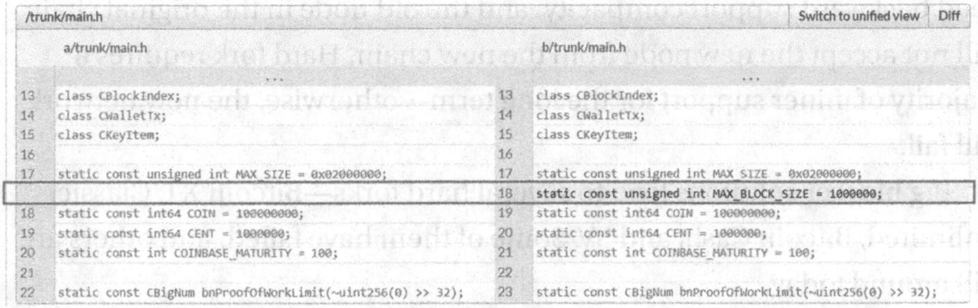

```
/trunk/main.h                                                            Switch to unified view   Diff

        a/trunk/main.h                                b/trunk/main.h
                        ...                                          ...
13   class CBlockIndex;                       13   class CBlockIndex;
14   class CWalletTx;                         14   class CWalletTx;
15   class CKeyItem;                          15   class CKeyItem;
16                                            16
17   static const unsigned int MAX_SIZE = 0x02000000;   17   static const unsigned int MAX_SIZE = 0x02000000;
                                              18   static const unsigned int MAX_BLOCK_SIZE = 1000000;
18   static const int64 COIN = 100000000;     19   static const int64 COIN = 100000000;
19   static const int64 CENT = 1000000;       20   static const int64 CENT = 1000000;
20   static const int COINBASE_MATURITY = 100;   21   static const int COINBASE_MATURITY = 100;
21                                            22
22   static const CBigNum bnProofOfWorkLimit(~uint256(0) >> 32);   23   static const CBigNum bnProofOfWorkLimit(~uint256(0) >> 32);
```

Figure 3-5. *Bitcoin max block size 1 MB*

It opened up a debated topic, "constitutional crisis," in the Bitcoin community over the years, even until today. During 2015 and 2017, a debate about increasing the limit size of Bitcoin's blockchain blocks heavily took place in the Bitcoin community.

To solve scalability issues, the community split into two major solutions:

One side (big blockers solution) was to increase the block size, allowing more transactions to fit into each block and making transactions cheaper. However, a larger block size also requires higher transmission time, and it is just a temporary solution. When users continue to increase in the network, the new block size will become a limitation again. It is not a long-term solution.

Because Bitcoin is decentralized, any proposed consensus changes must receive significant support from the Bitcoin community. When the Bitcoin community does not agree on the proposal, it will result in "forking." Blockchain has two kinds of forks—soft and hard. A soft fork applies newly implemented changes to an existing blockchain, and the modification will support backward compacity. The majority of the participating nodes agree on the changes. The old node will accept the new node after changes. Hard forks make a radical change to the Bitcoin protocol and lead to a chain splitting two ways. The new chain will not

91

need backward support compacity, and the old node in the original chain will not accept the new node from the new chain. Hard fork requires a majority of miner support for the long term—otherwise, the new network will fail.

Big blocker solutions lead to several hard forks—Bitcoin XT, Classic, Unlimited, Bitcoin Cash, and SV. Some of them have failed, and others are still around today.

The other solution (small blockers) is to remain at 1 MB block size and scale via layer-two solutions, giving end users the easy option to run a node. The solution includes SegWit soft fork Lighting Network. We will discuss this in more detail in a later section.

Bitcoin XT (August 2015) – Bitcoin XT was one of the first notable hard forks of Bitcoin Core.

On June 10, 2014, Mike Hearn published a Bitcoin Improvement Proposal (BIP 64) calling for "a small P2P protocol extension that performs UTXO lookups given a set of outpoints."

On June 22, 2015, Gavin Andresen published BIP 101, calling for "an increase in the maximum block size."

The changes would increase the block size from 1 MB to 8 MB and then double every two years until 2036. The block size would eventually be around 8 GB.

In August 2015, Bitcoin XT launched with an eight MB block size. In the first few months, more than 1,000 nodes ran in Bitcoin XT. However, the Bitcoin community hasn't widely supported Bitcoin XT protocol. As a result, block size debates gained media attention and were seen on various social media channels—especially Reddit. It started to bring the scaling debate over the years.

Many community members are worried that a larger block size will lead to Bitcoin's centralization, which, as one critic quotes, is "against the ethics of Satoshi Nakamoto." A few months later, the project lost users' and node operators' interest, essentially fell away, and was abandoned by its users.

The Lightning Network whitepaper (January 2016) – Joseph Poon and Thaddeus Dryja published the Lightning Network white paper on January 16, 2016. The white paper proposed a protocol called "the lightning network" that speeds up transactions by creating a second layer on top of the Bitcoin blockchain that uses user-generated micropayment channels to perform more efficient transactions. These transactions are very fast because no miners are involved, and transaction fees are much lower or even unnecessary without changing the block size. Small blockers support it as one of Bitcoin's scalability solutions.

Bitcoin Classic (January 2016) – In early 2016, a group of Bitcoin community members proposed increasing the maximum size of Bitcoin blocks from 1 MB to 2 MB, which is less aggressive than what was proposed by Bitcoin XT—8 MB. As a result, a group of developers launched Bitcoin Classic. At the beginning of 2016, Bitcoin Classic had hard forks from Bitcoin. It had about 2,000 nodes initially operated on the network, but Bitcoin Classic never reached massive adoption from the community. A year later, there were no more than 100 nodes in the network. Although Bitcoin Classic is still alive today, compared to Bitcoin's price today, $23,028, it is only valued at $0.027632.

The Hong Kong Agreement – SegWit proposal (February 2016) – In February 2016, developer Peter Wuille presented an idea called "segregated witness and its impact on scalability" (SegWitness or SegWit) at Hong Kong's Cyberport Bitcoin conference. Signature data is bulky compared to other transaction input and takes up 65% of the space. Therefore, it quickly filled up the block. SegWit is a mechanism that separates witness signature data from the input field of the block transaction by creating its own individual tree. It allows for the computation of transaction IDs without signatures, and light clients can skip the separated data entry entirely. Signatures will act as "witnesses" when needed to authorize transaction outputs from the original owners. Bitcoin includes a mechanism that validates these signatures using checkpoints. SegWit enables more transactions to be stored within a block.

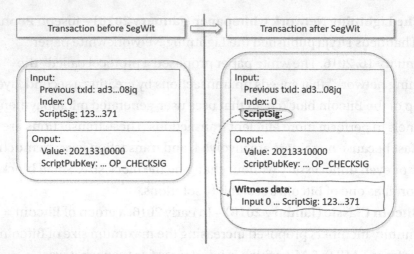

Figure 3-6. *Bitcoin SegWit*

SegWit immediately ignited a new discussion within the community. After the conference, the Bitcoin community agreed to use SegWit as a future soft-fork release and continue working on a safe hard fork based on SegWit improvements, including increasing the nonwitness data to be around 2 MB.

New York Agreement (NYA) (May 2017) – On May 23, 2017, 58 Bitcoin companies across 22 countries representing over 85% of the network computing power held a meeting to decide the future of BTC. The meeting aimed to resolve Bitcoin's scaling issues and the conflict by doing a soft and a hard fork. The NYA published a statement known as the SegWit2x upgrade (essentially the same as the Hong Kong agreement). The aims were:

- Activate Segregated Witness at an 80% threshold, signaling at bit 4

- Activate a 2 MB hard fork within six months

The solution was to compromise between people wanting SegWit and others a hard fork.

SegWit Activated (August 2017) – On August 8, 2017, 100% of the Bitcoin mining pools signaled support for SegWit. Segregated Witness was activated on August 24, 2017. According to buybitcoinworldwide.com data, around 84% Bitcoin nodes have adopted SegWit as of July 2022.

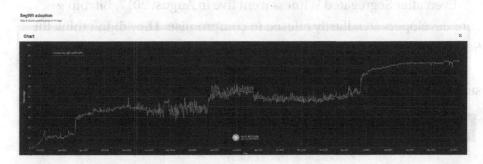

Figure 3-7. Bitcoin SegWit adoption

Bitcoin Cash (August 2017) – However, the NYA does not satisfy everyone. Some large blockers are unhappy with SegWit improvement and feel that this agreement will fail. A group of Bitcoin stakeholders, developers, and miners started to discuss new solutions by increasing the block size limit to 8 MB through a hard fork. In August 2017, Bitcoin Cash (BCH), led by entrepreneur Roger Verand, was launched, forking from Bitcoin. The network can process 24 transactions per second, and the cost is much lower at around 0.18 cents. The block size is 8 MB.

On August 1, 2017, Bitcoin Cash opened trading at about $400, while Bitcoin's value sat at about $7567. On December 19, 2017, it reached a historical high of $3,923, and Bitcoin Cash was $124 compared to Bitcoin's $22,532 on July 23, 2022.

SegWit2x canceled, NYA collapses – After NYA, many of Bitcoin's core developers, who maintain and contribute to Bitcoin's open source code, were furious about the development plans for the NYA because there was no representation from the small blockers and didn't involve them in this agreement. They highlighted that Bitcoin was supposed to be an open system; therefore, the changing consensus behind closed doors by a secret mailing list was a deal breaker, and they considered opposing Bitcoin, stating that the hard fork would deviate from the "real Bitcoin."

Even after Segregated Witness went live in August 2017, Bitcoin's core developers steadfastly refused to compromise. They didn't think the SegWit2x plan would succeed.

On August 18, 2017, Bitcoin Core announced a statement not to support the SegWit2x proposal.

Figure 3-8. *SegWit2x statement from Bitcoin Core* https://bitcoincore.org/en/2017/08/18/btc1-misleading-statements/

On November 8, 2017, BitGo CEO Mike Belshe sent an email signed by major companies originally supporting it. The statement meant a canceled SegWit2x hard fork, and NYA collapsed. At the time of the statement announcement, Bitcoin's price surged by 20% or more to reflect users and investors fleeing.

[Bitcoin-segwit2x] Segwit2x Final Steps

Mike Belshe mike at bitgo.com
Wed Nov 8 16:58:41 UTC 2017

- Previous message: [Bitcoin-segwit2x] Require a new Statement from NYA companies
- Next message: [Bitcoin-segwit2x] Segwit2x Final Steps
- **Messages sorted by:** [date] [thread] [subject] [author]

```
The Segwit2x effort began in May with a simple purpose:  to increase the
blocksize and improve Bitcoin scalability. At the time, the Bitcoin
community was in crisis after nearly 3 years of heavy debate, and consensus
for Segwit seemed like a distant mirage with only 30% support among miners.
Segwit2x found its first success in August, as it broke the deadlock and
quickly led to Segwit's successful activation. Since that time, the team
shifted its efforts to phase two of the project - a 2MB blocksize increase.

Our goal has always been a smooth upgrade for Bitcoin.  Although we
strongly believe in the need for a larger blocksize, there is something we
believe is even more important: keeping the community together.
Unfortunately, it is clear that we have not built sufficient consensus for
a clean blocksize upgrade at this time. Continuing on the current path
could divide the community and be a setback to Bitcoin's growth. This was
never the goal of Segwit2x.

As fees rise on the blockchain, we believe it will eventually become
obvious that on-chain capacity increases are necessary. When that happens,
we hope the community will come together and find a solution, possibly with
a blocksize increase. Until then, we are suspending our plans for the
upcoming 2MB upgrade.

We want to thank everyone that contributed constructively to Segwit2x,
whether you were in favor or against. Your efforts are what makes Bitcoin
great. Bitcoin remains the greatest form of money mankind has ever seen,
and we remain dedicated to protecting and fostering its growth worldwide.


Mike Belshe, Wences Casares, Jihan Wu, Jeff Garzik, Peter Smith and Erik
Voorhees

--

*Mike Belshe*
*CEO, BitGo, Inc*
```

Figure 3-9. *SegWit2x canceled* `https://lists.linuxfoundation.`
`org/pipermail/bitcoin-segwit2x/2017-November/000685.html`

Lightning Network (March 2018) – On March 15, 2018, Lightning
Labs announced the first beta release of the Bitcoin Lightning Network.
Twitter CEO, Jack Dorsey, endorsed the network. Bitcoin's Lightning
Network scaling solution has continued growth with increasing
commercial and user adoption, but it is in its early stages. As of April
2022, the lightning network capacity grew to around 3,600 BTC, with over
300 companies, projects, and apps using the Lightning ecosystem. The
Lightning transaction fee is around one Satoshi or $0.000301142. Event on-
chain fees reached near $60 at peaks in 2021.

Bitcoin SV – Hash War (November 2018) – History tends to repeat itself. In August 2018, Bitcoin Cash proposed an upgrade to the protocol: the introduction of noncash transactions to support smart contracts and oracle price prediction services on the blockchain.

Again, not everyone supported the changes in the source code, with opponents criticizing the prioritization of noncash transactions in a blockchain that they felt ought to deal with payments only. A group within the Bitcoin Cash community, led by Craig Wright and Calvin Ayre, disagreed with these changes in the source code and thought the update would corrupt Satoshi Nakamoto's original Bitcoin white paper's vision. Instead, Bitcoin as digital cash should deal with payments only, and the block size should be increased to 128 MB to deal with scalability issues in the future.

On November 15, 2018, the Bitcoin Cash network split into Bitcoin Cash ABC (BCH ABC) and Bitcoin SV (BCHSV). The split between two competing chains was a contentious one. Both chains battled to win the hash race by becoming the longest chain with more blocks. Bitcoin SV, led by Craig Wright and Calvin Ayre, spent a significant amount of hash effort against Bitcoin Cash, led by Roger Ver and Jihan Wu of Bitmain. The heated hash power contest lasted around ten days and ended as the Bitcoin SV team announced a permanent split from Bitcoin Cash. These periods were called a "hash war." As a cost, Bitcoin Cash miners lost $3.45 million, and Bitcoin SV miners lost $2.49 million.

On November 15, 2018, Bitcoin SV opened trading at about $122, while Bitcoin Cash valued at about $388. On April 15, 2021, it reached a historical high of $441.39, and Bitcoin SV was $58 compared to Bitcoin Cash at $124 on July 23, 2022.

Acceptance As a Mainstream Currency

CME to launch Bitcoin futures (December 2017) – The Chicago Mercantile Exchange (CME) Group Inc. is an American global markets company for trading futures and options. In response to increasing investors' interest in the evolving cryptocurrency markets, CME got clearance from the U.S. Commodity Futures Commission and introduced a Bitcoin futures contract trading on December 18, 2017.

CME Bitcoin futures will allow investors to bet on the future price of Bitcoin without the need to hold the underlying Bitcoin.

A futures contract is a legal agreement in which the buyer and seller agree to buy or sell a commodity or asset at a predetermined future date and price. For example, the Bitcoin price was $22,000 on July 1. If someone thinks the price will go higher, they will buy a Bitcoin future at $23,000 a month later. On August 1, if the Bitcoin market price is $23,500 and if the futures contract expires, the buyer will get the $500 difference.

Futures trading has a long history. The first modern futures exchange began in 1710 in Osaka, Japan, and cotton futures started on the New York Cotton Exchange in about 1870. Professional investors and firms typically trade futures. A Bitcoin future could open the door to bringing more Wall Street firms into the Bitcoin and other cryptocurrency space and help reduce volatility in the underlying Bitcoin market.

New Zealand legalizes crypto-salaries (September 2019) – On September 1, 2019, New Zealand Inland Revenue Department (IRD) officially declared that an employee could be paid a salary using cryptocurrencies such as Bitcoin and Ether. It means a company can directly pay workers in cryptocurrency as long as it is under an employment agreement. As a result, New Zealand became the first country to legalize crypto-salary payment options and brought cryptocurrencies into everyday payment methods.

MicroStrategy Bitcoin purchased (August 2020) – On August 11, 2020, a leading worldwide business intelligence company MicroStrategy Inc (NASDAQ: MSTR) announced that it had purchased 21,454 Bitcoins (worth $250 million at that time). MicroStrategy became the first public listed company to buy Bitcoin as a legitimate investment asset. The MicroStrategy purchase signifies Bitcoin's growing legitimacy and mainstream adoption.

PayPal launched Bitcoin payment service (October 2020) – On October 21, 2020, PayPal received a conditional BitLicense from the New York State Department of Financial Services (DFS). With approval from DFS, on November 12, 2020, PayPal launched a new payment service that allowed PayPal users to buy, hold, and sell cryptocurrency. PayPal has nearly 350 million users and over 26 million active merchants in the system. It almost took a decade to gain 100 million Bitcoin users. The payment giant's adoption meant an additional 300 million more users could start using Bitcoin and other cryptocurrencies as payment methods.

Cryptocurrency users reached more than 100 million (January 2021) – During COVID-19, global cryptocurrency users grew rapidly. According to a report from Crypto.com, more than 100 million people are now using cryptocurrencies worldwide for the first time ever.

Coinbase launch (April 2021) – On April 14, 2021, riding the wave of the overall cryptocurrency market boom as one of the most anticipated events on Wall Street, Coinbase Global Inc. went public on Nasdaq. Coinbase is the largest by volume and the most liquid-regulated cryptocurrency exchange in the United States. As the first major crypto exchange listing on Nasdaq, Coinbase sets a benchmark for other crypto exchanges, and the launch is a watershed moment for the digital asset industry. Coinbase (COIN) opened at around $340 per share and was valued at $86 billion.

El Salvador made Bitcoin legal tender (September 2021) – In June 2021, President Nayib Bukele announced his Bitcoin Law at a Miami Bitcoin 2021 conference.

On September 7, 2021, El Salvador became the first country in the world to accept Bitcoin as legal tender alongside the dollar. The new law required companies to accept Bitcoin as payment. The government also launched a national virtual wallet called "chivo" based on the Lightning Network protocol that allows no-fee transactions and fast payments.

First US Bitcoin exchange-traded fund (ETF) (October 2021) – An exchange-traded fund, or ETF, is exactly as the name implies: an investment fund that can be traded on exchanges. When you invest in an

ETF, you can buy and sell on the stock market, just like company stocks. ETFs generally track a specific index—for example, the "Spider" ETF (The SPDR S&P 500 – SPY) is the most widely known ETF that tracks the S&P 500 Index. ETF is one of the most popular investment options today throughout the world. The first US ETF (SPY) launched in 1993; iShares launched its first bond ETF LQD in 2002; the SPDR Gold Trust ETF is the first gold-backed ETF in the United States. On October 19, 2021, the first US Bitcoin exchange-traded fund (ETF), ProShares Bitcoin Strategy ETF (BITO), started trading. The ProShares Bitcoin Strategy ETF attracted more than $1 billion in assets in its first two days of trading. Compared to the gold ETF, GLD took three days to reach ten digits. BITO became one of the most heavily traded ETFs in market history.

NYSE   Listings   Trading & Data   Insights   About

Note: Quote Data is Delayed At Least 15 Minutes

PROSHARES BITCOIN STRATEGY ETF BITO

QUOTE   OPTIONS

QUOTE

PROSHARES BITCOIN STRATEGY ETF (BITO)

13.98   0.00 (+0.00%)

Figure 3-10. *NYSE-listed BITO*

Bitcoin ETF provides a way for institutional and retail investors to invest in the crypto market on traditional stock market exchanges instead of cryptocurrency trading platforms. As a result, investors who were previously frightened by the technical complexity of trading and other security concerns needn't create new crypto wallet accounts to hold the tokens and can indirectly invest in the Bitcoin market.

Bitcoin's price reached over $68,000 (November 2021) – On November 5, 2021, Bitcoin's price hit a new all-time high at $68,521. The soaring Bitcoin price pushed the cryptocurrency market capitalization to above $3 trillion. This indicates that Bitcoin is becoming a leading innovative payment model and is increasing mainstream adoption.

Taproot – Bitcoin privacy update (November 2021) – After SegWit was activated in August 2017 and SegWit2x was canceled three months later, it has been four years since Bitcoin had a major upgrade. Finally, on November 14, 2021, Taproot—Bitcoin community's most anticipated upgrade since 2017—went live. It is a milestone for Bitcoin, and Taproot received almost universal support from miners, developers, and users.

Taproot is a soft fork upgrade initially proposed by Bitcoin core developer Gregory Maxwell in January 2018. Since then, the proposal has been reviewed, discussed, and tested in numerous rounds in the community.

While SegWit and the Lightning Network's primary objective is improving transaction speed and reducing fees, Taproot aims to address Bitcoin's scalability, privacy, and transparency challenges.

The Taproot update includes three main improvements:

- BIP340 – Upgrading Bitcoin's core cryptography by replacing the legacy Elliptic Curve Digital Signature Algorithm (ECDSA) with Schnorr. Schnorr public keys are 32 bytes, and signatures will be 64 bytes long, compared to ECDSA public keys—33 bytes— and signatures 72 bytes long. The upgrade makes complicated Bitcoin transactions more secure, simpler, and cheaper.

- BIP-341 – Merkleized Alternative Script Trees (MAST), which introduces a Taproot feature, aims to enable the Bitcoin network to execute smart contracts. It brings the potential to support decentralized finance (DeFi) and NFT projects with BTC with Schnorr signatures.

- BIP342 – Introducing a new type of transaction script language called "Tapscript," it allows Bitcoin nodes the combination of the Schnorr signature and MAST in a single transaction. In addition, it also provides Bitcoin smart contracts more flexibility and control by removing the 10,000-byte size limit.

Bitcoin ETF (October 2021–July 2022) – In June 2013, Cameron and Tyler Winklevoss cofounded cryptocurrency exchange Gemini. Best known for their battle with Mark Zuckerberg over the ownership of Facebook, the twins proposed creating a Bitcoin exchange-traded fund with securities regulators. However, in March 2017, S.E.C. rejected the Winklevoss brothers' bid to create Bitcoin ETF.

Nearly eight years later, with long-awaited development for the cryptocurrency industry, investors, and securities issuers, S.E.C. approved the first Bitcoin ETF—BITO. BITO start to trade on the New York Stock Exchange (NYSE). Legitimacy is a crucial concern for Bitcoin trading in the finance industry. Gaining approval from the U.S. Securities and Exchange Commission (S.E.C.) opens the door for Bitcoin's acceptance as a mainstream digital currency. Since the first Bitcoin ETF was approved in October 2021, many other crypto ETFs have been approved by S.E.C. and are available to trade on the stock market. Here is the list of Bitcoin ETFs:

Table 3-2. *SEC-approved Bitcoin ETF*

Symbol	ETF Name	Asset Class
ARKW	ARK Next Generation Internet ETF	Equity
BITO	ProShares Bitcoin Strategy ETF	Currency
SPBC	Simplify US Equity PLUS GBTC	ETF
BITQ	Bitwise Crypto Industry Innovators ETF	Equity
BTF	Valkyrie Bitcoin Strategy ETF	Currency
XBTF	VanEck Bitcoin Strategy ETF	Currency
BITS	Global X Blockchain & Bitcoin Strategy	ETF
RIGZ	Viridi Bitcoin Miners ETF	Equity
SATO	Invesco Alerian Galaxy Crypto Economy ETF	Equity
BLKC	Invesco Alerian Galaxy Blockchain Users and Decentralized Commerce ETF	Equity
BTCR	Volt Crypto Industry Revolution and Tech ETF	Equity
CRYP	AdvisorShares Managed Bitcoin Strategy ETF	Multi-Asset

Getting to Know Bitcoin

In a centralized economy, the currency issued by a central bank is supposed to match the economy's growth and the number of goods exchanged at stable prices. A central bank controls the money supply, and there is no fixed formula to determine how much money a central bank should print. However, the money system may sometimes lose control.

Bitcoin's inventor, Satoshi Nakamoto, designed Bitcoin to resist inflation, limit its supply, and cap the number of coins at 21 million. As a result, the new number of Bitcoins is reduced by half every four years, and the last coins will be minted around 2140.

Limited supply makes Bitcoin a scarce asset, which can boost the coin's future price—one of the reasons Bitcoin is often referred to as "digital gold."

Bitcoin Unit

Today, one Bitcoin is around $25,000, and the total market cap is 455B. Like major centralized world currencies such as the US dollar and the Euro can be broken down into smaller units such as cents, Bitcoins can also be broken down into Satoshi. Satoshi is the smallest unit of a Bitcoin.

One Bitcoin equals 100 million Satoshi, divisible to the eighth decimal place.

Table 3-3 shows the Satoshi unit conversion in the Bitcoin system:

Table 3-3. *Bitcoin denominations and unit name*

Unit name	BTC
Satoshi	0,00000001 BTC
µBTC (Micro Bitcoin)	0,00001 BTC
MBTC (Milli Bitcoin)	0,001 BTC
cBTC (Centi Bitcoin)	0,01 BTC
dBTC (Bitcoin said)	0,1 BTC
BTC (Bitcoin)	1 BTC

Consider the payment of 1 BTC for $23,798.46. One MBTC is $ 0.001 23.8, and 1 µBTC is $ 0.24.

Bitcoin Halving

Bitcoin halving, also known as "the halvening," is a pivotal event in Bitcoin's history. Every four years, new Bitcoins are released into circulation, and the number of Bitcoin mining rewards is cut in half. The maximum total supply of Bitcoins is 21 million.

Here is a brief Bitcoin halving process in the past and future:

> 2009 – Bitcoin network rewarded miners, starting at 50 BTC per block every ten minutes.

> 2012 – After 210,000 blocks were mined, the first Bitcoin halving, the reward went down to 25 BTC.

> 2016 – After 420,000 blocks were mined, the second Bitcoin halving, the mining reward went down to 12.5 BTC.

> 2020 – After 630,000 blocks were mined, the third Bitcoin halving, the mining rewards dropped to 6.25 BTC.

> 2024 – The next Bitcoin halving will happen when 840,000 blocks are mined, and the mining reward will decrease to 3.125 BTC.

> 2140 – The 64th and last halving will occur, and no new Bitcoin will be produced.

Satoshi wrote the halving policy into Bitcoin's mining algorithm to lower Bitcoin's inflation rate by maintaining scarcity. When miners' rewards go down and they have less to sell, limited supply positively impacts price when demand increases.

Bitcoin Wallet

"Not your keys, not your coins" is one of the crypto world's most famous mantras. It means if you do not truly have control over your private keys, then you do not actually "own" your crypto/coins. In other words, if you lose your Bitcoin wallet's private key, you lose the funds in it.

In a traditional finance system, you have a wallet to store your cash. A Bitcoin wallet is similar to your regular wallet, but it is used for storing, sending, and receiving Bitcoins. It has two main functions:

First, storing the user's public and private keys, and second, performing transactions—for instance, receiving and sending Bitcoins.

How Bitcoin Wallets Work

We learned public and private keys in Chapter 2, "Cryptography." The chapter shows an example of using asymmetric encryption to generate a pair of private and public keys. After that, a blockchain address is derived from its public key.

In Bitcoin, when you create a blockchain wallet, private and public keys are associated with it. There is one private key per address. The Bitcoin address is publicly visible, represents your account in the blockchain, and is used for receiving and sending Bitcoins.

A private key is kept secret. It is used to verify transactions, account ownership, or spend the Bitcoins in your account. It can have many forms:

1. A 256-character-long binary code. Example:

   10101111001110000000111101100011110101111010010100100
   01011001111011110100011000010100011111100100010100011
   11000111010100011001111111000010100011000101011101000
   10100111111101010010100111101101101100000011011110100
   11000001110101101001000010001000010000100111.

2. A 64-digit hexadecimal code. Example:

    c2e44f51a0277e7bde2b244de3ac9afb62b528bf2f23
    4f0a0a085e963ef7134e
    associated address: 1Ghftir7isD9MsJVH6qc
    Tbm2nCBHTs3Csp

3. A QR code. Example:
    You can use an online Bitcoin QR code to
    generate one by giving the Bitcoin address: www.
    bitcoinqrcodemaker.com/.

Figure 3-11. *Bitcoin QR code*

4. Mnemonic phrase. Example:

Mnemonic Language	English	日本語	Español	中文(简体)	中文(繁體)	Français	Italiano	한국어

BIP39 Mnemonic	corn surge rate bridge mom wife enter whale useless riot magic detect same metal humble
BIP39 Seed	592390f5aef469435146ced1ee343a2e472fcb8fd537cd863d369a78f059f4bf518b449bb229a2f9b6f77dec7a785bc35250336ba90747b5c4c224234326c09c
Coin	BTC - Bitcoin
BIP32 Root Key	xprv9s21ZrQH143K3KfBvob7SrwBuJ6zSDeShrJ9oPcA2TMaHCV3NWjRTmY4tkkSaAz5pKYwnbXHY91WaXBY4oXZmE4BJ1nuXoJYgQhKQwy1UAc
Account Extended Private Key	xprv9xq8CZNQaVVoicKpv9obBbdJWXng9i6qMRdT12Cg5ffSAwEpoHhBUK6zBdFAZn2fMnEqSceWLndDGzD8k2hFm9WxjDaBF3NurVGo1SaWdJC
Account Extended Public Key	xpub6BpUc4uJQs46w6QJ2BLbYja34ZdAZApgieZ3oQcHe1C43jZyLq1S27RU2uRGBuGW7nmoiJX7DgoXACvtEeKTvm9cAUVH1LfUFnahx7bYhEb

The BIP32 derivation path and extended keys are the basis for the derived addresses.

BIP32 Derivation Path	m/44'/0'/0'/0
BIP32 Extended Private Key	xprvA2AeEzvVPEkY9XGyQkLgnh88umQmV61oAaSrZsLvsmkuuyHa38qjzb4BtrfhxA6m1UogyHeBiRRbTwLgQ1vETEAiXj8vzMu6d69v3JEYnqH
BIP32 Extended Public Key	xpub6F9zeWTPDcJqN1MSWmsh9q4sToFFtYjeXoNTNFkYS7Htnmciag9zYPNfk7nNitiAZ1ByQyvQpVY5kPrcbgBuXhnbcTB4Hqbhg.yYeqiajT2N

Derived Addresses

Path	Address	Public Key	
m/44'/0'/0'/0/0	1Bj5DYZfsAjtdPvx3Bq9yt9Z5ggrFTN5d5	0247986c22b87400c9a8a53bce0a3c894b66d2bb002be62041a6b506015e39dbe8	K
m/44'/0'/0'/0/1	1BZehw4DEiVo7yzwjmYM6o5mUAenEAeand	029bd68b673b8abbb18d742307db95f62372bb823a870d00d325498bb0df09b438	L
m/44'/0'/0'/0/2	1DFqCdYZqQArTE1GPwxycKiccw9BTQLpZ2	02fe6ded1e2ee4d573e6e00c6b72360c5a39bccaa41ce5e4d64831d0d9fb6b65b0	L

***Figure 3-12.** Mnemonic phrase*

When Alice wants to send one Bitcoin from her wallet to Bob, the process handled by the wallets can be described as follows:

Step 1 – Alice collects the transaction data to be sent. Once finalized, Alice uses Bob's public key to encrypt the transaction data.

Step 2 – Alice then uses her private key and signs the transaction as a digital signature. Alice then sends the transaction, the digital signature, and her public key to Bob.

Bob receives the transaction message. He must verify that the data sent from Alice has not been tampered and must have been sent from Alice.

Step 3 – Bob decrypts the transaction data using his private key.

Step 4 – Bob receives Alice's public key to verify the digital signature to ensure the message is from Alice.

If true, Bob knows the data is not altered and good to go.

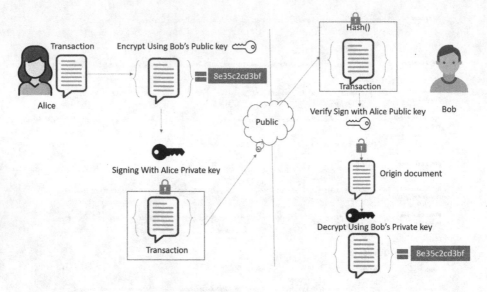

Figure 3-13. *How Bitcoin wallet works*

Types of Bitcoin Wallets

There are two categories of wallets: hot and cold. The difference between the two is that hot wallets require an Internet connection, while cold wallets store the crypto tokens offline.

Since hot wallets are always connected to the Internet, it is easy and convenient to use, and it is useful for beginners to learn or for traders to make a quick online payment. It is highly user-friendly. On the other hand, hot wallets are generally less secure and more vulnerable to hacking and online attacks. Several types of hot wallets are available; the most common are web wallets, mobile wallets, and desktop wallets.

Cold wallets are not connected to the Internet. It is highly secure. Stealing funds from cold wallets requires physical access to the cold wallet with the owner's passwords or PINS. It minimizes online hacker attacks.

At the same time, it is hard to access and less user-friendly, with transactions taking longer. It is suitable for storing a large number of crypto assets over a long period. Cold wallets include paper and hardware wallets.

Figure 3-14 illustrates the two types of Bitcoin wallets.

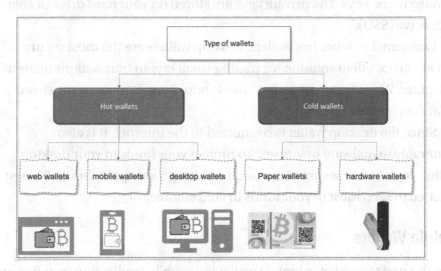

Figure 3-14. *Types of Bitcoin wallets*

Web Wallets

As the name implies, online wallets store your private keys, which are managed entirely online by a third party, typically centralized exchanges. Web wallet vendors are provided as a cloud service. The user-friendly web interface makes users smoothly handle their wallets and perform various operations, such as sending and receiving payments. You can access web wallets from anywhere through a web browser. However, web wallets are frequently targeted by hackers. Among hot wallets, web wallets are the least secure. Most exchanges store the majority of customer funds offline in cold wallets. For security reasons, users typically should not keep significant amounts of crypto in hot wallets.

An example of a popular web wallet is www.exodus.com/ or https://electrum.org/.

Desktop Wallets

Desktop wallets are downloaded computer software that runs on your desktop or laptop device. This wallet software generates a data file to manage users' keys. The private keys are stored on your hard drive or solid-state drive (SSD).

Compared to other hot wallets, desktop wallets are the most secure and are an excellent solution for trading small crypto transactions using a computer. When using the wallet, users should create a strong password for accessing the keys.

Since the desktop wallet is connected to the Internet, it is also vulnerable to malware or viruses. To protect your funds in your desktop wallet, you need to secure your computer using a safe passphrase. It's best practice to keep most of your funds in cold storage.

Mobile Wallets

Like the desktop wallet, a mobile wallet is a mobile application installed on your mobile phone.

Hardware Wallets

A Bitcoin hardware wallet is the most commonly used form of cold wallet and the most secure way of storing Bitcoins. The account's private keys are isolated from the Internet and stored in a secure physical device. Similar to portable devices, hardware wallets can be connected to the computer to make a transaction. The private key in the device will automatically sign cryptocurrency transactions without requiring you to enter the key, which effectively prevents hackers from stealing your private key.

Trezor (https://trezor.io) and Ledger wallets (www.ledger.com) are two of the most popular hardware wallet providers.

Paper Wallets

As the name implies, a paper wallet is a piece of paper containing a public and a private key associated with a wallet address. In addition, paper wallets are often printed in the form of QR codes, so you can quickly scan them to make a transaction.

As a type of cold wallet, paper is pretty safe to store your cryptos since your keys are entirely offline and out of reach of online hackers. It is the cheapest cold wallet option. Compared to hardware wallets like Trezor Ledger, the cost may range between $50 and $300.

Paper wallets are generated by downloading a wallet generator software.

Once downloaded, you must check to ensure the software doesn't contain malware. Then, to print out a paper wallet, you need to disable browser add-ons and extensions, disconnect from the Internet, and add a passphrase. Finally, follow the wallet generator instructions to complete the process, print the newly generated wallet, and delete the files. Just make sure no one is watching you create your wallet.

Avoid using public printers, such as in schools and offices; the wallet information could store in the printer's internal hard drive storage. A public unsecured Wi-Fi network could also leak your wallet information.

A paper wallet is easily damaged or lost. In case the app is uninstalled, you will lose your funds. Also, when using a wallet to receive the fund, a paper wallet won't tell you if you received Bitcoins and in what quantity; you will need to use another app to check.

Due to many drawbacks of the paper wallet, it is not currently widespread in use.

You can create your own Bitcoin paper wallet online from various service providers, such as https://bitcoinpaperwallet.com/, https://paperwallet.bitcoin.com/, or www.bitaddress.org/.

Bitcoin Network

Bitcoin is a peer-to-peer (P2P) network of nodes that operates on a proof-of-work protocol. Each node as a participant is simply a computer that runs the Bitcoin software. Nodes randomly select and connect with other peered nodes. Anyone can download and install the Bitcoin software to start a new Bitcoin node and join the network. The new nodes can come at any time, so the nodes in the network are dynamic and join and leave all the time.

The transaction will be broadcast to other nodes and miners in the network when the sender sends Bitcoins to a receiver signed using a Bitcoin wallet. Miners use computation power to run the mathematical process to verify transactions and add them into a block. After, the miner will broadcast the new block to the network. The nodes that received the new node will verify that the miners are following the network rules and add a block to their node. Miners are rewarded with minted Bitcoin for their contributions to the network. With the confirmed transaction, the receiver receives the Bitcoin from the sender.

There are different types of nodes on the Bitcoin network, of which there are three main types: full and super nodes, light nodes or SPV (Simple Payment Verification), and mining nodes.

Let us explore the different nodes in detail.

Full Nodes

A full node runs Bitcoin software to validate transactions and blocks from other full nodes. It can validate transactions all the way back to the genesis block, then relay them to further full nodes. Full nodes store a copy of the entire blockchain's history, including all blocks created. At the time of writing, running a Bitcoin full node requires at least 280 GB of free space.

A new full node installs the client's software and is connected to other peer nodes. The client's software then embeds the "genesis" block—the first node in the blockchain—and the new node will send the "version" message that provides a block header with block height.

The peer node will check block height by comparing it with its own copy of the entire blockchain data. If the new node block number is lower than its copy, the peer node will know how many blocks that new node is missing. The peer node can send the new node for the missing block to catch up with the latest block data. Each full node can have a maximum of 500 blocks per node connection.

When setting up a new node as a full node connected to the Bitcoin network, it will start an Initial Block Download (IBD) process.

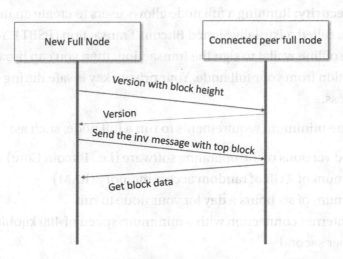

Figure 3-15. *Full node Initial Block Download (IBD)*

IBD refers to downloading and validating all blocks from the genesis block to the current block in the blockchain. Depending on the speed of node connection and hardware configuration such as CPU and memory, the entire IBD could take several hours to days. During the IBD process, a full node will not accept or send transactions.

Increase privacy: Connecting with a third-party node broadcasts your transactions. It could gather details about your transactions. Your transaction request is associated with your IP address, which can correlate to your name. To protect your privacy and stay truly anonymous, you need to connect to the full node you set up to broadcast and verify your own transactions.

The benefits of running a full node are as follows:

Maintain decentralization: By joining the Bitcoin network, you will help the network become more decentralized and secure. The full node will ensure that Bitcoin's consensus is followed by rejecting blocks and transactions that don't follow the consensus rule.

More security: Running a full node allows users to create an unsigned transaction, called a Partially Signed Bitcoin Transaction (PSBT). You can choose one offline wallet to sign the transaction, then you can broadcast the transaction from your full node. Your private key is safe during the entire process.

There are minimum requirements to run a full node, such as:

Updated versions of the operating software (i.e., Bitcoin Core)

A minimum of 2 GB of random access memory (RAM)

A minimum of six hours a day for your node to run

A fast Internet connection with a minimum speed of 400 kilobits (50 kilobytes) per second

A minimum of 280 GB of free storage space, with a minimum read/ write speed of 100 MB/sec.

Light Nodes or SPV

Light nodes or SPV (Simple Payment Verification) perform a similar function to full nodes but only download the block header of previous transactions and confirm the validity of the blockchain. Compared to full nodes, it saves a lot of storage space and allows for a faster and cheaper transaction. A block header is only 1/1000 the size of a block. The total size of the Bitcoin blockchain is 280 GB, then the total size of the block headers would be around 280 MB. Many mobile photos are larger than this. It is an affordable size for a mobile phone or tablet.

An SPV node or a wallet application needs to know about its user's unspent transaction outputs (UTXO)—the amount of Bitcoin that remains after a transaction. Since the SPV nodes only contain the header and don't have the full picture of all UTXOs available for spending, the SPV nodes must connect to other full nodes and query to find the related transactions by a given Bitcoin address. Once an SPV node gets all related transactions by a given Bitcoin address, the wallet application can find out the unspent transaction outputs.

Mining Nodes

Mining nodes pick up transactions and produce new blocks by performing proof-of-work consensus. Groups of miners can team up to build a mining pool. Utilizing combined miners' resources increases the probability of finding and generating blocks more quickly for Bitcoin. Once the mining pool is successful and receives a reward, that share of the reward is divided among participants by the miner's contribution.

Transactions

Transactions are at the heart of the Bitcoin ecosystem, which can be as simple as just transferring some Bitcoins to a Bitcoin address.

Suppose Alice wants to send Bob one Bitcoin. She uses her wallet's private key to create and digitally sign the transaction. In the next step, Alice's wallet will broadcast the transaction to the Bitcoin network. This transaction contains the sender's and receiver's addresses, the transferring amount, and Alice's digital signature. Any node in the network can pick up this transaction and add it to unconfirmed transaction pools known as a mempool. Now, the mining process starts. Miners pick up these unconfirmed transactions and solve the PoW problem. The mining process typically needs around ten minutes. Once transactions are validated, they will be added to a newly mined block and publicly broadcast to the network. Other nodes can verify and confirm the transactions for the new block. It typically needs three to six confirmations (the probability of double spending is ruled out after six confirmations) and adds them to the current block. The transaction is finalized, and Bob gets one Bitcoin in his wallet.

Figure 3-16 shows an example of a transaction detail.

Details ⓘ	
Hash	424135e848521733a7580670f98c827cfdf809111fdb635820e4ce9660ab099d
Status	Confirmed
Received Time	2022-08-04 23:04
Size	217 bytes
Weight	760
Included in Block	748021
Confirmations	5
Total Input	0.00000000 BTC
Total Output	6.29695864 BTC
Fees	0.00000000 BTC
Fee per byte	0.000 sat/B
Fee per vbyte	0.000 sat/vByte
Fee per weight unit	0.000 sat/WU
Value when transacted	$145,123.70

Figure 3-16. *Transaction detail*

Let's go over some concepts for a transaction data structure.

The Transaction Data Structure

Figure 3-16 shows typical transaction information. There are many other fields; we have chosen some of the most used ones and illustrated them in Table 3-4.

Table 3-4. *Bitcoin transaction detail*

Field name	Description
Transaction hash (Transaction ID (TxID))	A transaction hash is a unique string of characters given to every transaction verified and added to the blockchain. Bitcoin uses the SHA-256 hash algorithm to generate the transaction hash value.
Transaction status	It checks the status of the Bitcoin transaction confirmation.
Received time	The time when the sender's wallet broadcasts the transaction to the network.
Size	The total size of this transaction.
Block	Block number to which the transaction belongs.
Confirmations	The number of confirmations that succeed in hashing a transaction and adding it to the blockchain.
Fee/Byte	The total fee paid to process this transaction.

Alice sends Bitcoins to Bob. Alice's wallet will start to create a transaction. At a high level, the transaction has three main parts:

1. Inputs: contains Alice's Bitcoin address with the amount of Bitcoin Alice owns.

2. Outputs: Bob's Bitcoin address or public key.

3. Amounts: the amount of Bitcoins Alice sends to Bob.

Figure 3-17 shows an input and output example:

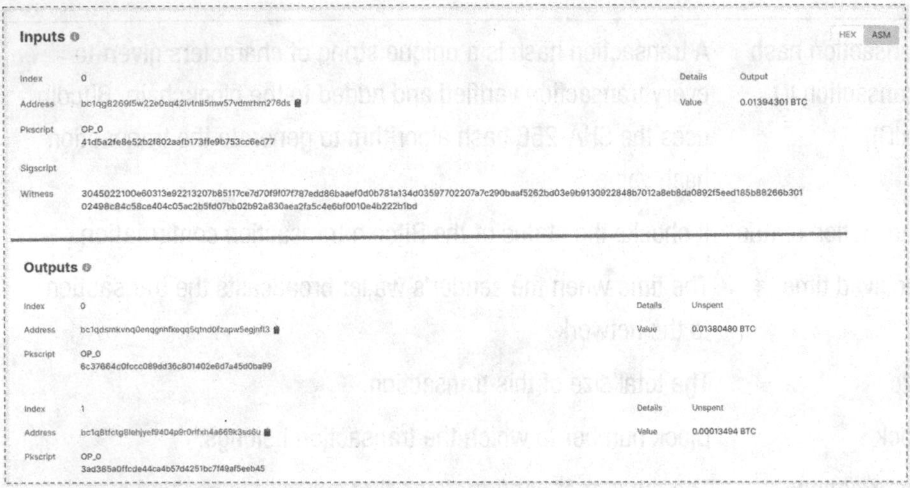

Figure 3-17. *Transaction input and output*

Input

Think of inputs as spending and outputs as savings to a Bitcoin account. Generally, each input spends a previous output. Each output is an **Unspent Transaction Output** (**UTXO**) until a later input consumes it.

A transaction can contain multiple inputs and outputs. The transaction will be valid if the input amount exceeds the associated output amounts, and the input amount also includes the transaction fee.

A UTXO is an unspent transaction output used for the next input spent for a new transaction. The transaction input data structure is described in Table 3-5.

Table 3-5. *Bitcoin transaction input*

Field name	Type (length)	Description
Transaction Hash/ Tx-ID	32 bytes	SHA-256 has a transaction ID. The previous transaction ID with UTXO.
Transaction Index	4 bytes	The previous transaction output index.
Unlock script length	2–9 bytes	Size of the unlocked script.
Unlock script	Variable	It contains the unlocked scripts.
Sequence	4 bytes	Sequence number. The default value is 0xffffffff.

Output

Outputs have three fields containing information about transferring Bitcoins. The first field is the amount of Satoshis to send, whereas the second field indicates the byte size of the lock script. Finally, the third field contains a locking script that defines the conditions that expect others in the future to spend that output. The transaction output data structure is explained in Table 3-6.

Table 3-6. *Bitcoin transaction out*

Field name	Type (length)	Description
Value	8 bytes	Amount to transfer in Santoshi.
Lock script length	2–9 bytes	Size of the locking script.
Lock script	Variable	It contains the lock scripts.

UTXO (Unspent Transaction Output)

Each output of a transaction, called Unspent Transaction Output (UTXO), is used as the input of the next spent transaction. UTXO can only be spent once in the Bitcoin network, so Bitcoin transaction outputs can be classified as either UTXOs or spent transaction outputs. Since the Bitcoin blockchain doesn't maintain each person's account balances, Bitcoin wallet applications can query the blockchain full node data and aggregate the total UTXO for the Bitcoin wallet address. Similar to how blocks are connected in blockchain, each transaction input is linked to the previous transaction's output, and each output points to the subsequent transaction's input.

Imagine Alice has received multiple payments from 08/01/22 to 08/05/22. Each transaction contains different values of BTC, as shown in Figure 3-18.

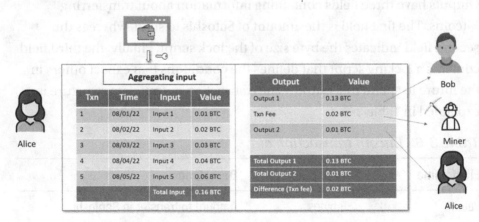

Figure 3-18. *Aggregating transaction inputs and generates output*

Alice's wallet address is 18AEg8g8VWxBfFGeWLqJURuw1DLK Qne8jV. Alice wants to send 0.005 BTC to Bob. Alice just needs to unlock any transaction between 08/01/22 to 08/05/22 because all of these transactions have a UTXO amount larger than 0.005 BTC. But if Alice wants to send 0.13 BTC to Bob, she must unlock all these transactions. To pay

0.13 BTC, Alice can't simply take transactions 1–4 and have 0.03 BTC from transaction 5. In other words, you can never use UTXO as partial spending; all these transactions need to be unlocked and added together to spend 0.16 BTC in the new transaction, pay 0.02 BTC for the miner as a transaction fee, and then send the remaining 0.01 BTC back to Alice.

Once a transaction is committed in the Bitcoin network, the Bitcoin transactions can't be reversible unless the recipient of that payment starts a new transaction and sends the Bitcoin back to your Bitcoin address.

Unlike traditional accounts, input value can be a bit more than output value. In the preceding example, Alice sends Bitcoins to Bob. It needs to aggregate five different transaction inputs and generate three outputs: one paid for Bob, one for the miner, and the remainder returned to Alice.

Let's have a look at the most common types of Bitcoin transactions.

One Input – Two Outputs

Two outputs of a transaction are the most common type of a Bitcoin transaction. For example, Alice sends 8 BTC to Bob, but her transaction UTXO has 10 BTC. She will get the remainder back to her address. This remaining amount will be the input of the next transaction from her address.

One Input – Multiple Outputs

123

Multiple outputs of a transaction could represent someone sending Bitcoins to many recipients. For example, if the account is a business account, it could be a payment for its employee.

Multiple Inputs – One or Two Outputs

The owner could move these funds to an address when they have many different wallet addresses with smaller amounts. Another case could be a business account receiving public Bitcoin payments.

Transaction Pool

Before transactions are added to the block, they are first added into a common transaction pool. These transactions are "unconfirmed." A transaction pool, also known as memory pools, contains all unconfirmed transactions that have been validated but not yet mined.

Miners then pick the unconfirmed transactions from the transaction pool based on the fee and their position in the order of transactions in the pool. Higher transaction fees will have a better chance of being selected.

Once transactions are mined or added to the blockchain, the transaction pool is cleared. Then, the miner broadcasts a new block to the network. Each network node has a copy of the transaction pool. When the node receives an update, it will adjust its transaction pool.

Transaction Fees

Transaction fees are used as an incentive reward for miners to encourage them to validate user transactions in the block and support network security. Mathematically, transaction fees are the difference between the amount of Bitcoin transaction input and the amount out.

When a Bitcoin wallet sends a transaction, it will usually display an option to select a fee rate in Satoshis per unit, abbreviated as sats/vByte. This transaction fee will be calculated based on transaction data size multiplied by this rate. A Bitcoin block can contain a maximum of 4 MB of data, and a larger transaction will occupy more block space. Thus, the larger transaction will pay more fees. If you want to speed up the transaction validation process with less waiting, you need to include more fee rates in the transaction, which makes it more likely to be included in the next block. However, if you do not care about waiting, pay a minimum fee like two sats/vByte. The transaction will typically be confirmed within a day or a week. A simple formula can be expressed as:

$$fee = sum(inputs) - sum(outputs)$$

A Bitcoin transaction at a high level contains three primary components: metadata (including headers), inputs, and outputs. Each of the preceding three components has its own specific size. The overall transaction size will be the sum of the size of these components, as shown below:

Txn Input	Txn Output	Metadata

Assuming a transaction has the following approximate sizes with a network fee rate of 10 Satoshis per vbyte:

- 120 vbytes per input
- 58 vbytes per output
- 22 vbytes for metadata

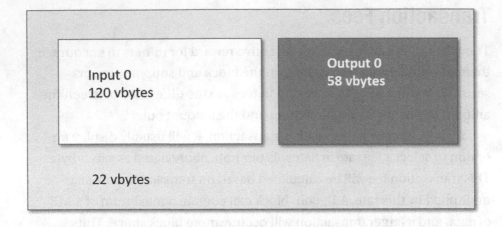

For each transaction, the total transaction size is:

120 (input) + 58 (output) + 22 (metadata) = 200 bytes

If the transaction fee rate is 10 Satoshi/vByte, then 2000 Satoshis are needed for sending 200 bytes.

1 Satoshi is 0.00000001 BTC; 2000 is 0.00002 BTC.

At the time of writing, the BTC price is $23,147.80, so the total transaction fee is:

$$23,147.80 * 0.00002 = \$0.462956$$

You need to pay $0.462956 for the above transaction.

Lighting Network

In Jan 2016, Joseph Poon and Thaddeus published a white paper titled *The Bitcoin Lightning Network: Scalable Off-Chain Instant Payments*. The Lightning Network is the solution to scale up Bitcoin outside the main Bitcoin network. The Lightning Network is a "Layer 2" decentralized payment protocol layered on top of the Bitcoin blockchain, allowing off-chain transactions. The transaction process only needs to be validated between two parties without committing them as a transaction to the

Bitcoin network. With Bitcoin adoption growing, Lighting Network has become a popular Bitcoin scaling solution. There are more than 20,000 active Lighting Network nodes with over 83,000 unique payment channels. Here are some of the benefits of the Lightning Network:

1. **Instant Payments:**

   The Bitcoin network can process around three to seven transactions per second (tps). Lightning Network builds a peep-to-peer payment channel in which two party nodes establish a bidirectional payment connection and allocate funds from a 2-of-2 multi-signature address by cryptographic protocol. Two parties in the channel can commit a transaction and pay each other directly without creating on-chain transactions for miner validation through the Bitcoin network—so the payment process is near-instant within the Lightning Network.

2. **Scalability**

   Channels on the Lightning Network are "bidirectional," as both participants can send and receive payments based on channel capacity.

   Channel capacity is the total balance each participant holds within a channel. For example, a payment channel is opened by Alice and Bob by making a 10 BTC transaction. If Alice sends 10 BTC across the channel to Bob, she can't receive any payments. Bob can receive 10 BTC from Alice but can't send any payments. However, if Alice sends 5 BTC to Bob, both parties can now send and receive up to 5 BTC within the channel. Depending on channel capacity, many transactions could happen within the off-chain payment channel without an on-chain miner involved, which can potentially scale to millions of transactions per second (tps) and dramatically scale the Bitcoin network capacity.

3. **Low Cost**

    There is nearly no transaction fee using the Lightning Network. The cost of a Lightning fee is approximately one Satoshi or $0.000233.

4. **Cross Blockchain Transactions**

    Lightning Network functionality is available on more than one blockchain as long as the blockchains can support a similar cryptographic hash function. Lightning Network could enable the ultimate decentralized exchange. The transactions could potentially be across numerous blockchains without needing a third party.

5. **Privacy**

    No blockchain records. The details of individual Lightning Network payment transactions are not publicly recorded on the blockchain directly. Payments may be routed through many sequential channels where each node operator will be able to see payments across their channels, but they will not be able to see the source or destination of those funds if they are nonadjacent.

A few limitations of the Lightning Network:

The Lightning Network is made up of bidirectional payment channels between two nodes, which, combined, create smart contracts. If at any time either party drops the channel, the channel will close and be settled on the blockchain.

Due to the nature of the Lightning Network's dispute mechanism, which requires all participants to always monitor their channel and track the state of offline ledgers broadcasted to the network, the concept of a "watchtower" has been developed.

How Lightning Network Works

Initially, Alice holds the A1 commitment transaction, and Bob holds the B1 commitment transaction.

The revocation key for A1, K_{A1}, is owned only by Alice.

The revocation key for B1, K_{B1}, is owned only by Bob.

Suppose Alice and Bob each own 5 BTC in their wallet. Alice wants to send 2 BTC to Bob.

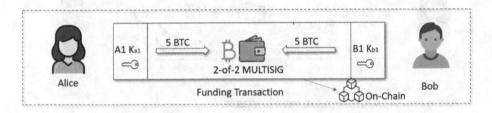

Alice and Bob are opening a payment channel on the Lightning Network by committing funds to a 2-of-2 multi-sig address and sending a transaction, also called a funding transaction or the anchor transaction, to the Bitcoin network. This transaction is mined to create the channel.

Alice and Bob both deposit equal amounts of money—in our case, 5 BTC—and each puts a lock on it.

After the payment channel is established, two parties can start signing and exchanging transactions. The transactions are called commitment transactions, which will alter the initial state within the channel.

Alice creates a new transaction, B2, which allocates 3 BTC to Alice and 7 BTC to Bob.

Alice signs B2 and sends it to Bob. Bob receives B2, signs it, and keeps it.

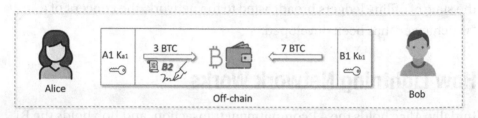

Bob creates a new transaction, A2, which allocates 3 BTC to Alice and 7 BTC to Bob.

Bob signs A2 and sends it to Alice.

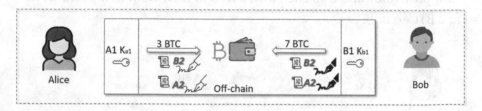

Alice receives A2, signs it, and keeps it.

Alice provides K_{A1}, invalidating A1; she can then delete A1.

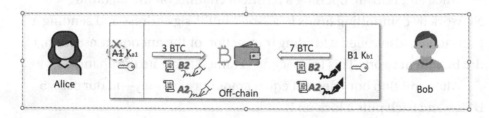

Bob provides K_{B1}, invalidating B1; he can then delete B1.

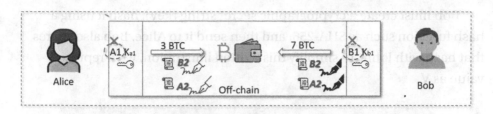

To sum up, a payment channel creates a combination of money pooling for both parties and then transfers the promise of ownership of the pooled-in money in an agreed-upon manner.

When either Alice or Bob, at some point, decides to close the payment channel, they can sign a closing transaction. Closing a channel means both sides take their money back and settle the final balance between the two parties. This transaction will then be mined in the Bitcoin network. No matter how many transactions are executed in the payment channel, the Bitcoin network will only mine two transactions—opening and closing channel transactions.

Hash time lock contracts (HTLC), as its name indicates, consists of two parts: hash verification and time expiration verification. It is a type of payment in which two parties agree to a financial arrangement, where one party receives from the other party a certain amount by generating cryptographic proof before a deadline. Otherwise, the money will return to the payer. Payment channels are time-locked by default. Extended with hash locks, payment can route through multiple payment channels connected end-to-end. The transaction can be sent between parties who do not have direct channel connections, so anyone connected to the Lightning Network is part of a single, interconnected global financial system.

Let's take a look at an example.

Alice wants to send payment to Bob, but she doesn't have a payment channel with him. Alice has a payment channel with John, who has a payment channel with Bob. How can Alice pay Bob?

Bob must create a cryptographic secret string (key), hash it using a hash function such as SHA-256, and then send it to Alice. Bob also shares that hash with John. To simplify this written illustration, we'll represent value as V.

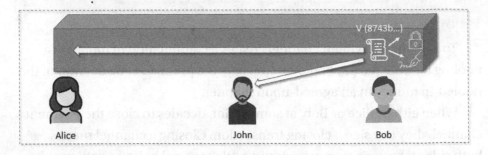

This hash V is the lock; the key is the code to unlock the HTLCs.

Alice creates a Hash Time-Locked Contract (HTLC) with John and tells him that she will pay him if he can produce the preimage of V within two days. Alice signs a transaction with a lock time of two days after it is broadcast. John can redeem it with knowledge of V, and afterward, it is redeemable only by Alice. HTLC allows Alice to make a conditional promise to John while ensuring that her funds will not be accidentally burned if John never knows what V is.

John does the same, making an HTLC that will pay Bob if Bob can produce V within a day. However, Bob does, in fact, know V. Because Bob can pull the desired amount from John by using his key, Bob can consider the payment from Alice completed. Now, he has no problem telling V to John so that they can collect their funds too.

Bob discloses his key to John within one day, and Bob gets paid by John.

John discloses his key to Alice within two days, and John gets paid by Alice.

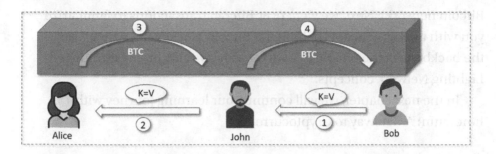

After everyone cooperates, all of these transactions occur inside the Lighting Network. Everyone gets paid in a mechanical manner. The Lightning Network is almost atomic in nature and bidirectional, meaning that everyone gets paid or nobody gets paid.

In the Lighting Network, when the payment transaction is broadcasted, all the individual transactions will be verified first, and they must match the transaction history to avoid broadcasting fake or incorrect transactions. There is also a penalty imposed on fraudulent transactions, where if the Lighting Network detects a bad actor in the system, they are immediately charged with a penalty. This way, the entire network ensures credibility and consistency while discouraging bad behavior.

Summary

The main purpose of this chapter was to present the basic concept of the Bitcoin network. Although it only scratches the surface of entire Bitcoin blockchain, this chapter was an opportunity to enrich your Bitcoin knowledge. The chapter started with a discussion on the history of Bitcoin, then we learned basic Bitcoin concepts (including Bitcoin wallet and

Bitcoin network). Next, we went over Bitcoin transactions to familiarize you with the key concepts behind the Bitcoin blockchain, which form the backbone of the Bitcoin network. Lastly, we also briefly introduced Lighting Network concepts.

In the next chapter, we will continue our learning journey with Ethereum: A Gateway to Cryptocurrency.

CHAPTER 4

Ethereum: A Gateway to Cryptocurrency

Alan Turing, a mathematician, logician, and computer scientist, is widely considered to be the father of computer science. In the 1930s, he invented the Universal Turing Machine. Assuming enough memory is available, the Turing Machine could calculate anything using only two symbols (0 or 1) arranged in a potentially infinite one-dimensional sequence. This is the basis for the first computer. Turing-completeness, therefore, refers to any computation problem that can be solved and implemented in a Turing-complete environment, no matter how complex.

Ethereum, the second-largest cryptocurrency after Bitcoin, is considered a distributed Turing machine. It introduced a built-in Turing-complete programming language—smart contract, which can be used for creating various decentralized applications (also called Dapps).

The previous chapter introduced Bitcoin as the first embodiment of blockchain technology and the world's most popular cryptocurrency.

In this chapter, we'll continue exploring the Ethereum blockchain, built as a Turing-complete blockchain. The chapter begins with the history of Ethereum. From there, we cover many Ethereum basic concepts and elementary operations, including Ether, Gas, and Ethereum Account. Then, for a deeper and more comprehensive understanding of Ethereum, we explore a big-picture overview of the Ethereum Virtual Machine (EVM). We will also see the important Ethereum clients and node

B. Wu and B. Wu, *Blockchain for Teens*, https://doi.org/10.1007/978-1-4842-8808-5_4

implementations. Finally, we discuss how Ethereum works and explores the internal Ethereum architecture.

One of this chapter's goals is to help you acquire the necessary technical background to understand Ethereum mechanics and get you ready to develop your first decentralized application in the next chapter.

This chapter is organized around a few major topics:

- The history of Ethereum

- Getting to know Ethereum

- How Ethereum works

The History of Ethereum

Vitalik Buterin is a Russian-Canadian writer and programmer who has been involved in Bitcoin and crypto since 2011 just two years after Bitcoin was created. Vitalik became a writer, earning 5 Bitcoins for every post for the Bitcoin Magazine website. Soon, he became the co-founder of *Bitcoin Magazine*. Having improved his understanding of Bitcoin, Buterin became a Bitcoin expert and realized the limited functionality of Bitcoin. In 2013, for six months, Vitalik traveled around the world to learn, meet, and speak with Bitcoin developers. He recognized that he could build a new, potentially better version of blockchain by iterating on the Bitcoin.

Whitepaper Released (November 2013)

In November 2013, Vitalik, just 19 years old, published a white paper entitled *Ethereum: A Next-Generation Smart Contract and Decentralized Application Platform*, exploring the general idea of Ethereum.

The white paper explaining the concept of Ethereum that includes the following:

- It provides a built-in Turing-complete programming language that can be used to create a "smart contract"—simply a self-executing program that runs on the blockchain.

- It establishes peer-to-peer transactions in the blockchain. The platform can create and build a smart contract and decentralized application, allowing anyone to define, create, and exchange types of value: cryptocurrencies, shares, and many other assets.

Yellow Paper Released (April 2014)

In April 2014, Dr. Gavin Wood published the Ethereum yellow paper, giving a technical definition of the Ethereum protocol—Ethereum: a secure decentralized generalized transaction ledger, which describes a technical definition of the Ethereum protocol.

The Birth of Ethereum (July 2014)

Ethereum was publicly announced at the North American Bitcoin Conference in Miami in January 2014. Ethereum Foundation, as a nonprofit organization, was formed on July 6th, 2014, in Zug, Switzerland. Ethereum's founding members were Vitalik Buterin, Gavin Wood, Charles Hoskinson, Anthony Di Iorio, Mihai Alise, and Joe Lubin.

Launching the Ether Sale (July–September 2014)

On July 20th, 2014, the Ethereum Foundation launched a 42-day crowdfunding campaign. On September 2nd, 2014, the public crowd sale ended. Ethereum foundation raised 31,591 Bitcoin, that's about $18 million at the time of the sale's close.

Ethereum Released (June 2015)

During 2014 and 2015, many proofs-of-concept were developed. "Olympic" was the ninth and last prototype. On June 30, 2015, Ethereum went live, and the first "genesis block" was created.

DAO Attack (July 2016)

In May 2016, a Decentralised Anonymous Organisation (DAO) was created on the Ethereum blockchain by developers. The DAO uses a smart contract to self-govern and automate decisions without a typical centralized management structure. Anyone has the right to participate and vote regardless of their location. The first DAO crowd sale is very successful. It raised a record 12.7M Ether (worth around $150 million at the time) to fund the project.

However, on June 17, 2016, a hacker exploited some vulnerabilities in the smart contract of the DAO. The hacker was able to invoke the DAO smart contract to give the Ether back multiple times before the smart contract could update its balance. The hackers managed to steal more than 3.6 million ETH (worth around $50 million at the time).

Because of the huge amount of funds lost among DAO investors, the Ethereum community decided to reverse the attack to refund the lost money, which lead to Ethereum forked into two blockchains. One is the current Ethereum blockchain. The token owners were given an exchange rate of 1 ETH to 100 DAO tokens, the same rate as the initial offering. The lost funds of the DAO investors were recovered. In September 2016, digital exchange currencies de-listed the DAO token. In the meantime, part of the Ethereum community did not agree with the hard fork and decided to continue to maintain the old blockchain, which is now known as Ethereum Classic.

Ethereum 2.0 (The Merge)

In recent years, the Ethereum community started to migrate from Ethereum 1.0 to Ethereum 2.0, also known as Eth2, The Merge, or Serenity. Ethereum 1.0 was created based on a proof-of-work blockchain. Compared to Ethereum 1.0, 2.0 has several major advantages. Table 4-1 shows these differences.

Table 4-1. *Comparing Ethereum 1.0 and 2.0*

	Ethereum 1.0	Ethereum 2.0
Consensus	Uses proof-of-work (PoW) consensus.	Uses proof-of-stake (PoS) consensus.
Speed	The network can process around 15 transactions per second (15 TPS); it often causes network congestion and delay.	The ETH 2.0 network will scale up to a potential 100,000 TPS, compared to Visa, 30,000 TPS.
Energy	Proof-of-Work requires miners to consume large amounts of computing power to solve a complex mathematical puzzle.	Ethereum 2.0 use PoS Consensus by staking its tokens as a collateral asset to check and validate the transactions and add block. It requires minimum hardware power, which can reduce 99% fewer resources than the proof of work consensus.

(*continued*)

Table 4-1. (*continued*)

	Ethereum 1.0	Ethereum 2.0
Security	Some powerful group of miners could control more than 50% of the network's activities which could lead to vulnerabilities like a 51% attack.	In Ethereum 2.0, it is more decentralized. The network requires around 16,384 validators. The user just needs to stake 32 ethers to participate in validating the Ethereum network. Even with less ether, users can join a mining pool that enables everyone to stake together and share the rewards. There are no miners controlling the blockchain.
Gas fee (transaction fees)	As the network can only handle a limited number of transactions per second, leading to high transaction fees known as "gas," and slow transactions. Typically, avg gas fee per transaction is around $12. With demand rising sharply, the gas fee could be much higher, such as $100.	The Ethereum 2.0 uses PoS consensus to process transactions that require a nearly zero gas fee. So, it just charges some basic fee to avoid malicious activities on the Network.

There are three phases to launching Ethereum 2.0, it will take several years to completely roll out Ethereum 2.0 as Figure 4-1 shows.

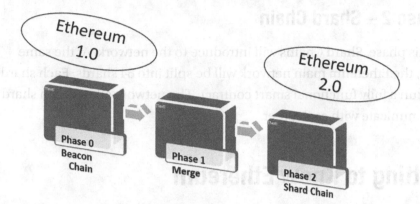

Figure 4-1. Three phases of Ethereum 2.0

Phase 0 – Beacon Chain

Phase 0 started with the official launch of Beacon Chain in December 2020. Beacon Chain builds based PoS in the Ethereum network and manages the registry of validators.

Phase 1 – Merge

The Ethereum main net merged with the Beacon Chain in this phase. It officially ends the POW consensus on the network and starts with PoS. On September 15, 2022, Ethereum switched from the original proof-of-work mechanism to proof-of-stake, called "the merge." The merge reduced Ethereum's energy consumption by ~99.95%.

Users who staked Ethereum on the Beacon Chain can become validators.

Transactions and Dapps will continue to run the same behavior as before.

Phase 2 – Shard Chain

In this phase, Shard Chains will introduce to the network. At the same time, the Ethereum main network will be split into 64 shards. Each shard can run a fully functional smart contract. The network allows each shard to communicate with each other.

Getting to Know Ethereum

In the Bitcoin network, Bitcoin is digital gold, designed as a medium of exchange and a way to store value. Bitcoin provides a payment way for people who can transfer value from one to another using a decentralized way without a central bank. On the other hand, the Ethereum network is built as a Turing-complete blockchain. The network was built in a Turing-complete programming language called Solidity, which can run in the Ethereum Virtual Machine (EVM). Users can create and run decentralized applications (Dapps) in EVM. EVM is where all Ethereum accounts and smart contracts live. As the native currency in the Ethereum blockchain, Ether was used internally by Dapp in the Ethereum network to process transactions. For example, when a smart contract executes a transaction, Dapp must pay a gas fee (Ether) for the miner to perform mining work.

Ether (Unit)

Each blockchain has its own native currency. Similar to Bitcoin, the native currency is called Ether (ETH) in the Ethereum blockchain.

Ether acts as the "fuel," to pay for the execution of smart contracts on the EVM. When miners solve the computational puzzle, they will get Ether as a currency reward. Ether can also be used for payments and users can send ether to other users as payment.

Like the US dollar, which come in seven denominations: $1, $2, $5, $10, $20, $50, and $100, Ether is broken into denominations. The smallest denomination unit of ether is called Wei, named after a digital money and cryptography pioneer, Wei Dai. Wei created Crypto++ cryptographic library and invented B-money. Other units include a Gwei, Mwei, Kwei, microether, and milliether. They are known by other names as well. For example, a milliether is also called Finney, named after another digital money pioneer, Harold Thomas Finney II, who in 2004 implemented the world's first reusable proofs of work system (RPOW) before Bitcoin. In January 2009, Finney was the recipient of the Bitcoin network's first transaction. Table 4-2 lists the named denominations of Ether and other units:

Table 4-2. *Ether denominations and unit name*

Unit Name	Value (in Wei)	Ether
Wei	1 wei	10^{-18} ETH
Kilowei (Babbage)	1,000 wei	10^{-15} ETH
Mwei (Lovelace)	10^6 wei	10^{-12} ETH
Gwei (Shannon)	10^9 wei	10^{-9} ETH
Microether (Szabo)	10^{12} wei	10^{-6} ETH
Millether (Finny)	10^{15} wei	0.001 ETH
Ether	10^{18} wei	1 ETH

Gas, Gas Price, and Gas Limit

Like Bitcoin, Ethereum currently uses a proof-of-work (PoW) consensus mechanism. It required miners to compute and solve complex mathematical puzzles, verify transactions, and create a block of transactions to be added to the blockchain. A miner is rewarded with Ether (ETH). When users submit transactions, they need to pay Ether for the miner to execute such work.

According to coinwarz.com, assume you use a machine with a hash rate of 750.00 MH/s (Megahashes per second) and 1350 power consumption in watts. You need about $20,000. Assume the cost of electricity is $0.10 per kWh (depending on your location, the average is $0.14/kWh in the United States). It will take up to around 103 days to mine one Ether. The current ether price is around $1100, it will take a while to become profitable. Figure 4-2 shows the result of the Ethereum mining calculator.

♦ Ethereum Mining Calculator

ETH Mining Calculator

Enter your Ethereum mining hashrate, power consumption in watts, and costs.

Ethereum Mining Hashrate ⓘ

750.00   MH/s ✓

Power Consumption in Watts ⓘ

1350.00

Electricity Costs in $ / kWh ⓘ

0.10

Pool / Maintenance Fees % ⓘ

0.00

Mining Revenue $10.88

Mining Fees $0.00

Electricity Costs $3.24

0.00040418 ETH
Ethereum mined per hour

0.00970022 ETH
Ethereum mined per day

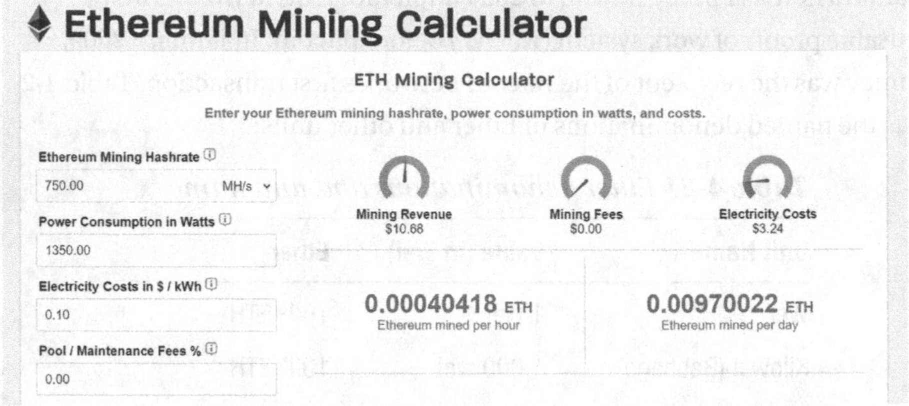

Figure 4-2. *Ethereum mining calculator*

Gas refers to such fees required to execute a transaction on Ethereum successfully, that is, the fees that need to be paid to miners for processing transactions.

One of the commonly used Ether units is Gwei. It is used to specify Ethereum gas prices and pay for transaction fees. For example, one Gwei is the same as 0.000000001 ETH. If a transaction cost is 0.000000050 ETH, we can say that the cost was 50 Gwei.

In the current Ethereum blockchain, the standard transaction fee is 21,000 Gwei. The gas fee can be calculated using the following formula:

Total Fee = Gas unit (limits) * (Base fee + Tip)

Gas units (limits) – This refers to the maximum amount of gas you want to spend to execute a transaction.

Base fee – It refers to a minimum amount of gas fee that requires a user transaction to be included in a block. The base fee amount is automatically dynamic and calculated by Ethereum based on market demand at any given time.

Tips – Also known as a priority fee, a miner tip. It is an optional fee, determined by the user and directly paid to miners. The priority fee helps your transaction can be picked and processed faster by the miner.

Let's take a real Ethereum blockchain transaction as an example (see Figure 4-3, the data is from etherscan.io) and calculate the cost of an Ethereum transaction today.

⑦ Status:	✅ Success
⑦ Block:	14998670 1 Block Confirmation
⑦ Timestamp:	⏱ 28 secs ago (Jun-20-2022 09:06:10 PM +UTC) | ⏱ Confirmed within 30 secs
⑦ Value:	0.000000000000057349 Ether (< $0.000001)
⑦ Transaction Fee:	0.006961592286951576 Ether ($7.82)
⑦ Gas Price:	0.000000034630135688 Ether (34.630135688 Gwei)
⑦ Gas Limit & Usage by Txn:	500,000 | 201,027 (40.21%)
⑦ Gas Fees:	Base: 33.529135687 Gwei | Max: 47.579327056 Gwei | Max Priority: 1.101000001 Gwei

Figure 4-3. *Ethereum transaction cost (etherscan.io)*

From the preceding example, a transaction's gas limit is 201,027 units, the base fee is 33.529 Gwei, and the priority fee is 1.101 Gwei; the total transaction fees to execute the transaction would be 0.006961 ETH (201,027* (33.529 + 1.101) = 2,310,000 Gwei). In the current market, one Ether is around $1100 so this transaction fee is about 0.006961* 1100 = $7.65.

It's important to note that if you pay less than the required transaction fee, the transaction will be reverted, and you won't receive your gas fee back because the miners have done the amount of mining work to process your transaction. They would collect the fee for their work even if the transaction failed. On the other hand, if you pay more gas fees, the extra gas fee will return to you once the transaction is complete. In the preceding example, there is field "usage by Txn" indicated that only 40.21% gas fee was used, the remaining fee will return to the user (500,000 - 201,027 = 298,973).

Ethereum Account

Each Ethereum account has an Ethereum address. Ethereum has two types of accounts: Externally Owned Account (EOA) and Contract Account.

Externally Owned Account (EOA)

An Externally Owned Account is controlled by a public/private key pair owned by a user. In Chapter 2, we have learned how the Ethereum address is derived from the public key using Keccak-256 hashes. Each Ethereum addresses are 42 hex string characters starting with 0x, representing a hexadecimal format. There is no cost to create an Ethereum account. The Externally Owned Account can be used for fund (Ether) transfer or send transactions to smart contracts. You need the private key to access your fund or send funds to other people.

Contract Account (CA)

A contract account is controlled by code executed by the Ethereum Virtual Machine. These codes are typically referred to as the smart contract code. Creating a contract account is costly because it will use network storage. A contract account can do Ether transfers and create Smart Contract accounts.

Figure 4-4 highlights the USDT token smart contract creator address, which is a contract account:

Figure 4-4. *USDT Contract account (etherscan.io)*

All accounts have four common fields:

- **Nonce** – Each address has a nonce, which represents the transaction count of an account. Different account addresses can have the same nonce. The number used in nonce is unique to prevent double-spending situations.

- **Balance** – It is the Ether owned by this account.

- **Storage hash** – Sometimes it is called storageRoot. Each Ethereum contract account has its own storage trie (ordered tree data structure) where the contract data is present. StorageRoot is a Merkle Patricia trie of the current contact state as a mapping between 32-byte integers. A 256-bit hash value is calculated based on these contract data. The hash value will change anytime when its state charges. It could be used to verify the past state. Storage hash is only for contract accounts. Figure 4-5 represents Ethereum account storageRoot.

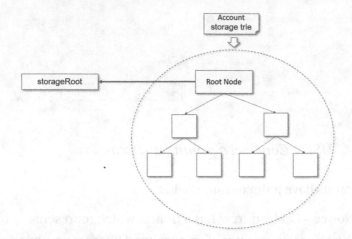

Figure 4-5. *Ethereum account storageRoot*

- **Code hash** – It refers to your contract's code under this account on the EVM. It's immutable.

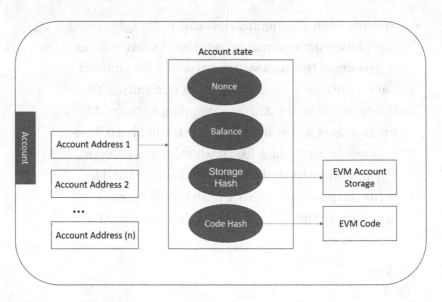

Figure 4-6. *Ethereum account structure*

Smart Contract

A contract is a written and oral arrangement between two or more parties to do certain things.

Here are just a few examples in our everyday life:

> **House rental contract** – A lease agreement between a landlord who rents a property to a tenant in exchange for monthly payments.

> **Landscaping contract** – An obligation between the landscaper and the client.

> **Software license agreements** – An agreement between the software company and customers to offer the right to use software legally.

> **Personal loan** – A written agreement between a lender that lends money to a borrower in exchange for a refund plus interest.

An effective contract will describe the formal requirements in detail, the responsibilities each party must follow, when and how contract items ought to be performed, and what happens when these rules are not followed. As a result, contracts act as a reliable document for each party expected to meet as planned.

Smart contracts are very similar, but the contracts are implemented for these detailed agreements by using computer code. They can't be changed once created in a decentralized blockchain network. When the conditions are met, smart contracts will be executed automatically instead of by a third party. Since blockchain is decentralized, immutable, and transparent, everyone in the network can publicly verify the smart contract transaction result.

Nick Szabo was the first person to describe smart contracts. He published a paper *The Idea of Smart Contracts* in 1997. He imagined converting contracts into code to achieve self-enforcing contracts that removed the need for trust among the parties. To illustrate his concept, Nick used a vending machine to explain how smart contracts work. When you insert the correct amount of money into the machine, you get the desired product. The software instructions inside the vending machine guarantee that the contract will be fulfilled as intended. Today, this idea has now spread all over the world.

Ethereum is the most popular smart contract platform. Anyone can create smart contracts in the blockchain. The code is transparent and publicly verifiable. Everyone can see what kind of implementation logic is for smart contracts. Here is an example of SHIBA INU from etherscan.io.

Figure 4-7. *Ethereum SHIBA INU contract example*

In Ethereum, smart contracts are written in a variety of programming languages, including Solidity and Vyper. Solidity is the most popular Smart contract language used in Ethereum as we will explore more in a later section.

Each network computer node stores a copy of all existing smart contract codes and their current state alongside transaction data. A user is typically required to pay a gas fee to execute the function of the smart contract and include the transaction in a new block.

Ethereum Virtual Machine (EVM)

A "Virtual Machine" or "VM" is a simulated computer system you can use to run software on a physical computer. Virtual machines are essentially establishing an isolate level between a simulated computer system and the running operation system like Windows, macOS, or Linux. For instance, using "Parallels Desktop for Mac," you can run Windows on your Apple Mac computer, as shown in Figure 4-8.

Figure 4-8. *VM example – Window runs on Mac*

The Ethereum Virtual Machine (EVM) is a Turing-complete virtual machine that allows EVM Byte Code runs on an isolated and sandboxed runtime environment. Bytecode is compiled from a high-level smart contract programming language such as Solidity.

On Ethereum, smart contracts are typically written in a high-level programming language called Solidity. Solidity compiler compiles smart contract into low-level binary machine code (Bytecode). A user just needs to send an Ethereum transaction containing these Bytecodes, and this transaction doesn't need to specify any recipient. Once the contract transaction is committed to the blockchain, a new Ethereum account is created. The contract account stores the contract balance, the contract nonce, the code, and the data. The contract account storage hash is effectively a hash of the smart contract's data. The creation of a contract address is determined based on the sender's EOA address and nonce. RLP encoded nonce and EOA address data and hashed with keccak-256 algorithm. RLP (Recursive Length Prefix) is the way of encoding arbitrarily nested arrays of binary data. When you call a smart contract function, you interact with this contract address, and the contract storage Opcode will instruct EVM to execute the operation. The contract deployment process is illustrated in Figure 4-9.

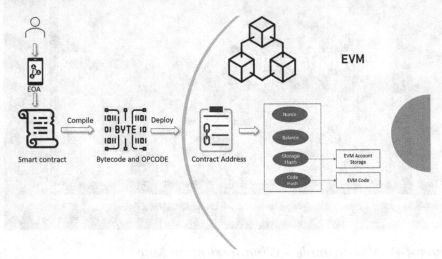

Figure 4-9. *Smart contract deployment*

Once the contract is compiled, the compiler will generate Abi, Bytecode, and Opcode. ABI (Application Binary Interface) is a JSON (JavaScript Object Notation) file that describes the deployed contract and its functions. It allows us to call contract functions externally. Bytecode and Opcode (operation code) are compact binary representations. They are stored on the blockchain and associated with a contract address.

152

EVM runtime environment will interpret Bytecode to correspond to a series of Opcode as a set of instructions and execute the Opcode when the user calls smart contracts. Figure 4-10 shows compiled contract Bytecode and Opcode example.

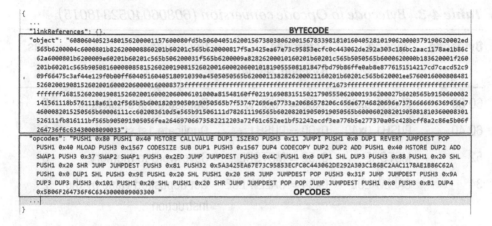

Figure 4-10. *Solidity compiled Bytecode and Opcode example*

You can find the Opcodes reference for each Bytecode from Ethereum's official website (`https://ethereum.org/en/developers/docs/evm/opcodes/`). There are around 148 unique Opcodes, which enable EVM to compute almost any task to make it a Turing-complete machine.

The Opcodes can be divided into the following categories:

- Arithmetic operations, comparison, and bitwise logic operations (ADD, SUB, GT, LT, AND, OR, etc.)

- Execution context inquiries (CALL, DELEGATECALL, CALLCODE, etc.)

- Stack, memory, and storage access (POP, PUSH, UP, SWAP, LOAD, STORE, MSSTORE 8, M SIZE, etc.)

- Control flow operations (STOP, RETURN, REVERT, etc.)

- Logging, calling, and other operators (LOG0, LOG1, LOG2, etc.)

153

Let's use the preceding Bytecode example to simulate EVM interpreter. We will focus on the first 16 bytes of the contract Bytecode: 6080604052348015. Based on Opcode reference, we can translate Bytecode to Opcode, as shown in Table 4-3.

Table 4-3. *Bytecode to Opcode conversion (6080604052348015)*

Bytecode	Opcode	Reference (Opcode, Name)	Description	Gas
60 80	PUSH1 0x80	0x60 = PUSH1,	Duplicate 1st stack item	3
60 40	PUSH1 0x40	0x60 = PUSH1	Duplicate 1st stack item	3
52	MSTORE	0x52 = MSTORE	Save word to memory	3*
34	CALLVALUE	0x34 = CALLVALUE	Get deposited value by the instruction	2
80	DUP1	0x80 = DUP1	Duplicate 1st stack item	3
15	ISZERO	0x15 = ISZERO	Simple NOT operator	3

The EVM is a simple stack-based execution machine that will execute Opcode instructions. Stack (sometimes called a "push-down stack") is a linear collection of items where the new element is inserted into the last position (referred to as the "top"), and the removal of existing items always takes place at the top position. It is also called Last In First Out (LIFO). In the preceding interpreted Opcode example, we will expect EVM will execute standard stack operations sequentially:

PUSH1 ➡ 0x80 ➡ PUSH1 ➡ 0x40 ➡ MSTORE ➡ CALLVALUE ➡ DUP1 ➡ ISZERO ➡ ⋯

EVM stack has a depth of *1024* items, each item contains a 256-bit (32 bytes) word or 32 chunks where each chunk is 8-bit (1 byte) size. The reason for 256 bits is mainly to apply the Keccak-256 cryptographic hash function to any number of inputs and convert it to a unique 256 bits hash. In EVM, contract can store and read data in the above items. The EVM has three places where it can store items—storage, memory, and stack.

Memory is the location to hold temporary values for the short term. It will be erased between smart contract function calls.

When reading data from memory, EVM will use MLOAD. To write 32 bytes (256-bit) of data, Opcode MSTORE will be used. When writing 1 byte (8-bit) of data, EVM will use MSTORE8. Figure 4-11 represents how EVM uses Opcode to read and write contract memory.

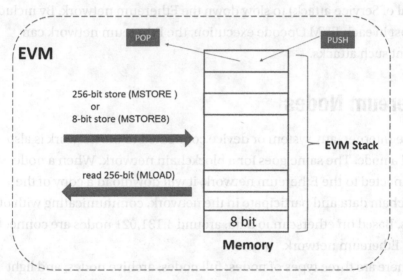

Figure 4-11. *Opcode read and write contract memory*

Storage is where you save data permanently. When a smart contract running in EVM uses permanent storage, these data will be part of the Ethereum state. You can consider storage as an array in which each array item is 256 bits (32 bytes). There are no fees for externally reading the storage value. However, it is very expensive to write data into storage, Opcode is SSTORE and the current cost per one 32-byte word is 20,000 Gas. Let's look at how much it costs.

First, convert gas (Gwei) to ETH - 20,000 * 0.000000001 ETH = 0.00002 ETH,

Then, calculate cost: $1100*0.00002 = $0.022.

Writing to storage is more than 6000x the cost compared to writing to memory.

In the previous table (Table 4-3), we list the first few steps of Opcode instruction with gas cost, and every Opcode has its own base gas cost. All Ethereum contract executions are run publicly. Attackers could create a contract to perform massive, expensive operations (DDoS – Distributed Denial of Service attack) to slow down the Ethereum network. By including gas cost in each EVM Opcode execution, the Ethereum network can prevent such attacks.

Ethereum Nodes

On the Internet, any system or device connected to the network is also called a node. The same goes for a blockchain network. When a node is connected to the Ethereum network, it will download a copy of the blockchain data and participate in the network, communicating with other nodes. Based on etherscan.io data, around 4,131,021 nodes are connected to the Ethereum network.

There are three types of nodes: full nodes, archive nodes, and light nodes. Each type of node consumes data differently.

Full Node

Full nodes will store all the recent blockchain data, run their own EVM environment, and can operate EVM instructions. They can be helpful when participating in blockchain transaction validation and maintaining the current state of the blockchain. When transactions in a new block do not comply with the rules defined in the Ethereum specifications, they will be discarded. For example, if Alice sends 50 ETH to Bob, but Alice's account doesn't have enough ether or pays a very little gas fee when a full node verifies transactions, it will mark this transaction as invalid and revert it. A full node can directly deploy a smart contract and interact with any smart contract in the network.

A full node stores a limited number of most recent blocks. The default is 128 (or 64 if you use the fast sync option). Each Ethereum block is typically around 80KB in size or around 4 MB in ten minutes. The 128 blocks are about a recent one week of trace data. When you query historical block data that is not accessible from a full node, you will generally get the "Missing trie node" error. The error means you need an archive node.

When a full node is the first time connected to the network, syncing full node data can be very time-consuming, it may take weeks to sync! After that node needs to stay online for block data upgrade and maintenance. Otherwise, it has to repeat the full synchronization process. It typically takes 13 seconds to create a new block. When new data arrives, a full node could delete old blockchain data to conserve disk space.

Hardware requirements to run a full node with fast sync:

Fast CPU with 4+ cores

16 GB+ RAM

Fast SSD with at least 500 GB of free space

25+ MBit/s bandwidth

Archive Node

Archive nodes run with a special configuration called "archive mode." Archive nodes will store all the blockchain data since the genesis block. It also builds an archive of historical states.

Current archive Ethereum blockchain sizes are ~12 TB.

Typically, in most cases, we don't need archive node data. A full node can provide most data, such as check account balances, transfer funds, etc. But sometimes, you may need to check last year's account balance, assets you owned, or transactions. The full node prunes data periodically and only stores the most recent 128 blocks of data (about 25 minutes). The node has to resync to get earlier data, which would be too slow to extract. The archive node has all data locally, which can quickly get past data.

Archive node data are often used for blockchain services such as block explorers, data analysis, etc. Syncing full archive node data will be much longer than full node syncing. It may take at least one month.

These are the hardware requirements to run a full archive node:

Fast CPU with 4+ cores.

16 GB+ of RAM.

Fast SSD drive with at least 6 TB+ of space.

25 MBit/s+ bandwidth.

Light Node

Light nodes only download the minimum block headers information and use it to verify the data validity by checking the state roots in the block headers. Light nodes are designed to interact with full nodes as intermediaries and rely on full nodes to perform blockchain operations, from requesting account balance to smart contract interaction. So, light nodes don't need to keep running online and store large amounts of Gigabytes of data locally. Light nodes can be very useful for running on low memory and computational devices, like mobile, IoT devices, and laptops.

Ethereum Clients

As we just learned, Light Clients are mostly implemented on mobile devices. Although setting up a full node or archive node will take a long time to sync, there are multiple benefits to running your own node:

1. Your node can be a network validator to verify all the transactions and blocks.

2. You can verify your application client transaction data by yourself, without the need for a third party to verify a transaction—"Don't Trust. Verify."

3. You will have a consistent view of the current network state and not need to rely on other public nodes or services where data could be delayed or untrusted.

4. You have more data privacy. When you use third-party software or tool to submit a transaction, these services could read your IP address along with your account information. IP addresses will reveal your current location.

To sync and communicate to the Ethereum network, you need to install Ethereum client software. The most used Ethereum clients are Geth. etherscan.io show that 90.3% of Ethereum node install Geth as an Ethereum client to join the network and establish a p2p communication channel with other nodes. Diagram 4-12 shows overall Ethereum client usage.

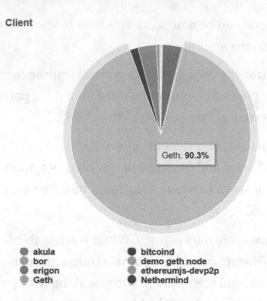

Client

akula
bor
erigon
Geth

bitcoind
demo geth node
ethereumjs-devp2p
Nethermind

Figure 4-12. *Overall Ethereum client usage*

Geth (Go Ethereum) is an open source command line interface (cli) for running an Ethereum node written in Google's programming language Go.

The Ethereum community built and maintained Go Ethereum.

Using Geth allows the node to perform transactions, mining, transfer ether between accounts, and deploy and interact with smart contracts on the Ethereum blockchain. Geth can be directly downloaded from Geth's official website—https://geth.ethereum.org/downloads/. The site provides a standard installation guide.

Once installed Geth, you can run Geth in sync mode to become a full, light, archive node.

Geth command to sync full node:

geth --syncmode full

When sync mode is a full mode, Geth will download all blocks and replay all transactions from the genesis block. The state for full nodes will keep the last 128 blocks in memory.

Geth command to sync light node:

geth --syncmode light

When sync mode is a light mode, Geth will download the most recent 2,300 blocks and replay related transactions. As a result, the sync process for light mode is much faster than in full mode.

Geth command to sync archive node:

syncmode full`--gcmode archive

Geth will download all blocks and replay all transactions from the genesis block and write all intermediate states to the archive disk.

There are many other Ethereum clients that are available in the Ethereum community. These clients are developed by different teams and implemented in different programming languages. All of these clients are actively used in the industry. Table 4-4 summarizes the different client's usage.

Table 4-4. *Ethereum clients*

Client	Programing language	Disk size (fast sync)	Disk size (full archive)
Geth	Go	400 GB+	6 TB+
OpenEthereum	Rust	280 GB+	6 TB+
Besu	Java	750 GB+	5 TB+
Nethermind	C#, .NET	200 GB+	5 TB+

Geth has a JavaScript console built using the GoJa JS Virtual Machine.

Geth has a built-in JavaScript console and supports all standard web3 JSON-RPC APIs, called web3. js, which is compatible with ECMAScript 5.1. You can use JSON-RPC APIs to interact with your node. Geth supports multiple ways to let client applications send raw JSON objects to the node. One of the most widely used protocols is called JSON-RPC over HTTP. JSON stands for JavaScript Object Notation. It is an open standard file format that transmits data between a server and web application. The data are in key/value pairs separated by a comma in the JSON file. Here is an example:

```
{
    'name': 'Alice',
    'gender': 'Female',
    'account': 12345
}
```

RPC stands for "Remote Procedure Call" and is used for other remote system processes. When client applications use JSON-RPC over HTTP to send JSON data to Geth, Geth will execute specific tasks provided by Web3 API in the blockchain. Web3 is run on top of the RPC layer, as shown in Figure 4.13.

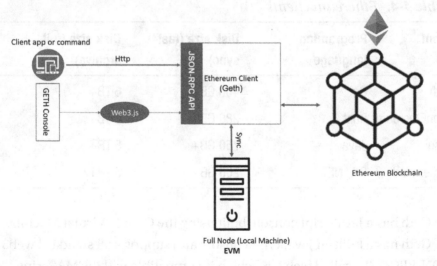

Figure 4-13. *Call Ethereum client via JSON-RPC*

Geth Console

To start Geth JavaScript console, you can run the command—Geth attach with IPC. IPC (Inter-Process Communication) provides unrestricted access to all Web3 APIs. You can use IPC to connect when the Geth console is running on the same machine as the Geth node.

They opened the console from the running Geth instance, the result will look like this:

```
$ geth attach geth.ipc
Welcome to the Geth JavaScript console!

instance: Geth/v1.10.17-stable-25c9b49f/linux-amd64/go1.18
coinbase: 0x2c752051c8a839015cde43388f81458c09487486
at block: 518413 (Mon Jun 27 2022 04:25:16 GMT+0000 (UTC))
 datadir: /home/ubuntu
 modules: admin:1.0 debug:1.0 eth:1.0 ethash:1.0 miner:1.0 net:1.0 personal:1.0 rpc:1.0 txpool:1.0 web3:1.0

To exit, press ctrl-d or type exit
>
```

To get support for web3 APIs including eth,personal, admin, and miner, Geth console provide web3 command. Let's take a look at eth related API. Type eth in Geth console. It will show all supported eth commands.

```
> eth
eth._requestManager          eth.getBlockUncleCount        eth.getWork
eth.accounts                 eth.getCode                   eth.hashrate
eth.blockNumber              eth.getCoinbase               eth.iban
eth.call                     eth.getCompilers              eth.icapNamereg
eth.coinbase                 eth.getGasPrice               eth.isSyncing
eth.compile                  eth.getHashrate               eth.mining
eth.constructor              eth.getMining                 eth.namereg
eth.contract                 eth.getPendingTransactions    eth.pendingTransactions
eth.defaultAccount           eth.getProtocolVersion        eth.protocolVersion
eth.defaultBlock             eth.getRawTransaction         eth.resend
eth.estimateGas              eth.getRawTransactionFromBlock eth.sendIBANTransaction
eth.filter                   eth.getStorageAt              eth.sendRawTransaction
eth.gasPrice                 eth.getSyncing                eth.sendTransaction
eth.getAccounts              eth.getTransaction            eth.sign
eth.getBalance               eth.getTransactionCount       eth.signTransaction
eth.getBlock                 eth.getTransactionFromBlock   eth.submitTransaction
eth.getBlockNumber           eth.getTransactionReceipt     eth.submitWork
eth.getBlockTransactionCount eth.getUncle                  eth.syncing
```

To list all of your current accounts in the network, simply run the following:

`eth.accounts.`

The listed account output should be similar to the following:

> eth.accounts
["0x2c752051c8a839015cde43388f81458c09487486", "0x88437244acbb6276de36175740a8d686a9531ba7", "0x54c37ed7cabac60dde894c6260c59f24695ade53",
"f2b3f849ec6462bcc370e90378"]

To check the account balance, covert wei to ether, run the following command:

`eth.getBalance('0x88437244acbb6276de36175740a8d686a9531ba7')`
`to get wei`

Or, we can directly convert to ether:

`web3.fromWei(eth.getBalance('0x88437244acbb6276de36175740a8d68`
`6a9531ba7'),'ether')`

> eth.getBalance("0x88437244acbb6276de36175740a8d686a9531ba7")
99996902986000000000
> web3.fromWei(eth.getBalance("0x88437244acbb6276de36175740a8d686a9531ba7"),"ether")
99.996902986

To get the latest block number of the blockchain, run the following command:

> eth.blockNumber
518560

Then, you can display a matching block summary information by calling:

`eth.getBlock (blockNumber)`

```
> eth.getBlock(518560)
{
  difficulty: 895127,
  extraData: "0xd683010a11846765746886676f312e3138856c696e7578",
  gasLimit: 8000000,
  gasUsed: 0,
  hash: "0x5d0d2201f7fd6a7b7472562cc243d10126cac0374d68c050ddc9018d02136718",
  logsBloom: "0x0000000000000000000000000000000000000000000000000000000000000000000000000000000000000000000000000000000000000000000000000000000000000000000000000000000000000000000000000000000000000000000000000000000000000000000000000000000000000000000000000000000000000000",
  miner: "0x2c752051c8a839015cde43388f81458c09487486",
  mixHash: "0x8636e19c73e4ba469764d7cc6b68decd1e8789da75714d254c61e7a9c4aea744",
  nonce: "0x717d1dc685266c0ca",
  number: 518560,
  parentHash: "0xb54662211d6b20571e27673f9a784f780949057e75a4a01fcfeafb8c6db7b804",
  receiptsRoot: "0x56e81f171bcc55a6ff8345e692c0f86e5b48e01b996cadc001622fb5e363b421",
  sha3Uncles: "0x1dcc4de8dec75d7aab85b567b6ccd41ad312451b948a7413f0a142fd40d49347",
  size: 537,
  stateRoot: "0x7d8071b7bb11ae997e62194bf8644b41bcc4d18b5030852353ecbd2eb06aa4b3",
  timestamp: 1656305590,
  totalDifficulty: 486691900015,
  transactions: [],
  transactionsRoot: "0x56e81f171bcc55a6ff8345e692c0f86e5b48e01b996cadc001622fb5e363b421",
  uncles: []
}
```

To exit the Geth console, just simply run exit or press CTRL-C.

Geth JSON-RPC via Command

cURL stands for "Client URL" and is a command-line tool for transferring data using various supported protocols (HTTP, IMAP, SCP, SFTP, SMTP, LDAP, FILE, and many others). The curl syntax is

```
curl [options] [URL...]
```

For example, you can open a window or mac terminal, type the below curl command, you will see HTTP response from the remote server:

```
curl -k www.apress.com/us
```

To start Geth in http mode, you can use the --http flag as follows:

```
geth –http
```

The default port is 8545. Once the Geth node starts, we can run the curl command to query some useful blockchain information.

To get the web3 client version, run the following curl command:

```
curl -X POST -H 'Content-Type: application/json' \
--data '{'jsonrpc':'2.0','method':'web3_clientVersion','params':[],'id':11}' \
http://localhost:8545
```

Here id - 11 is blockchain Id. The response result shows that web3_ clientVersion is Geth/v1.10.17-stable-25c9b49f/linux-amd64/gol.18

```
> curl -X POST -H "Content-Type: application/json" \
> --data '{"jsonrpc":"2.0","method":"web3_clientVersion","params":[],"id":11}' \
> http://localhost:8545
{"jsonrpc":"2.0","id":11,"result":"Geth/v1.10.17-stable-25c9b49f/linux-amd64/gol.18"}
```

To check account balance, we saw in the previous Geth console example, running the following curl command:

```
curl -X POST \
-H 'Content-Type: application/json' \
--data '{'jsonrpc':'2.0','method':'eth_getBalance','params'
:['0x88437244acbb6276de36175740a8d686a9531ba7','latest'],'
id':11}' \
http://localhost:8545
```

```
> curl -X POST \
> -H "Content-Type: application/json" \
> --data '{"jsonrpc":"2.0","method":"eth_getBalance","params":["0x88437244acbb6276de36175740a8d686a9531ba7","latest"],"id":11}' \
> http://localhost:8545
{"jsonrpc":"2.0","id":11,"result":"0x56bbc5d759fba6400"}
```

We get hex result - 0x56bbc5d759fba6400

By converting Hex value to decimal (www.binaryhexconverter.com/ hex-to-decimal-converter),

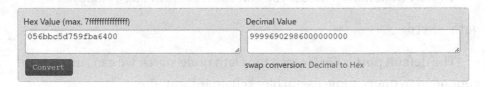

Hex Value (max. 7fffffffffffffff)	Decimal Value
056bbc5d759fba6400	99996902986000000000
Convert	swap conversion: Decimal to Hex

And then, we convert Wei to Ether and divide the decimal number by 10^{18}. The final result is 99.996902986 Ether, which is matched to the previous result we run in Geth console.

Geth Folder Structure

Once Geth installed, it stores the default Geth local data directory based on operating systems:

Mac: ~/Library/Ethereum

Linux: ~/.ethereum

Windows: %LOCALAPPDATA%\Ethereum

It is structured as shown in Figure 4-14.

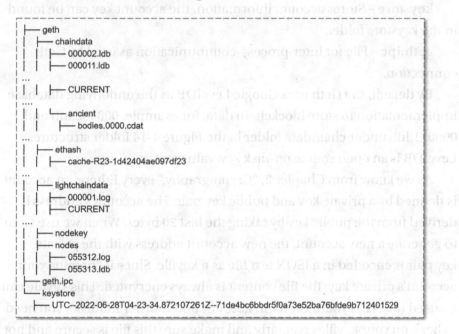

```
├── geth
│   ├── chaindata
│   │   ├── 000002.ldb
│   │   ├── 000011.ldb
...
│   │   ├── CURRENT
....
│   │   └── ancient
│   │       ├── bodies.0000.cdat
...
│   ├── ethash
│   │   ├── cache-R23-1d42404ae097df23
...
│   ├── lightchaindata
│   │   ├── 000001.log
│   │   ├── CURRENT
....
│   ├── nodekey
│   ├── nodes
│   │   ├── 055312.log
│   │   ├── 055313.ldb
├── geth.ipc
└── keystore
    ├── UTC--2022-06-28T04-23-34.872107261Z--71de4bc6bbdr5f0a73e52ba76bfde9b712401529
```

Figure 4-14. *Geth folder structure*

chaindata – Directory of the downloaded blocks data and EVM state data.

ancient – When chaindata passes approximately 100k blocks, the past blocks are moved to the ancient directory.

ethash – Ethash is Ethereum's Proof of Work hashing algorithm, the files under this location are part of the Ethereum mining computation. It can be regenerated and deleted safely.

lightchaindata– Contain a light version of the blockchain, just the receipts (not data) and content.

nodekey – File of public key used for other public peer nodes to connect or add a peer node to network.

nodes – Contains peer connection data, used to establish network at the start.

keystore – Stores account information, the account key can be found in the keystore folder.

geth.ipc – File for inter-process-communication as used by Geth connection.

By default, the Geth uses Google LevelDB as the underlying database implementation to store blockchain data, for example, 000002.ldb and 000011.ldb under chaindata folder in the Figure 4-14 folder structure. LevelDB is an open source on-disk key-value storage.

As we know from Chapter 2, "Cryptography," every Ethereum account is defined by a private key and public key pair. The account's address is derived from the public key by taking the last 20 bytes. When we use Geth to generate a new account, the new account address with the private key pair is encoded in a JSON text file as a keyfile. Since it contains your account's private key, the file content is always encrypted. This keyfile can be used to access your Ethereum account and transfer fund. So, you need to back up your keyfiles regularly and make sure this file is secure and not accessible by others.

Let's use Geth console to generate a new account address by running command personal.newAccount() and enter a passphrase:

```
> personal.newAccount()
Passphrase:
Repeat passphrase:
"0x0b1400031bea2def60a9d8f28fa373ab95d641f6"
```

The account address 0x0b1400031bea2def60a9d8f28fa373ab95d641f6 is generated. Now check keystore directory, there is a new JSON text keyfile generated for this account:

```
└── keystore
    ├── UTC--2022-06-28T04-14-13.945107969Z--0b1400031bea2de
f60a9d8f28fa373ab95d641f6
```

The content of this keyfile is encrypted, as displayed in the following:

```
{
    "address":"0b1400031bea2def60a9d8f28fa373ab95d641f6",
    "crypto":{
        "cipher":"aes-128-ctr",
        "ciphertext":"3b186d62d4d8d67eaaa719f54eaed52f42cd2e28660b410fd5c24e7c982e60b1",
        "cipherparams":{
            "iv":"01bf4c3d5f4154cd96503c5f7ab72b4a"
        },
        "kdf":"scrypt",
        "kdfparams":{
            "dklen":32,
            "n":262144,
            "p":1,
            "r":8,
            "salt":"420cc880ba93409169209ab004bf660ebd2ed024603b0202288d6d7ae4b86a55"
        },
        "mac":"da91971e8da7e5873330203ec3a46ded4425097c7a39e36ddc54e33d5c2453c7"
    },
    "id":"239e15ca-a4dc-4772-9b0b-33f92297653c",
    "version":3
}
```

We have now learned Ethereum client—Geth and clarified how remote clients (command line or web app) can call the Ethereum client via web3j API and interact with the Ethereum blockchain.

Ethereum Network

Typically, when people are discussing the Ethereum network and ETH prices, they are talking about the Ethereum mainnet. The mainnet is the primary public Ethereum production blockchain. When we deploy a smart contract to mainnet, we have to pay gas fees, and these gas fees cost real money. Since the nodes connected in Ethereum run a protocol, there are many other similar controlled public environments that run the similar or same protocol to simulate the mainnet environments. Contract developers can run and test smart contracts in these production-like environments to ensure that the result is working as expected. These public networks we call Ethereum testnet.

In testnet, you don't spend real money when testing your smart contracts. Ethereum testnet provides free ethers you can use to pay for gas fees. These ethers can only use in testnet, not for any other environments, and they have no value in the real world. As the best practice, you should test your smart contract code in the testnet before deploying it to the mainnet.

Many testnets use a proof-of-authority consensus mechanism. A smart number of nodes are chosen as a validator to do consensus work and create new blocks. Testnets do not incentivize proof-of-work mining. There are a few Ethereum test networks available. You can choose your own favorite testnet. Since the Ethereum 2.0 merged on Sep 15, 2022, few public proof-of-work and proof-of-authority testnets became proof-of-stake. Some popular testnet will soon be deprecated, like Ropsten, Rinkeby, and Kovan. We will not discuss these testnets here. Goerli testnet is a proof-of-authority testnet. It merged to proof-of-stake and is expected to be maintained long-term as a proof-of-stake testnet.

The Görli test network was established in March 2019. It is a Proof-of-Authority testnet using the Clique consensus mechanism for Ethereum, originally proposed by Chainsafe and Afri Schoedon. You can use the official Goerli Testnet Faucet (`https://goerli-faucet.slock.it/`) to acquire free ETH. In a later section, we will use Goerli Testnet to get some ether to our wallet.

Now, we have covered most of the basic Ethereum fundamentals. In the next section, we will go over how Ethereum works.

How Ethereum Works

As we learned earlier, there is a multi-phased upgrade that aims to switch from a current proof-of-work (PoW) consensus mechanism to a proof-of-stake (PoS) model. In PoW, the miner verified transactions and added transactions to a new block. The new block is broadcast to the entire network, and validators will verify and eventually commit to the Ethereum network. The process typically takes at a constant rate of between 10 and 20 seconds. In ETH 2.0 PoS, the network could speed up to 100,000 transactions per second capacity.

In Ethereum, a transaction is initiated and securely signed by a user's EOA account. For example, Alice wants to send one Ether to bob. Alice will initiate a transaction for this transfer. Next, the Ethereum network transmits the transaction. Once the transfer completes, Bob's account will be debited one Ether and Alice's must be credited. Ethereum is a singleton world state machine. Transactions are the only things that can trigger a change and update the state of Ethereum. Figure 4-15 depicts the changing state of Ethereum in a transaction.

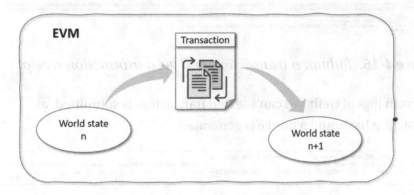

Figure 4-15. *The state of Ethereum changing through a transaction*

171

There are three types of transactions in Ethereum:

1. Transactions that transfer funds between two EOAs (e.g., Alice sends one Ether to Bob).

2. Transactions that deploy a contract.

3. Transactions that interact and execute a deployed contract function (e.g., update a total token supply).

The Structure of a Transaction

The blockchain requires a gas fee for miner mining and verifying when a user submits a transaction.

Let's use Geth console to submit one transaction by transfer 0.05 Ether and then, get the transaction receipt from the returning transaction hash as shown in Figure 4-16.

```
> eth.sendTransaction({from:'0x2c752051c8a839015cde43388f81458c09487486', to:'0x88437244acbb6276de36175740a8d686a9531ba7', value: web3.toWei(0.05, "ether"), gas:21000});
"0x6b08a9ef2041f98f296310718dfca928f2ed67455db674e1b8b39c61902b33be"
> web3.eth.getTransactionReceipt("0x6b08a9ef2041f98f296310718dfca928f2ed67455db674e1b8b39c61902b33be")
{
  blockHash: "0xa3ee94542512f e80106e13467974ca11cb20a69a800185a7d17bb5447b0c19e7",
  blockNumber: 528152,
  contractAddress: null,
  cumulativeGasUsed: 21000,
  effectiveGasPrice: 1000000000,
  from: "0x2c752051c8a839015cde43388f81458c09487486",
  gasUsed: 21000,
  logs: [],
  logsBloom: "0x0000000000000000000000000000000000000000000000000000000000000000000000000000000000000000000000000000000000000000000000000000000000000000000000000000000000000000000000000000000000000000000000000000000000000000000000000000000000000000000000000000000000000000000000000000000000000000000000000000000000000000000000000000000000000000",
  status: "0x1",
  to: "0x88437244acbb6276de36175740a8d686a9531ba7",
  transactionHash: "0x6b08a9ef2041f98f296310718dfca928f2ed67455db674e1b8b39c61902b33be",
  transactionIndex: 0,
  type: "0x0"
}
```

Figure 4-16. *Submit a transaction and get a transaction receipt*

From logs of Geth, we can see that transaction is submitted, a transaction hash, and a nonce is generated:

```
INFO [06-28|14:38:43.605] Looking for peers          peercount=1 tried=185 static=0
INFO [06-28|14:38:50.645] Submitted transaction                                      hash=0x6b08a9ef2041f98f296310718dfca928f2ed67455db674e1b8b39c61902b33be
from=0x2c752051c8a839015CDe43388F81458c09487486 nonce=76 recipient=0x88437244aCbb6276DE36175740a8d686A9531bA7 value=50,000,000,000,000,000
```

Figure 4-17 shows an example of the transaction detail from etherscan.io.

Figure 4-17. *Submit a transaction and get a transaction receipt*

A transaction detail contains the following data:

From – The sender's Ethereum address.

To – The receiver's Ethereum address.

Nonce – The sequence number of a transaction. The Nonce is issued by the originating EOA, which initiates the transaction. It is a unique number and prevents to replay of the same transaction.

Gas Price – The required transaction fee in the price of gas (in Gwei) that the transaction creator pays.

Gas Limit – Maximum limit of gas that would be consumed for the transaction.

Value – The amount of ether to send to the recipient.

Data – Transaction input binary payload data that is only used for sending a message call and executing functions of the contract.

Signature – v, r, s. It is the identification of the sender. The sender uses EOA to sign the transaction via its private key. It uses a cryptographic ECDSA digital signature. v, r, and s are the values for the transaction's signature.

Take your time to read this long list. You don't need to memorize each one of the fields. We describe each field to help you to understand what they mean. These terms may quite often appear when you work on more in Ethereum.

Transaction Receipt

In Figure 4-16, we see the transaction receipt output after running web3. eth.getTransactionReceipt(transactionHash). When the transaction receipt becomes available, it means that the transaction is added to a block. When a transaction is a pending status, the receipt returns null.

Here are the fields that the transaction receipt contains:

BlockHash – Hash of the block where this transaction was in.

BlockNumber – This transaction block number.

TransactionHash – String, 32 Bytes—hash of the transaction.

TransactionIndex – The transactions index position in the block.

From – The sender's Ethereum address.

To – The receiver's Ethereum address. Null when it's a contract creation transaction.

CumulativeGasUsed – The total amount of gas used by this transaction and all previous transactions in the same block.

GasUsed – The total amount of gas used by this specific transaction.

ContractAddress – The contract address is associated with this transaction. If the transaction was a contract creation, otherwise null.

Logs – Log information for this transaction.

Status – "0x0" indicates transaction failure, "0x1" indicates transaction succeeded.

Block

As we learned from Chapter 1, each block has header and body. Block body contains a list of transactions. This is true for both Bitcoin and Ethereum. Ethereum block structure is shown in Figure 4-18.

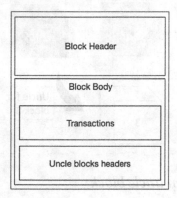

Figure 4-18. *Ethereum block structure*

Ethereum block body also contains "ommer" blocks, usually called "uncle" blocks. Uncle blocks are created to help reward miners when multiple block solutions are found.

When there are multiple miners who solve a cryptographic puzzle and propose a new block for a chain, only one of the blocks will be accepted in the network. Since other miners did the same work, the network will reward them. Those stabled blocks will be attached to the new accepted block. We call it uncle block, as shown in Figure 4-19.

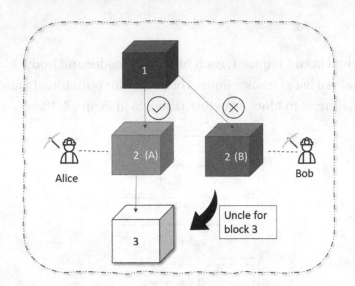

Figure 4-19. *Ethereum uncle block*

For example, in Figure 4-19, there are two blocks that were proposed by miner Alice and miner Bob. Alice's block (A) is eventually accepted and added as a new block #2. Bob's block (B) is ultimately rejected. Then, a miner in the network created a block (#3) using Bob's block (B) and specified that Alice's block is the parent block and Bob's block is an uncle/ommer block. This way, Alice will get the full reward, but Bob still gets a partial reward.

As we mentioned later, each block body contains the list of transactions, here is an example of a block from etherscan.io. We can see there are 374 transactions in this block as shown in Figure 4-20.

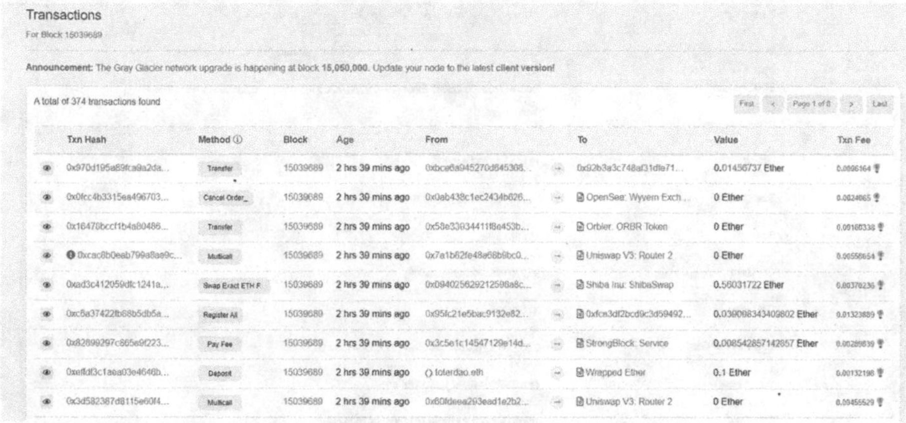

Figure 4-20. *A block: a list of transactions*

The block number is 15039689. Let's take a look at other block detail as in Figure 4-21.

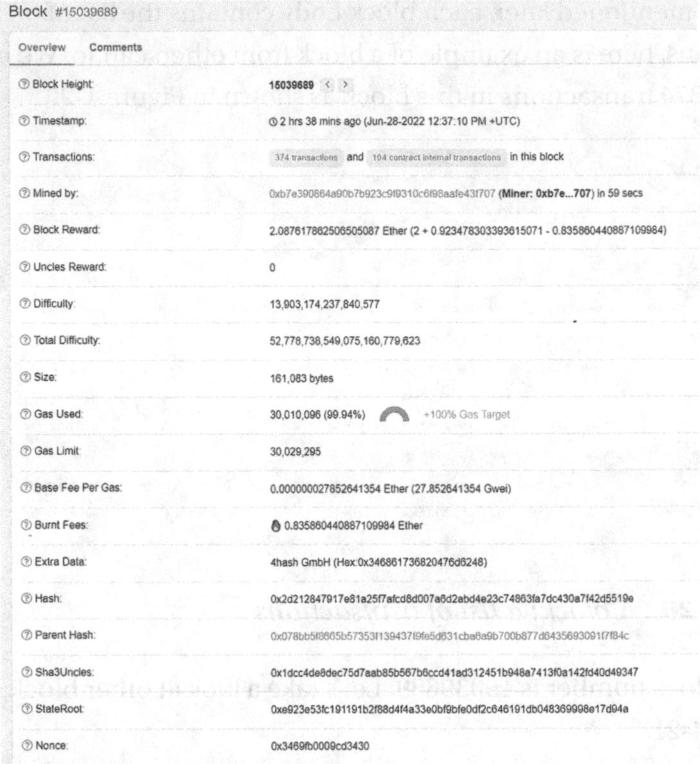

Figure 4-21. *Ethereum block detail*

The Block Header contains some key information about an Ethereum block. Each block header has the following important fields:

> **Block number** – Also called block height. The length of the blockchain ancestor blocks. The first block (genesis block) has the number zero. This number represents the height of the chain.
>
> **Difficulty** – Indicating how hard for hashing or staking effort to mine a block.
>
> **Total difficulty** – Indicating how hard it was to chain up to a specified block by an integer value.

Timestamp – A UNIX timestamp for when the block was mined.

Nonce – Please check the Ethereum Account section.

Parent hash – Also called previous hash. The hash came from the previous block (or the parent block). Each block contains a previous hash. By the way, we can link back to the first block in the chain.

Beneficiary – Also called "Mined by." It is the beneficiary miner address that receives a mining reward.

Gas price – Please check the Gas, Gas Price, and Gas Limit section.

Gas limit – Please check the Gas, Gas Price, and Gas Limit section.

Size – The block size in bytes.

Hash – A unique Keccak hash of the block.

Extra data – A field containing additional data from a block. When miners are creating a block, they can add anything in this field.

State root: Hash of the root node of a specialized kind of Merkle tree that stores the entire network state, also known as world state. It contains the Keccak hash of all account balances, contract storage, contract code, and account nonces. If any piece of the data changes, the entire state root value will also change.

> **Transactions root**: Hash of the root node of the transactions trie that stores all transactions in this block body.

> **Receipt root**: Hash of the root node of the transactions receipt trie that stores all transactions receipt in this block.

At this stage, we have deep dive into how Ethereum works, and especially we are anatomizing Ethereum block, transaction, account, and state. The relation between these Ethereum block structures. Let's summarize what we have learned and link it all together, as shown in the Ethereum architecture diagram (Figure 4-22).

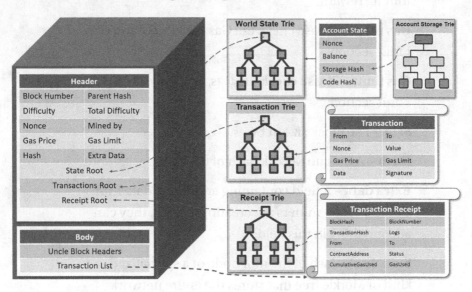

Figure 4-22. *Ethereum architecture: block, state, transactions*

We've now described most of the important concepts about Ethereum.

Summary

The main purpose of this chapter was to introduce the key concepts of Ethereum. We've started to learn about the history of Ethereum as well as the key components and elements behind Ethereum, including accounts, contracts, and gas. So, now you know the fundamentals of how Ethereum account works. We went over Ethereum node and Ethereum clients— geth technologies with some examples. We delve into the Ethereum architecture, understand how the Ethereum Virtual Machine (EVM) works, how smart contract Opcode is executed within the EVM, the structure of the block, state, and transactions in EVM. At this stage, you should be ready to go for the next chapter and start with developing your first smart contracts and end-to-end decentralized applications. We will show you how to build it step-by-step. Stay tuned.

CHAPTER 5

Smart Contracts and Dapps: From Theory to Practice

Brian Kernighan, a computer scientist, wrote the first "Hello, World!" program in 1972 for the language B to be used internally at Bell Labs. Brian wrote a manual titled *A Tutorial Introduction to the Language B* to demonstrate how to use B's language. From there, this popular text spread quickly. It was used in a Bell Laboratories memo in 1974, as well as *The C Programming Language* in 1978. "Hello, World!" remains popular to this day. It became a standard for new programmers for their first program. This particular piece of code proves your code syntax, compiles, and executes to consistently produce the desired output. "Hello, World!" offers the code in more than 60 programming languages.

In the previous chapter, we have theoretically explained the Ethereum network, including Ethereum key components, EVM, architecture, etc. The best way to better understand what we learned so far is to start practicing and writing a smart contract and Dapps for the Ethereum blockchain.

By using the online Remix tool, you'll learn how to write HelloWorld code in Solidity with all needed syntax. You'll start from the very beginning, line by line. You will also learn how to compile and deploy your smart contract locally as well as on a globally distributed testnet. Then,

B. Wu and B. Wu, *Blockchain for Teens*, https://doi.org/10.1007/978-1-4842-8808-5_5

we will install and connect our Metamask wallet to testnet. After setting up all that is required in your local Dapp development environment, you will start developing your own Dapp with minimal effort to connect the contract in testnet. By taking control of your Ethereum wallet at the end of this chapter, you should be able to run end-to-end HelloWorld Dapp.

This chapter will help you to achieve the following practical goals:

- Introducing Remix

- Writing your first smart contract

- Taking control of your first Ethereum wallet

- Decentralized Applications (Dapps)

- Tokens standard

In the last section, we talk about token standards with the two most important tokens—ERC-20 and ERC-721. ERC-721 is the NFT token standard that we will go over in the next chapter.

This will help make you more familiar with smart contracts and Dapps.

Introducing Remix

Gavin Wood proposed Solidity programming language in August 2014. Alex Beregszaszi, Christian Reitwiessner, and other Ethereum core contributors created Solidity. It is a high-level object-oriented programming language that is inspired by JavaScript, C++, and Python. The purpose of solidity is to execute smart contracts on EVM-based blockchain networks.

Many tools are available for creating and developing Solidity smart contracts. Remix, HardHat, Truffle, and others are popular tools used by Solidity developers. Remix is a powerful online integrated development environment (IDE) for coding, compiling, testing, and debugging smart contracts in Solidity. We don't need to install any other special software, apart from your web browser.

You can type the Remix IDE in your browser URL box using the following URL:

`https://remix.ethereum.org`. You'll then be navigated to the Remix home page as shown in Figure 5-1.

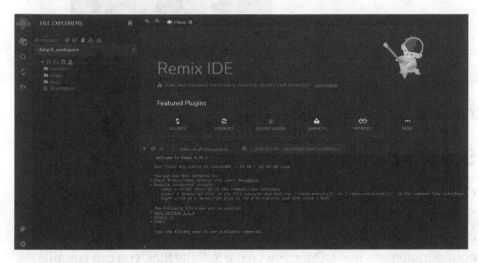

Figure 5-1. *Remix home page*

You will notice that there is a left toolbar menu on the Remix screen. When you click each menu icon, you will see different modules provided.

File Explorers

On File Explorer module, you can manage your workspaces and create contract files under workspaces. When you work on multiple projects, workspaces can help organize your files in different project workspaces. You can create smart contract files, create folders, and upload local files to the current workspace. It is very similar to other cloud browser-based tools, like google drive, dropbox, etc. Under contracts folder, Remix creates three default contracts for you. If you don't use, you can delete them.

185

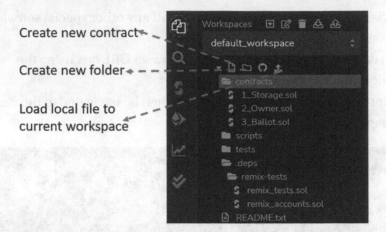

Figure 5-2. *Remix File explorer page*

Solidity Compiler

On the Solidity compiler module, you can select a different version of the Solidity compiler, the current version at this writing is 0.8.7. Since Solidity evolves quite frequently, you need to pay close attention to choosing the configuration you need. Once you create Solidity files, you can compile files by clicking the compile button. The Remix contract section will display a file compilation information, for example, error and warning. The Remix will auto-save the current file change continuously every 5 seconds.

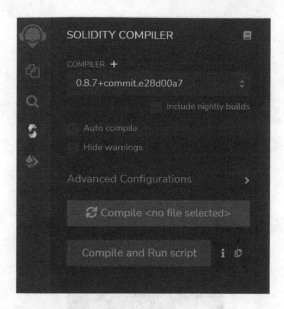

Figure 5-3. *Remix Solidity compiler page*

Deploy and Run Transactions

After you have compiled a smart contract, you can use deploy and run transactions module to deploy the contract. You need to select one contract in the Contract Editor to deploy if you have multiple contracts compiled.

Figure 5-4. *Remix Deploy and Run Transaction module*

This module provides multiple EVM Environments:

JavaScript VM – JS VM has its own sandbox blockchain simulated Environment running in your browser. It runs transactions very fast (no mining). When you execute transactions, the data is only saved temporarily in the browser. Once you close or reload the page, all transaction data will be lost. You will have to start from scratch. It is very useful for a quick try and tests simple contracts.

***Figure 5-5.** Remix EVM environments*

Injected Provider – Remix will connect to a web3 provider injected in the browser (commonly known as a browser extension for your wallet). Metamask is currently the most popular Injected Provider. You can also use other popular wallets like Coinbase wallet, Trust Wallet, and Ledger. You can connect to Ethereum's main network or various testnets through the provider. This allows the Remix to interact with a real network.

Web3 Provider – Remix will connect to a remote node. You will need to provide the URL for the selected provider. Infura, Alchemy, and QuikNode are some popular Web3 providers.

Other Modules

We have introduced the important remix modules, which we typically use often. Other modes like plugin module allow you to install the needed plugin like debug plugin, Solidity static analysis module, Solidity Unit test module, and Settings module. If interested, you can refer to the remix document for detail (`https://remix-ide.readthedocs.io`).

At this stage, we should have the basic knowledge of Remix.

Let's start to learn Solidity by writing "Hello, World!" smart contract.

Writing Your First Smart Contract

According to dune.com, the total number of smart contracts created in the second quarter of 2022 was 0.93 million. In Q2 2021, nearly 6 million smart contracts were created, as shown in Figure 5-6. In the current Ethereum blockchain, most smart contracts use Solidity programming language.

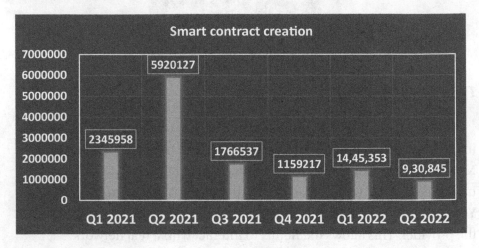

Figure 5-6. *Number of Smart contract creation from Q1 2021 to Q2 2022*

Write a Contract

On Remix File Explorer module, under contracts folder, click the create new contract icon (page icon) or use context menu by right-clicking to add our first contract. We will name our first smart contract HelloWorld.sol. Solidity Smart contracts will always have an extension of .sol as file type.

Software License

On the first line of a smart contract, you will write your smart contract license. SPDX License Identifiers indicate relevant license information. The MIT License grants anyone who uses this software the right to copy, modify, merge, distribute, and so on:

```
// SPDX-License-Identifier: MIT
```

Here Comments (//) is a line of text that appears in a Solidity program but is not executed by the program.

Pragmas

The second line is Pragmas like the following:

```
pragma solidity ^0.8.15;
```

The pragma keyword is similar to the C language, which provides the current Solidity compiler. Here 0.8.15 is the Solidity compiler version. The ^ symbol means this file will only support compiler version starting from 0.8.7 till future break changes, which will cause this file to not compile. For example, pragma solidity >=0.4.0 <0.6.0 such as the contract won't compile in 0.6.0 because of a major solidity change. In that case, you need to modify the related syntax in the file to use the newer version.

Define Contract

To make the code cleaner, you typically leave a blank line after the pragma entry. Then, in the following line of code, you start to declare the contract. In Solidity, we use the **contract** keyword followed by the name of the contract. In our case, it will be HelloWorld. The contract name should match the filename you created. The contents of the contract will be enclosed within curly braces {}:

```
contract HelloWorld {
}
```

So far, the contract should look like Figure 5-7.

Figure 5-7. *HelloWorld Empty contract*

Declare Contract Variable

In the next line, we enter **string public message**.

Here the **string** keyword is a state variable type. State variables are values permanently stored in contract storage and are used to maintain the contract's state.

The visibility of a state variable can be defined as public, private, or internal. In our case, because we set the visibility to public, the message field can be publicly accessed outside of the smart contract.

Define Contract Constructor

The next thing is to create a constructor function:

```
constructor(string memory initMessage) {
  message = initMessage;
}
```

The HelloWorld.sol will be like Figure 5-8.

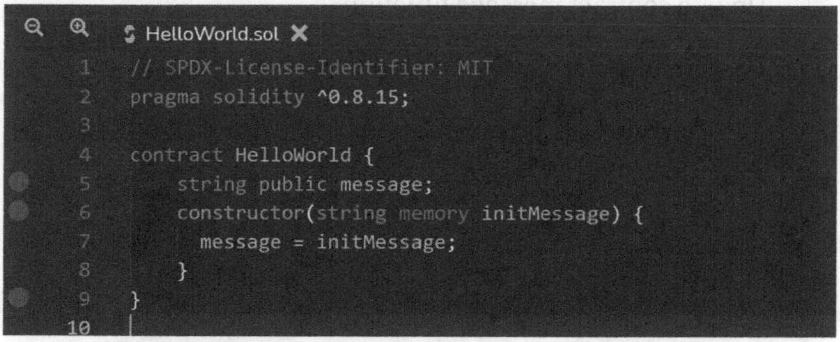

```
$ HelloWorld.sol  ✕
1   // SPDX-License-Identifier: MIT
2   pragma solidity ^0.8.15;
3
4   contract HelloWorld {
5       string public message;
6       constructor(string memory initMessage) {
7         message = initMessage;
8       }
9   }
10
```

Figure 5-8. *HelloWorld contract constructor*

The constructor is a function that can be compared to a factory machine. Once given an input, they can run a specific task to return a result.

To declare a constructor, we use the constructor keyword. Once we create our constructor, we can create many different contracts using the same constructor. Whenever a new contract is created, the system automatically calls on the constructor; they only need to use the constructor once to create the contract. If a constructor is not defined explicitly, the Solidity compiler will create a default constructor, which does not require any input.

Most often, you may need a constructor that passes one or more parameters. Inside the {}, we add the initialization logic. In our example, we pass "string memory initMessage" input. The memory keyword we use here indicates that we want initMessage parameter to be mutable, or changeable, and the initMessage value is assigned to message variable and initialized during contract creation time.

Define Functions

HelloWorld contract will have two functions. One to update message and the other to get message:

1.   Update contract message function

     Update function will be like as follows:

     ```
     function update(string memory newMessage) public {
       message = newMessage;
     }
     ```

2.   Get contract message function

     ```
     function getMessage() public view returns (string
     memory) {
         return message;
     }
     ```

A Solidity function is defined with the function keyword, followed by

- The name of the function. Here "update" is the function name.

- A list of parameters to the function is enclosed in parentheses and separated by commas (parameter1, parameter2, ...). It could be empty (). (string memory newMessage) are parameters in the HelloWorld function.

- Function visibility – public, private, internal, and external.

- Functions behavior – pure, view, and payable.

- Followed by optional returns keyword and return value type (type1, type2, ...) when the function has return values. In our update function, we don't have a return value. But in getMessage, we return (string memory)

- A statement block that defines the function, surrounded by curly brackets, {...}.

Syntax

The basic syntax is shown as follows:

```
function function_name(<parameter types>…)
{internal|external|private|public}
[pure |view|payable] [returns(<return types>…)] {

     //statements

}
```

Function Visibility

A function's scope of visibility can be set by one of these four modifiers:

- **Public** – It can be called internally or externally.

- **Internal** – Internal functions can only be accessed from inside the current contract and related deriving contracts.

- **External** – It can be called from other external contracts, but cannot be called internally (inside the current contract).

- **Private** – Like internal visibility, but the function cannot be accessed from related deriving contracts.

Functions Behavior

The pure, constant, view, and payable keywords dictate a Solidity functions behavior.

If the function behavior is not specified, it will read and modify the state of the blockchain.

Pure Functions: It ensures that the caller can't read or modify the state.

View Functions: View functions are read-only functions that ensure that state variables will not be modified after calling them.

Payable: A payable fallback function is also executed for plain Ether transfers.

Once you completed HelloWorld.sol, you should have 15 lines of code, as shown in Figure 5-9.

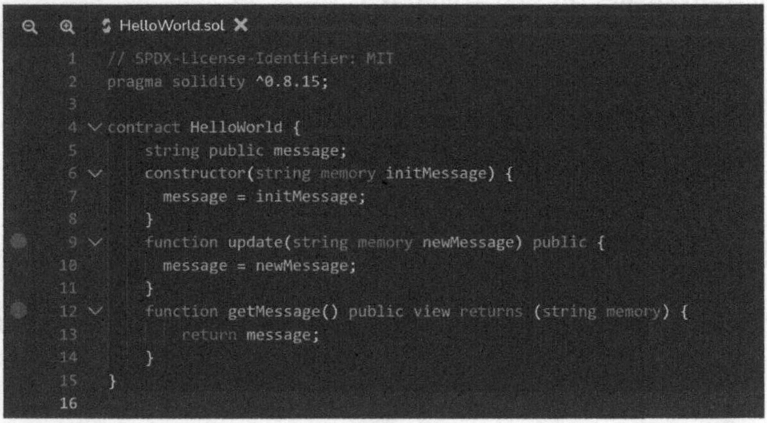

Figure 5-9. *HelloWorld completed contract*

Compile a Contract

As we learned in the EVM section, the smart contract needs to be compiled to Bytecode, before it can be deployed to the blockchain. In this step, we will compile our HelloWorld smart contract.

Remix IDE allows us to compile our Solidity smart contracts directly from our browser. Click on the compiler icon in the navigation. On the Solidity compiler page, select 0.8.15 compiler version; click the compile button to compile HelloWorld smart contract. If it compiles successfully, you will see a green checkmark on the compiler icon in the navigation. Notice also that compilation details button with Application Binary Interface (ABI) and Bytecode will show up after compiling. ABI contains JSON format data which encodes smart contract information that EVM understands and provides the standard way for Dapp to interact with contracts. You can check compilation detail by clicking the button, as shown in Figure 5-10. The result will have Bytecode, Abi, Assembly (Opcode), and other useful compiled contract information. You should copy abi content to some place; we will use this abi String in Dapp section to call with smart contract.

Figure 5-10. *Compiled HelloWorld contract*

Deploy and Run a Contract

To deploy our contract, click on deploy and run transactions module on the left menu. You should see a dropdown menu listing all the available smart contracts under the Contract Heading, HelloWorld. HelloWorld.sol will be the default selected contract, with an orange Deploy button directly beneath it.

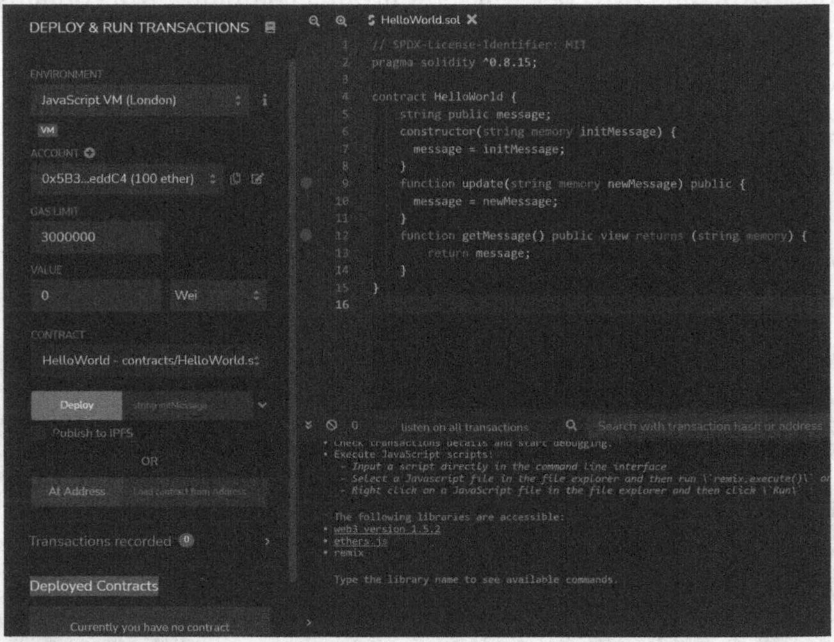

Figure 5-11. *HelloWorld contract deployment*

So far the contract hasn't been deployed yet. So, to deploy HelloWorld, we need to provide the string initMessage just beside the Deploy button.

We can leave Environment as default selected JavaScript VM, default selected account, Gas limit, and value. Let's enter Hello Solidity and click the Deploy button.

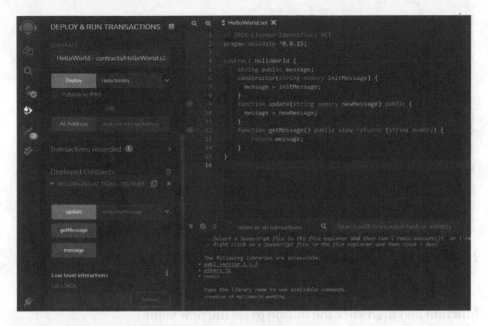

Figure 5-12. *Deployed HelloWorld contract*

The built-in terminal console shows deployment information. The default account amount was reduced by a small amount of gas fee, or a transaction fee, from 100.00000 ETH to 99.99999 ETH.

Under deployed contracts panel, you will see deployed HelloWorld contract with the contract address.

If you expand the deployed HelloWorld contract entry, it will show all contract items—state variables or functions—defined as *public* in your smart contract.

We can see the update, getMessage function, and message variables in our case.

When you click the message button, you should see "Hello Solidity" under the message button. The same thing happens when you click the getMessage button.

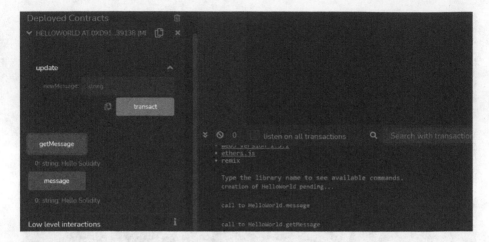

Figure 5-13. *Call HelloWorld contract message*

To change the message, enter "Hello Ethereum" for the update function and then click the button to set the new value.

You can validate that the message variable was updated by clicking on the getMessage function or message variable.

Figure 5-14. *Update HelloWorld contract message*

Congratulations! You have successfully written your very first Hello World smart contract in Solidity and deployed it to the blockchain. To learn more about Solidity, you can visit the Solidity Official Documentation (https://docs.soliditylang.org/en/v0.8.15/contracts.html).

Taking Control of Your First Ethereum Wallet

In Remix, when we use Injected Provider, Metamask is one of the most widely used wallet providers. MetaMask was founded in 2016 by Aaron Davis and Daniel Finlay and is currently owned by ConsenSys. As of March 2022, Metamask has over 30 million monthly active users. As a free browser extension for Chrome, Firefox, Brave, and Edge, MetaMask allows your regular browser to behave as a web3 browser for storing and exchanging cryptocurrencies, as well as interacting with Ethereum Dapps without running an Ethereum node. Simply put, MetaMask is a mobile crypto wallet you can access in your browser. To manage Metamask access, the user needs only a password and a 12-word recovery phrase, also known as a seed phrase. The seed phrase can be made up of any real words, such as dog, cat, or chicken.

If you forget or lose wallet recovery phrase, there is no way to recover your crypto wallet password. It is very important that you back up these seed phrase in a safe and secure place, maybe a hard disk, USB drive, or paper. Don't store it where it'll be vulnerable, like an email, online storage, etc.

MetaMask may not be the best place to store large amounts of crypto or valuable crypto assets, such as NFTs. When connecting to the mainnet for trading, use MetaMask as the only tab in that browser and avoid connecting to social media accounts in the same browser—some social media sites have plugins that can steal your data.

Install MetaMask from `https://metamask.io`. Then download the MetaMask wallet software onto your chosen browser. Select the "Create a Wallet" option, read the terms and conditions, and create a password. Once installed, you will see a fox on the top right of your browser. Open MetaMask, enable the test network, or testnet, by clicking Settings➤ Advanced ➤ Show test networks and select on button for "Select this to show test networks in network list." Transactions on a testnet are meant to only simulate mainnet transactions, or real blockchain transactions.

Figure 5-15. *Update Metamask setting for testnet*

Now you can switch to the Goerli test network from MetaMask's network list settings.

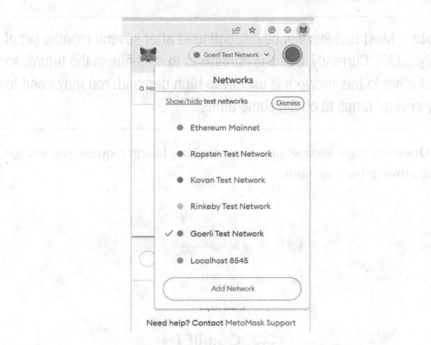

Figure 5-16. *Connect Metamask with Goerli test network*

You will see there is default account in account 1 without any ether.

We will get some free test ether from the Goerli test network. Copy account 1 Ethereum address and use one of Goerli Testnet Faucet to get the ether through your Ethereum account address:

> Official Goerli Testnet Faucet: `https://goerli-faucet.slock.it/`
>
> Starknet Faucet : `https://faucet.goerli.starknet.io/`
>
> Goerlifaucet: `https://goerlifaucet.com/`

> **Note**   Most testnets will be discontinued after several months (as of
> July 2022). Currently, Goerli is confirmed to continue in the future, so
> test ether in this network is usually in high demand. You may need to
> try several times to obtain some ether.

Once you have successfully submitted the faucet request, you will get
some ether in your account.

Figure 5-17. *Get ether from Goerli test network faucet*

With these Ethers, you have done all the hard work of bringing your
smart contract to life. Now it's time to share your first smart contract with
the world! Let's deploy our HelloWorld smart contract to the Goerli test
network from Remix.

In Remix, deploy and run the transaction module, select Injected Web3
environment. A popup from Metamask will ask to connect with Account
1 in Metamask in the Goerli test network.

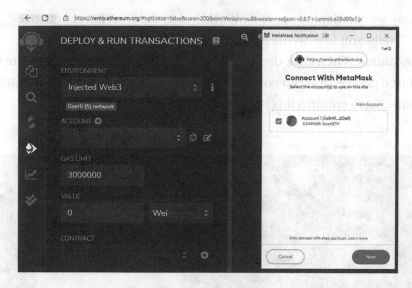

Figure 5-18. *Connect Remix to Goerli test network*

Click next and connect. It will connect remix IDE with Metamask in the Goerli test network. As shown in the following screenshot, you should see a green button showing a connected status.

Figure 5-19. *Connected Metamask Goerli test network*

Now we can deploy our HelloWorld.sol to the Goerli test network. Enter "Hello Solidity" as the initial message to the right of the orange deploy button. Then click deploy. Metamask will dynamically calculate the estimated gas fee. You can confirm or reject this request before submitting to testnet. Let's confirm this deployment transaction.

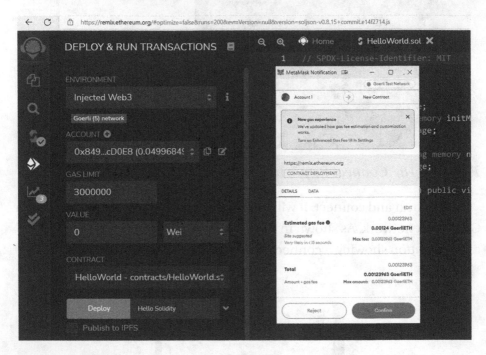

Figure 5-20. *Deploy contract to Goerli test network*

In the Remix console, you will see a block transaction confirmation message which returns the transaction hash and other transaction information. Here is the transaction hash: 0x7f773384290cff58ff6bb6e4f0411bfb625d3c1aa957208c6 e8b8abeeed9d710

Figure 5-21. *Deployed contract with transaction receipt*

In Metamask, we can see a new contract deployment information is displayed under the Active tab. Notice that the account ether value was deducted by the transaction gas fee. The original value is 0.05 ETH. Now it is 0.0487 ETH.

Figure 5-22. *Deployed contract with gas fee*

When you click Contract deployment, it will display details of deployment information.

Figure 5-23. *Contract deployment detail*

You can click the "View on the block explorer." The link will lead to the etherscan.io page and show this contract deployment detail. You can see that contract was deployed to address 0xe02cfad8b29d0aad478862facb2e6a9b1fed7bc9 (Note: it will display a different address number when you deploy it). This address is publicly accessible for everyone.

Now that you have deployed your first blockchain smart contract, the transaction hash matches the value we see in the Remix console. You can search the address from the etherscan search bar.

Figure 5-24. *Deployed contract in etherscan*

Great! You have published the HelloWorld contract in the Goerli test network, which is open to the public and accessible from anywhere. Next, let's build a simple Dapp to interact with our smart contract.

Decentralized Applications (Dapps)

Generally, a Dapp is a three-tier application comprised of three main components:

> **A front-end layer** – A web browser with web servers to host a web page.

> **Web3 Provider layer** – The middle layer between the frontend and the smart contracts, that is, Metamask wallet.

> **A backend (smart contract)** – Contracts run in the blockchain network.

209

Figure 5-25 shows a typical DApp layer architecture:

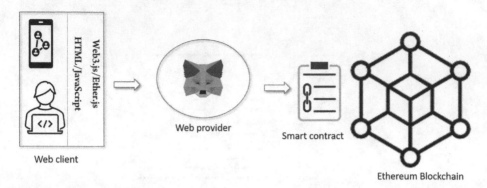

Figure 5-25. *Dapp layer architecture*

In the Ethereum client section, we use web3 API to query some blockchain information from the geth console. In this section, we will explore another Ethereum JavaScript Open source library—Ether.js, which also enables web clients to communicate and interact with the Ethereum network.

Getting Started

Before proceeding with this section, you need to install the following:

Installing node.js

Follow the node office installation guide, download and install node.js:

`https://nodejs.org/en/download/`

Installing Git

Follow the git office installation guide to install Git:

`https://git-scm.com/book/en/v2/Getting-Started-Installing-Git`

Git clone HelloWorld Dapp Project

Once you install node and Git, you need go to this book's Apress website, git clone chapter 5 HelloWorld Dapp source code:

```
git clone https://github.com/Apress/Blockchain-for-Teens.git
```

Install HelloWorld Dapp Project

Open terminal, navigate to helloworld project location. Run npm install

```
D:\>cd D:\documents\publish\Blockchain for Teens\helloworld

D:\documents\publish\Blockchain for Teens\helloworld>npm install
```

This will install node library needed to run Helloworld Dapp

The project structure should be similar to the one shown in Figure 5-26.

Figure 5-26. *Dapp project structure*

Note, the source code points to the Goerli test network contract address at:

0xe02cfad8b29d0aad478862facb2e6a9b1fed7bc9

You can use this address for testing or you modify this address to your own deployed contract address.

Open client.js, update line 3 of your own address. If you modified the contract and have different contract abi, replace line 4 with your own contract abi.

Run HelloWorld Dapp Project

Run the following command shown after the helloworld folder from terminal:

```
node index.js
```

This will bring up node server to host HelloWorld Dapp. The port number is 3000.

```
D:\documents\publish\Blockchain for Teens\helloworld>node index.js
Example app listening on port 3000
```

Figure 5-27. *Start Dapp node server*

Open HelloWorld Dapp from Browser

Now you can open Dapp from the browser by entering http://localhost:3000. You should see the HelloWorld Dapp page. You can see the top right corner has connect button, which will connect to Metamask. On the middle of the page, there is a blue message button that can be used to retrieve the blockchain message. The red update button with a Message input field will update contract message content.

212

Figure 5-28. *Dapp initial page*

Connect to Metamask

Ether.js use Web3Provider api to connect Metamask wallet:

`ethers.providers.Web3Provider(window.ethereum)`

Click the connect button. If you are not signed in, it will prompt you to sign in:

`await provider.send("eth_requestAccounts", []);`

Once connected, we can get user wallet, network, and account information from the provider. `provider.getSigner()` will get Ethereum Accounts from Metamask wallet. `provider.getNetwork()` returns current Ethereum Network that wallet connected.

Here is a snippet of the code:

```
/**
 * A Web3Provider wraps a standard Web3 provider, which is what MetaMask injects as window.ethereum into each page
 * @return
 */
async function connectToMetamask(){
        const provider = new ethers.providers.Web3Provider(window.ethereum, "any");
        // Prompt user for account connections
        await provider.send("eth_requestAccounts", []);
        const signer = provider.getSigner();
        const account = await signer.getAddress();
        const balanceInWei = await provider.getBalance(account);
        const balanceInEth= ethers.utils.formatEther(balanceInWei);
        const network = await provider.getNetwork();
        $('#network').text(network.name);
        $('#chainId').text(network.chainId);
        $('#accounts').text(account);
        $('#balance').text(balanceInEth + " ETH");
}
```

Since you are running Dapp for the first-time and are not connected to Metamask yet, the Dapp page connect button will be orange. So let's click the connect button to connect to Metamask. Once again, if you are not signed in, you will see a popup from Metamask asking you to sign in.

Figure 5-29. *Dapp connect to Metamask*

Login to Metamask. The page will automatically connect to Metamask and display related account and network information on the green display area across the top.

Figure 5-30. *Dapp connected to Metamask with blockchain data*

Get Contract and Call Get Message

In Remix smart contract compile and deployment, we have gotten abi and contract address information. Ether.js is provided below api to get contract information and you can use new ethers.Contract(contactAddress, abi, provider) API to get deployed contract instances.

```
function getContract() {
    const provider = new ethers.providers.Web3Provider(window.ethereum, "any");
    const signer = provider.getSigner();
    const contract = new ethers.Contract(contactAddress, abi, signer)
    return new ethers.Contract(contactAddress, abi, provider);
}
```

With ether contract object, you can start "call getMessag" function:

```
async function getMessage() {
    let message = await getContract().getMessage();
    $('#disPlayMessage').text(message);
}
```

You will get the Hello Solidity message from the Goerli test network:

Figure 5-31. *Dapp get First message*

Get Contract and Call Update Message

When you need to call state-changing methods, such as an update message, you must connect to the signer and pay a gas fee to send the state-changing transaction:

215

```
function getContractWithSigner() {
    const provider = new ethers.providers.Web3Provider(window.ethereum, "any");
    const signer = provider.getSigner();
    const contract = new ethers.Contract(contactAddress, abi, signer)
    return new ethers.Contract(contactAddress, abi, signer);
}
```

With the signer contract object, you can now pass input message to update contract:

```
async function updateMessage() {
  var messageInput = $('#messageInput').val();
  console.log(messageInput);
  const transaction = await getContractWithSigner().update(messageInput);
  const transactionReceipt = await transaction.wait();
  if (transactionReceipt.status !== 1) {
      alert('error message');
      return;
  } else {
      alert(JSON.stringify(transactionReceipt))
      await connectToMetamask();
  }
}
```

Let's update our message, enter "Hello Ethereum."

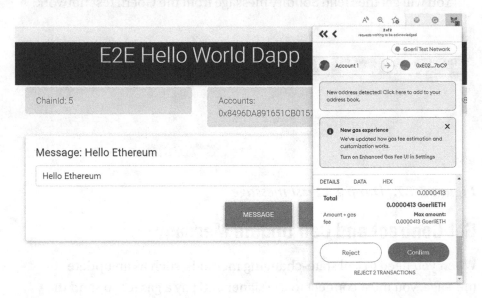

Figure 5-32. *Dapp update message*

Metamask will popup and ask to confirm transaction with an estimated gas fee. You review the transaction and submit. The block explorer allows you to view transactions.

Figure 5-33. *Dapp update message transaction detail*

Click view on block explorer to see your transaction in etherscan.

217

Figure 5-34. *Dapp update message transaction in etherscan*

Once the transaction is confirmed, you will get transaction receipt in page popup.

Figure 5-35. *Dapp with response transaction receipt*

Finally, verify your updated message by clicking the message button. "Hello Ethereum" should show on the page.

Figure 5-36. *Dapp verify updated message*

Congratulations, you have successfully published your first smart contract to the public testnet and built a Dapp to call and update the message content! You have now completed an end-to-end Dapp development cycle, which is a huge accomplishment. Pat yourself on the back, because that was a lot of work.

Despite the fact that we have spent enough time exploring Ethereum Dapp and Solidity principles to get you to build a Dapp, this book only provides a basic introduction. There are a lot of good online documentation covering all aspects of Javascript, JQuery, express.js, and ether.js.

Here are some useful links:

ether.js: the document can be found at `https://docs.ethers.io/v5/`

JQuery: the document can be found at `https://jquery.com/`

express.js: the document can be found at `https://expressjs.com/en/starter/hello-world.html`

Node.js: he document can be found at `https://nodejs.org/en/docs/guides/getting-started-guide/`

Tokens Standard

In Chapter 1, we learned Mohammad Bin Tughlaq invented token money—Tanka, which used copper currency to represent the same value as a silver coin. In a blockchain, the coin represents the native currency. For instance, ether is the coin in Ethereum. And a token is created by a smart contract, which defines basic token properties, then builds and operates.

A crypto token is a virtual currency token representing programmable assets or shared ownership with access rights to an entity with a specific value. The token is managed by a smart contract, which allows for the efficient and secure purchase or sale of an item such as an art collection, the exchange of token ownership, the transfer of token balance, the storage of token value, and the verification of transactions on the blockchain.

To assist developers in standardizing token creation, the Ethereum community has developed many token standards through the Ethereum Improvement Proposal (EIP) process.

EIPs contain standard technical specifications for potential new Ethereum features or processes, including core protocol specifications, improvements, client APIs, and contract standards. It acts as the "source of truth" for the community. Anyone can create an EIP by following standards guidelines in the EIP-1, published in 2015 (`https://eips.ethereum.org/EIPS/eip-1`). As stated in EIP-1, Ethereum Request for Comment (ERC) is the application-level standards and conventions. If the specific ERC is approved in the Ethereum community, it becomes a new token standard rule which will be outlined in the document through a related smart contract.

There are many token standards, including:

> Standards of token (ERC-20, ERC-721, ERC-1155, ERC-777)
>
> Name registries (ERC-26, ERC-137)

URI schemes (ERC-67)

Library/packet formats (EIP-82)

Wallet formats (EIP-75, EIP-85)

There are many other tokens still in draft and review status. You can check all token ERC through this link: `https://eips.ethereum.org/erc`

Let's take a look at the two most popular ERC standards, ERC-20 and ERC-721.

ERC-20

ERC-20 is the most popular Ethereum token standard and was proposed on November 19, 2015 by Fabian Vogelsteller. Most ICOs (Initial Coin Offering) that have issued their tokens on the Ethereum platform or EVM-based blockchain (like Binance) are ERC-20 tokens. The ICO is cryptocurrency version of the IPO (initial public offering), which is used in the stock market to raise capital or participate in investment opportunities. There are around 508k ERC-20 tokens in the Ethereum mainnet on March 2022. The total market cap of all ERC-20 tokens is around $18.7 billion, and there are more than 160K ERC-20 in Binance.

20 is a unique identification number to distinguish the ERC-20 standard from others.

The ERC-20 token has several optional fields such as name and symbol and defines the following rules in the smart contract:

```
contract ERC20Interface {
    function totalSupply() public view returns (uint);
    function balanceOf(address tokenOwner) public view returns
    (uint balance);
    function allowance(address tokenOwner, address spender)
    public view returns (uint remaining);
```

```
function transfer(address to, uint tokens) public returns
(bool success);
function approve(address spender, uint tokens) public
returns (bool success);
function transferFrom(address from, address to, uint
tokens) public returns (bool success);

event Transfer(address indexed from, address indexed to,
uint tokens);
event Approval(address indexed tokenOwner, address indexed
spender, uint tokens);
}
```

totalSupply(): Gets the total number of token supply.

balanceOf(): Gets the account balance for the specified address.

allowance(): Returns the amount of tokens which the spender is allowed to withdraw from the owner.

transfer(): Transfer the balance from the owner's account to another specified address and must fire the transfer event.

transferFrom (): Send the amount of tokens from address `from` to address `to`. The transferFrom method is used for a withdraw workflow, allowing contracts to transfer tokens on your behalf.

approve(): Allows spender to withdraw the specified amount of tokens from your account multiple times.

If you ever find yourself working on a project that requires creating and deploying an ERC-20 token, you can create a smart contract by implementing these ERC-20 functions. Here is a simple example:

```
MyToken is ERC20 {

// implement the functions required by ERC20 interface standard
// other functions...
}
```

In Etherscan, you can find many ERC-20-compliant tokens that have been deployed mainnet. Here is a real-world example of an ERC-20 token transaction on the Etherscan.

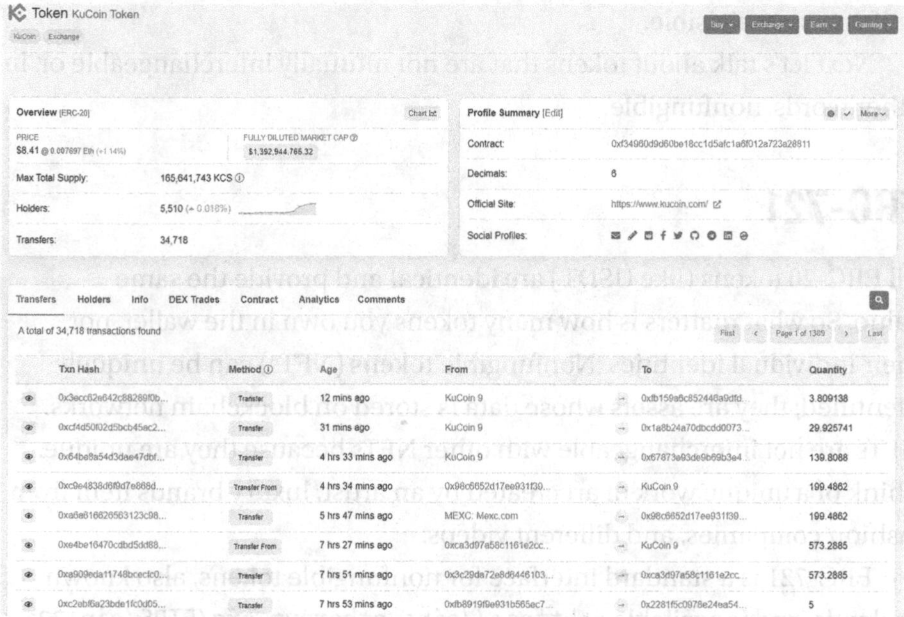

Figure 5-37. *ERC-20 example*

The screenshot shows the amount of ERC-20 tokens being transferred from one address to another address by the transfer or transferFrom method.

In ERC-20 token, tokens are fungible, meaning that each token has exactly the same type and value as another token. If you swap one ERC-20 for another, there will be no difference in authenticity or value; they are interchangeable and represent a single entity.

For example, Tether (USDT) is an ERC-20 Token. It is a stablecoin—a crypto asset value pegged to the US dollar at a 1 to 1 ratio and 100% backed by Tether's equivalent reserves. These reserves are a mix of assets, including cash. USDT is similar to the ETH, meaning that 1 Token is and will always be equal to all the other USDT Tokens. They are the same type, represent the US dollar, and are mutually interchangeable. USDT is also divisible, which can be broken down into smaller units like cents.

So fungible tokens have the following properties: interchangeable, uniform, and divisible.

Next let's talk about tokens that are not mutually interchangeable or, in other words, nonfungible.

ERC-721

All ERC-20 tokens (like USDT) are identical and provide the same value. So what matters is how many tokens you own in the wallet, not their individual identities. Nonfungible tokens (NFTs) can be uniquely identified; they are assets whose data is stored on blockchain networks. NFTs are not interchangeable with other NFTs because they are unique. Think of a unique work of art created by an artist, luxury brands item from fashion companies, and different videos.

ERC-721 is a standard interface for nonfungible tokens, also known as deeds, and is available at https://eips.ethereum.org/EIPS/eip-721. The proposal for the creation of this new standard was created in Jan 2018, proposed by William Entriken, Dieter Shirley, Jacob Evans, and Nastassia Sachs. According to a Bloomberg report, NFT Market surpassed $40 Billion in 2021 and over $37 billion in NFT marketplaces in 2022 on May 1.

Similar to the ERC-20 token standard, the ERC-721 specification provides details and defines functions and events that a derived contract should implement to develop an NFT, shown in the following code block:

```
interface ERC721 {
    event Transfer(address indexed _from, address indexed _to,
    uint256 indexed _tokenId);
    event Approval(address indexed _owner, address indexed _
    approved, uint256 indexed _tokenId);
```

```
    event ApprovalForAll(address indexed _owner, address
    indexed _operator, bool _approved);
    function balanceOf(address _owner) external view returns
    (uint256);
    function ownerOf(uint256 _tokenId) external view returns
    (address);
    function safeTransferFrom(address _from, address _to,
    uint256 _tokenId, bytes data) external payable;
    function safeTransferFrom(address _from, address _to,
    uint256 _tokenId) external payable;
    function transferFrom(address _from, address _to, uint256
    _tokenId) external payable;
    function approve(address _approved, uint256 _tokenId)
    external payable;
    function setApprovalForAll(address _operator, bool _
    approved) external;
    function getApproved(uint256 _tokenId) external view
    returns (address);
    function isApprovedForAll(address _owner, address _
    operator) external view returns (bool);
}
balanceOf: Gets the account balance for the specified address.
```

ownerOf: The function returns the unique address of the owner of a token based on the provided tokenId.

safeTransferFrom: Transfers the ownership of an NFT from one address to another address. It is required that msg.sender is the current owner, an authorized operator, or the approved address for this NFT.

transferFrom (): Send the amount of tokens from address `from` to address `to`. The transferFrom method is used for a withdraw workflow, allowing contracts to transfer tokens on your behalf.

approve(): Allows spender to withdraw the specified amount of tokens from your account multiple times.

setApprovalForAll: Assign or revoke approval rights for the given operator to manage all of `msg.sender`'s assets.

getApproved: Get the approved address for a single NFT

isApprovedForAll: Check if the given operator address has access right to operate for the given owner's tokens.

The most known example of ERC-721 is the CryptoKitties game, the first NFT token. In the game, there are thousands of CryptoKittie. Each cat has their own profile, which includes unique genes, name, color, shape, price, and other profiles. The game player can collect and breed adorable kittens. As shown in Figure 5-38, each cryptoKittie as a collectible digital asset can be traded, sold, and bought by the player:

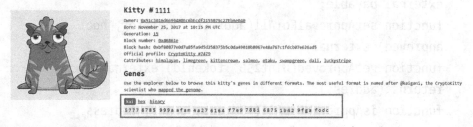

Figure 5-38. *ERC-721 CryptoKitties example*

We can find CryptoKittie in etherscan. These tokens are bid and trade daily by game player. Some individual cryptokitties have sold for more than $300,000 a piece.

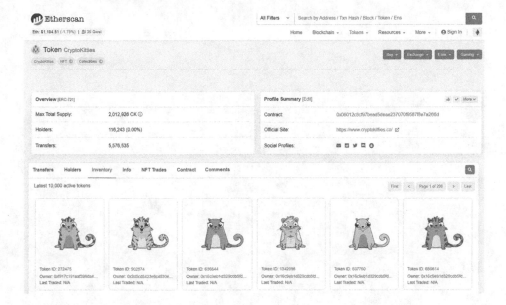

Figure 5-39. *ERC-721 CryptoKitties in Etherscan*

NFT collectibles market continues to grow as fan engagement increases, which will likely increase mainstream adoption. NFTs can have only one owner at a time. True ownership is one of the key characteristics of any NFT, and it has the potential to play a critical role in bringing the digital and physical worlds closer together than they have ever been.

Summary

You have written your first smart contract through Remix IDE, and deployed HelloWorld Solidity file to the Goerli test network. We demonstrated the basics of Dapp and web3.js and how Dapp interacts with smart contract by connecting with Metamask wallet.

But our journey doesn't end here—in the next chapter, we will cover more exciting details on the NFT.

CHAPTER 6

NFT: Crypto As Collectibles

The term "NFT" has amassed popularity on social media and has been discussed in major news and journals. But what exactly is an NFT, and why is it important? Why are NFTs so valuable?

In this chapter, we will address those and even give you a tutorial on how to create your very own NFT.

In this chapter, we cover the following specific topics on NFTs:

- What is an NFT?

- Fungible vs. nonfungible

- A brief history of NFTs

- Applications of NFTs

- Examples of NFTs

- Selling points of NFTs

- Creating your own NFT

- NFT market place

- The future of NFT

© Brian Wu and Bridget Wu 2023
B. Wu and B. Wu, *Blockchain for Teens*, https://doi.org/10.1007/978-1-4842-8808-5_6

What Is an NFT?

NFT stands for "nonfungible token." It represents ownership of unique items and cannot be replicated on a blockchain. In Chapter 5, we introduced ERC-721 token standard. The initial ERC-721 specification was proposed by Dieter Shirley, William Entriken, Jacob Evans, and Nastassia Sachs in January 2018 as an Ethereum Improvement Proposal (EIP) for the Ethereum network. It defines the standard smart contracts interface, which can represent real-world items from digital collectibles to music, artwork, sports, and many other real-world assets.

When you acquire ownership of an NFT, you don't get physical copy of the NFT. In fact, if the NFT is a form of media, anyone can still get a copy of it. But the important thing is that a smart contract is created to verify the buyer's ownership of an NFT. Anyone can see transaction and contract history for NFTs on the Ethereum network, similar to how cryptocurrency transactions can be viewed and traced by anyone.

The NFT itself, however, is typically not stored in the blockchain. The owner, hash, token name and symbol, and link to file are stored in blockchain. So, although anyone can make a copy of the NFT, that does not mean they will own or have rights to it. But it is important that the buyer is not always granted all rights to the NFT. The creator may keep copyright and licensing rights, and can earn royalties from resells of the NFT, as well as choose to sell multiple replicas of an NFT.

Fungible vs. Nonfungible

In economics, fungibility refers to something that is easy to exchange or trade and cannot be distinguished from another. Before a good or a commodity can be traded or exchanged, it must be fungible. For example, the US dollar is fungible. Therefore, a person holding one bill can exchange it for another bill without changing its stored value.

Every $1 bill has the same value, uniform, and usability as another quantity of the bill. Divisibility is another essential feature of fungibility, and it refers to the property of a good or a commodity that can be broken into smaller units without losing value. Just like a $10 bill can purchase the same amount of goods as two $5 bills or ten $1 bills. In the blockchain, Bitcoin (BTC), Ether (ETH), and many other cryptocurrency units have the same highly divisible. One Bitcoin should carry the same purchasing value as a medium to buy or sell goods regardless of whether it is split into fractions of one, two, or ten UTXOs. Most daily transactions will cost less than one Bitcoin, and divisibility will make cryptocurrency easier to exchange for other like items.

In the previous chapter, we learned about ERC-20, which introduces a standard way to create fungible tokens. ERC-20 defines an interface with a property, and each token can be exchanged the same (in type and value) as another token. Some popular examples are Tether Tether (USDT), USD Coin (USDC), Shiba Inu (SHIB), and Wrapped Bitcoin (WBTC).

In contrast, nonfungible assets are unique and not interchangeable assets that a person or group owns, like art, car, book, real estate, diamonds, copyright, collectible, and game items.

If a lender lends a borrower his house, it is not acceptable for a borrower to return to a different house and have the same ownership, even if both houses have the same market value. Each house has its own uniqueness. The value is judged across multiple complex criteria, including location, home size, usable space, neighborhood, and sold history.

In addition, nonfungible assets are not divisible and cannot be broken up and sold in multiple pieces. The whole of the item determines the value of a nonfungible asset. In the blockchain, a non-fungible token (NFT) is a unique digital asset representing real-world items. People can buy and sell NFT from marketplace based on the value they believe in. Every NFT has a unique digital signature stored in an NFT smart contract, which provides proof of ownership to ensure they cannot be duplicated or destroyed in the blockchain. The blockchain will keep track of ownership of the NFT assets.

Table 6-1 shows the differences between fungible and nonfungible tokens.

Table 6-1. *Comparing fungible and nonfungible*

	Fungible token	Nonfungible token
Interchangeable	Fungibles are interchangeable. A token can be exchanged with any other token of the same type. A person holding one bill can exchange it for another bill without changing its stored value. One Bitcoin value can be exchanged with other Bitcoin, which makes no difference for holders.	Nonfungibles are not interchangeable. A token cannot be replaced with any other token of the same type. If a lender lends a borrower his house, it is not acceptable for a borrower to return to a different house.
Uniform	Fungible tokens are uniform and have the same properties and are non-unique	Each token is unique and different from all other tokens of the same type.
Divisible	Fungible tokens are divisible and can be broken down into smaller units as long as the value remains the same. For example, one Bitcoin is divided into units as small as 0.00000001 BTC. One Ether can be divisible up to 18 decimal places.	Nonfungible tokens can't be divided, and each token has its own value. NFT assets on a blockchain are cryptographically unique identification codes and metadata, which provide proof of ownership to ensure they cannot be duplicated or destroyed.

(continued)

Table 6-1. (*continued*)

	Fungible token	Nonfungible token
EIP standard and example of tokens	Well-known EIP for Fungible token standard is ERC-20. Some popular examples are Tether Tether (USDT), USD Coin (USDC), Shiba Inu (SHIB), and Wrapped Bitcoin (WBTC). Blockchain native cryptocurrencies such as Bitcoin (BTC) and Ether (ETH) are fungible tokens.	ERC-721 is a nonfungible token standard. Some popular examples are artwork, cars, books, domain names, real estate, diamonds, copyright, collectible, and game items.

A Brief History of NFTs

On December 4, 2021, a paper published by Meni Rosenfield introduced the concept of "Colored Coins." The paper described colored coins as a Bitcoin but with a mark that allows people to prove ownership of and manage real-world assets.

On May 3, 2014, Kevin McCoy created the first known "NFT," which was known as Quantum. The artwork features an animation of a pulsing octagon that changes colors. In June 2021, Quantum was sold for $1.47 million at that time; NFTs were referred to as "monetized graphics."

In October 2015, the first NFT project built on Ethereum is launched at the DEVCON 1 conference, which was three months after the Ethereum network was launched. Players can make real money from the virtual world.

In September 2016, the first Rare Pepes were being sold and traded on Counterparty. Pepe the Frog is a character that became a popular meme across the Internet.

In 2017, one of the most successful NFT collections of all time was launched by the Larva Labs studio. Each CryptoPunk is a 24x24 size and pixel-art image that was generated by an algorithm, with a total of 10,000 CryptoPunks minted.

On November 28, 2017, CryptoKitties was launched. CryptoKitties is a virtual game that allows players to buy, breed, and trade cats.

From 2018 to 2020, Decentraland became increasingly influential in both the Metaverse and NFT industries. Decentraland is a virtual world where users can buy parcels of land. After users own a plot of land, they can lease it out to other people or do whatever they want with the virtual environment, such as build structures in the land. The platform was launched in 2017, but was opened to the public on February 20, 2020.

In 2020, NBA Top Shot launched, which is a marketplace for users to buy highlights and videos of NBA moments and players. Each moment is minted in a "pack," similar to a trading card set. When users buy a Top Shot NFT, they gain access to Top Shot challenges and can win prizes and other items from the marketplace.

In 2021, the most expensive NFT to date was sold. Mike Winkelmann, a digital artist known as Beeple, sold an NFT artwork file titled "EVERYDAYS: The first 5,000 days" for $69.3 million. It was sold at Christie's, a major auction house that deals with NFTs, making it the first digital artwork to be sold at a major auction house.

On April 22, 2022, RTFKT and Nike announced Nike Cryptokicks, which is a set of sneakers. RTFKT later released a set of skins that could upgrade the Nike Dunk Genesis and give them customizations.

Applications of NFTs

NFTs are very versatile. Generally, they can come in many different forms and be used for many different purposes, hence why NFTs are growing in popularity and creators are finding increasing uses for NFTs. Here are some possible ways to use NFTs.

Images

Most NFTs come in the form of still images which can be photographs or works of art. There are some NFT marketplaces that limit the size of the file that is being minted, but most of the time it is better to provide a higher-resolution image. There are two main types of images: raster, or bitmap images and vector graphics. Raster images are composed of pixels and support more depth of color than vector graphics, but lose their image quality as they are scaled up. On the other hand, vector graphics use equations to draw lines, curves, and points to create the photo, allowing the photo to scale without losing image quality.

Here are some examples of NFT images:

- "Everydays: The First 5000 Days" by Beeple is a collage of the first 5000 vector images and gifs created by Beeple for his Everydays series. The piece was sold for $69 million in Christie's, a major auction house.

- "Doge" is a picture of a Shiba Inu dog that became popular across the Internet and became easily recognizable. The "Doge" picture was sold for $4 million.

Videos

NFTs can come in the form of videos, which are often very popular. YouTube is an established platform for uploading videos and allows its users to sell their videos as NFTs. Other popular places to look for NFT videos are NFT marketplaces, where users directly upload their files. The benefit of having video NFTs is that they can have audio, animation, and videos with very high quality and resolution.

Here are some examples of NFT videos:

- CROSSROAD by Beeple is a 10-second video that was originally bought for $67,000 and was resold 5 months later for $6.6 million.

- "Earth" and "Mars" by Grimes are both short videos that were sold for $7500 per video. In total, almost 700 videos were sold, generating $5.18 million in 2 days.

- "Auction Winner Picks the Name" by 3LAU created an auction of an NFT music video before it was created. The winner of the auction brought the opportunity to name the music video for $1.33 million.

- "Charlie Bit Me" by Davies-Carr Family was a YouTube video from 2010 that was bought by 3F music for $760,999.

- "Lebron James 'Cosmic' Dunk" by NBA Top Shot was the largest sale on the NBA Top Shot marketplace. The video was bought for $387,600.

GIFs

Graphic Interchange Format, or GIF, is a type of file format that is used to create a short video that loops. The way GIFs work is that multiple images are stored in one file, allowing animations or still images—however, people prefer to use other file formats for still images like PNG and JPEG. A benefit of using GIFs is that unlike videos, which are displayed with a thumbnail and play button, GIFs automatically play and loop. GIFs are also easy to create and can play in most browsers.

However, GIFs have existed since 1987 and do have some outdated properties. GIFs only support 256 colors and do not support audio. They also have larger file sizes, so many GIFs are usually only a few seconds, have a low frame rate (how many images are shown per second), or have small dimensions.

Here are some examples of NFT GIFs:

- Nyan Cat by Chris Torres is a GIF of a cat that became widely recognized across the Internet. The original creator of the GIF sold the NFT for 300 ETH, or $583,464 on Foundation.

- Finite by Pak is a GIF of a spiraling coil that was sold for 444 ETH, which was $864,507 when the piece was sold on Foundation.

- War Haul by Jake is a GIF of barrels of oil being set on fire that was sold for 69 ETH, or $223,627 on SuperRare.

- Lova Park by OSF is a GIF of an amusement park where a roller coaster passes through a Ferris Wheel. The GIF was sold for 82 ETH, or $267,878 on SuperRare.

- Welcome Home Coldie is a GIF of a man moving on a color-changing path toward a sign that says "Welcome." The piece was sold for 75 ETH, or $242,761 on SuperRare. This is the first time the NFT GIF piece was sold, it sold for only 6 ETH.

Audio

Many music artists have found success in selling music NFTs. Major and independent artists have posted their works as NFTs to sell their music and attract new audiences. Different audio types include .mp3 files and .wav. In some marketplaces like OpenSea, audio NFTs require a preview image or GIF.

Here are some examples of NFT music artists:

- Grimes has sold around $5.8 million in NFTs. Her main success came from selling thousands of copies of two short videos with music called "Earth" and "Mars," as well as a video titled "Death of the Old" for $389,000.

- Steve Aoki said he has made more profit in one year from selling NFTs than streaming royalties for decade. Through selling NFT collections, he has made millions.

- Kings of Leon was a band that made over $2 million by selling tickets that gave their buyers front-row seats. They sold an album titled *When You See Yourself* as a collection of NFTs.

Digital Real Estate

Virtual property is a sector that will most likely grow in the future as the Metaverse becomes increasingly popular. Players can purchase property in a virtual world for them to "live" in or to sell at a greater profit later. NFTs make keeping track of the ownership of the virtual land simple and also prevent the need for a middleman—the buyer can directly buy the property from the marketplace. The record of purchase and information about the land will automatically be included in the blockchain instead of an office or paper document.

Here are some examples of NFT real estate:

- Sandbox is a virtual world where players can use building blocks to customize their gaming experience. Users can have complete control over their experience and can add assets on their land.

- Mars House by Krista Kim was sold for 288 Ether, or $514,557 at the time of selling. The home is completely virtual and is designed to be visited in the Metaverse.

Trading Cards

Trading cards have always been a physical phenomenon, but they have been gaining popularity in the world of NFTs. Storing the trading card as an NFT makes it easier to exchange cards and proves the authenticity of the card. Often, trading cards have no intrinsic value and most of their success comes from scarcity and a desire to collect.

Here are some examples of NFT trading cards:

- Gods Unchained is a blockchain-based multiplayer game that uses decks of trading cards. Players can earn in-game items as NFTs and sell them for real-world cash.

- Curio Cards is a set of 30 trading cards. Each card has a varied amount of supply, but the total amount of cards minted was 29,700.

- Candy Digital is an NFT platform where players can trade and collect official Major League Baseball NFTs. The platform also includes signatures, jerseys, images, video content, and other exclusive items.

Video Game Items

Many video games let players to collect in-game items, such as equipment, consumables, and skins, to customize their experience and progress in the game. However, earning items may be time-consuming or difficult, which is why when game developers give players the option to purchase their gear, they often make large amounts of profit.

Listing these in-game items as an NFT can help developers and players keep track of an item's status and properties. This is especially beneficial because the owner can prove the item's authenticity and the buyer can show their ownership. Creating in-game items as NFTs can also help players sell their items once they no longer need or want the item. It also eliminates the need for a secondary market, which often has scammers and may not always be allowed in the game.

Here are some examples of NFT video game items:

- Genesis Land Plots from Axie Infinity includes digital land in the game. 9 plots of land were bought for $1.5 million USD.

- Dragon Kitty from Crypto Kitties is one of the unique Kitties available in the pet breeding game. The pet was sold for 600 Ethereum, or around $1.3 million USD.

- Mobile Legends is a mobile game that launched an NFT collection called The Aspirants Mystery Box. The collection has 12 boxes, and each box has a digital figure and animations of in-game characters.

- Summoners Aerna is an MMORPG built on a blockchain. The heroes and in-game items are all NFTs.

Fashion

Individual designers and large brands alike have found interest in fashion NFTs. There has even been a Crypto Fashion Week and a Metaverse Fashion Week with virtual collections and digital clothing items. NFT fashion items can include wearables that users can wear in virtual environments or digital avatars, or digital models of physical fashion items.

Here are some examples of NFT fashion:

- Balmain x Barbie collaboration by Balmain and Barbie featured three dolls with pink garments. Purchasing a Barbie avatar gives the buyer ownership of the avatar and a real-life Barbie-sized outfit.

- MANGO is a fashion group that created three NFTs for the Metaverse Fashion Week in Decentraland. The collection was displayed in a virtual space and uploaded to OpenSea but was not made for sale.

3D Models

3D models can be designs or representations of abstract or real-world objects. The 3D model itself can be viewed, rotated, moved, and interacted with on a screen or with virtual or augmented reality headsets. The model itself can also be printed out with a 3D printer. 3D models are important to industries such as virtual and augmented reality, medicine, engineering, video games, scientific imaging, architecture, movies, advertising, and illustration.

Text

Text, such as ones in books, poems, articles, and quotes, has been branded and sold as NFTs.

Here are some examples of NFT text:

- "Source Code for the WWW" by Sir Tim Berners-Lee is 9,555 lines of code that created the original World Wide Web that was sold for $5.4 million USD.

- "Buy This Column on the Blockchain!" by Kevin Roose is an article about NFTs that was auctioned off as an NFT itself. The article was sold for around $560,000 at the auction.

Domain Names

A blockchain domain is an address you can purchase and own to allow someone to send crypto to an easy-to-remember address. For example, a typical Bitcoin address has 34 characters and an Ethereum address has 42, so addresses may look something like ac1qw508d6qejxtdg4y5r3zarvary0c5xw7kv8f3t4. Buying a blockchain domain allows users to simplify their address to example.crypto and will be easier to remember. And unlike website domains such as .com and .org, blockchain domains do not require an annual renewal fee to be paid.

Now that we have covered the different usages of NFTs, let us review the highlights of each application of NFT in Table 6-2.

Table 6-2. *Comparing different applications of NFT*

Application	Summary
Image	• Images have no motion • Can be photographs or art • Raster vs. vector graphics
Video	• Can have audio and animation • Can be very high resolution
GIFs	• Sequence of images • Automatically loops • Large file sizes
Audio	• Sometimes requires a preview image
3D models	• Can be viewed on a 2D screen or headsets • Can be interacted with • Essential to many industries
Text	• Examples include books, poems, articles, and quotes
Domain names	• Allows users to simplify their blockchain domain • Does not require a renewal fee
Real estate	• Virtual property can increase in value • Advantages over traditional real estate practices
Trading cards	• Easy to trade as NFTs • Collected because of market value
Video-game items	• Help developers and players keep track of items • Allows players to easily resell items
Fashion	• Can be virtual or have real-life value • Can be more useful in the future as the virtual world expands

Examples of NFTs

There have been many successful stories when it comes to NFTs. Here are some of the most iconic NFTs that have been sold:

Bored Ape Yacht Club (BAYC)

Yuga Labs, a blockchain technology company, created a collection of 10,000 NFTs of "Bored Apes." The most expensive unit, Bored Ape #2087, was sold for 769 ETH, or about $2.3 million. Owning a Bored Ape gives members exclusive benefits such as community events, a members-only Discord server, a graffiti board called "The Bathroom," airdrops, and more. Owners of Bored Ape NFTs can even rent out their NFT to an NFT museum or use it for high returns. Many celebrities have demonstrated interest in the BAYC.

William Shatner's Memorabilia

William Shatner sold items from his 60-year acting career as an NFT collection. 125,000 units sold out in just 9 minutes, which included headshots of himself, a photo of Shatner hugging fellow Star Trek actor Leonard Nimoy, and an X-ray of his teeth.

Grimes WarNymph

Grimes, a singer and songwriter, sold a video called "Death of the Old" for $389,000, which was part of a collection of 10 NFTs. In total, he made $5.8 million selling the collection.

Nyan Cat

Chris Torres sold the original Nyan Cat GIF in an online auction for 300 ETH (around $600,000 at the time) in February 2021. The creator said he was "very surprised with the success," but also "glad knowing that [he's] basically opened the door to a whole new meme economy in the crypto world."

Twitter CEO's First Tweet

Jack Dorsey, the co-founder of Twitter, sold his first tweet from Twitter's launch in March 2006 as an NFT for $2.9 million. Dorsey converted the money to Bitcoin then donated to the GiveDirectly charity organization.

NBA Top Shot

Top Shot is an NFT marketplace where users can trade and purchase videos of NBA highlights. NBA Top Shot sales were valued at over $338 million in October 2020. Currently, the most valuable asset on Top Shot is a video of LeBron James dunking against the Houston Rockets that was sold for $387,000.

RTFKT sneakers

RTFKT creates virtual sneakers for online gaming avatars that sell up to $10,000 a pair. In March 2021, RTFKT collaborated with an artist Fewocious to produce a series of sneakers that earned him $3.1 million in several minutes.

Taco Bell GIFs

Taco Bell, a fast food corporation, sold a series of GIFs based on food items from their menu as NFTs. After minutes, the GIFs sold out and Taco Bell proceeded to donate all of the earnings to the Taco Bell Foundation, which is their charity organization.

Reddit NFT avatars

Reddit, an online social platform where users can create posts and message each other, is inviting artists to create NFTs avatars. These NFTs are then sold on the official website for amounts from 15 to $100, and users can use these NFTs as their avatars.

The NFT Magazine

There is a project called the NFT Magazine by the Cryptonomist that allows people to read about different insights into the Crypto world, including important people, market trends, and advice on where to invest. However, to access the magazine, users must collect NFT magazine covers.

Selling Points of NFTs

Although some NFTs have no intrinsic value, NFTs do offer many advantages that non-NFTs cannot provide. The success of NFTs can be attributed to many factors, some of which include the following:

Scarcity

A creator can mint a limited number of NFTs, which will bring up the value of individual assets and make people more willing to buy. The number of copies available is also public. Combined with a favorable reputation of the creator and high market demand for a certain NFT, NFTs can fetch market prices of over millions.

Authenticity

The unique digital signature allows anyone to verify the originality of the NFT and prevents forgery, which is a common problem when it comes to physical art. It also helps the buyer avoid scams because it is easy to see who created the NFT, and the owner does not have to worry about proving whether they made the work or not.

Easy to Use with Cryptocurrency

NFTs can be easily traded with cryptocurrency integration because NFTs exist on a blockchain. The most popular cryptocurrency by far is ETH on the Ethereum network, but SOL crypto on the Solana network and ADA on the Cardano network.

Ownership

NFTs make it easy to change ownership. It is also possible to share ownership of NFTs, which is called "fractional ownership." Ownerships are also listed as public records, so there is no need for a middleman or physical document to prove an ownership.

Permanence

NFTs do not have limitations that physical items have and do not degrade over time. Physical items are subjected to ultraviolet radiation from the sun, accumulation of dust, damage from humidity, rust in the case of metal, and rough handling or other accidents. However, the owner of an NFT can permanently destroy the NFT if they want to, which is called burning.

Efficiency

Using a digital asset eliminates third parties. The buyer and seller can directly interact with each other without the need for a middleman. This can help save time, prevent miscommunication, and help businesses track where their products are reaching.

Royalties

After selling NFTs, the original artist can receive a share of the profit whenever their art is resold. This is a large improvement from current practices in the art and music industry, where many companies, streaming services, and other middlemen reap a large portion of profits. NFTs allow creators to have full control over their own work and manage their sales.

Cheap to Create

While gas fees may be high depending on the blockchain—notably Ethereum gas fees—minting an NFT can be free or only require several dollars. Solana, Tezos, Avalanche, WAX are cheaper blockchains and Polygon allows the user to create an NFT for free.

Creating Your Own NFT

Getting started with your first NFT may seem daunting, but the options are endless. Many associate NFTs with only digital art, but you can mint anything that's digital—from music to trading cards to memes to videos to tweets—as an NFT. Of course, it's important to remember to abide by all ownership and copyright laws. Creating your own work and using that as an NFT will prevent you from getting into legal complications and attract supporters.

A recommendation would be to start a collection. Making a collection can help you gain experience and can also help generate interest in traders. In the end though, no matter what you choose to create as an NFT, make it your own unique style.

Be aware, however, that just because some people have met astounding success when dealing with NFTs, does not mean that anyone who creates an NFT will instantly generate millions. Analyze the market to see what is popular and what gets ignored. Also note that minting an NFT requires you to pay for service and gas fees. And be sure to price your NFTs fairly—sometimes, NFT are sold at a low value and the buyer will resell the NFT for a significantly higher price.

Now, onto the actual process. If you haven't already, setup a crypto wallet and create an account. Popular options to download include MetaMask, WalletConnect, and Rainbow. Setting up a crypto wallet is free, but you should know the different types of wallets available. There are hosted wallets and self-custody wallets. Hosted wallets are managed by a third party, similar to a bank. While there may be less functions related to managing cryptocurrency, your money will be more secure. Self-custody wallets, on the other hand, give the user complete control over their wallet, but is less secure. The best option depends on what you are looking to use your wallet for, but for minting and trading NFTs, a hosted wallet is better.

No matter which option you choose, keep your password key safe— if you lose this key, you will lose access to your crypto assets. We also recommend purchasing a hardware or physical wallet.

It is also important to note that different types of blockchains use different crypto wallets. The top blockchain for crypto is Ethereum as of 2022, but Binance, Smart Chain, and Polkadot are becoming more popular.

Then, buy a form of cryptocurrency from a reputable trading platform, such as CoinBase or Gemini. ETH is the most popular cryptocurrency for NFT purchases, but SOL and XTZ are also notable options.

After your wallet is set up, sign up on an NFT marketplace, such as OpenSea, and connect your cryptocurrency wallet to your account. If you need a walk-through setting up a wallet, you can refer back to Chapter 5 to set up a MetaMask wallet. We will cover different marketplaces in the next section.

Now, you can upload your digital files and sell them either for a fixed amount or in an auction. Once they are moderated and approved, they will be listed for sale and buyers will be able to purchase the NFT. When a purchase is made or the auction concludes, the NFT owner will receive the top bid.

Now that you know the general procedure, let us go through the steps:

First, go to testnets.opensea.io. Note that we are using a testnet for our demo. Click on the create button.

Then, connect your wallet. We will be using MetaMask for our walk-through:

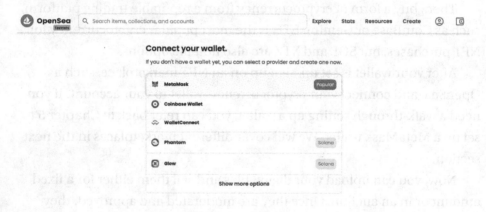

Once you choose the wallet you want to connect, you should see the screen as follows:

Great! You have now connected your wallet. Now, we can create our NFT. Upload your digital file and give your NFT a name:

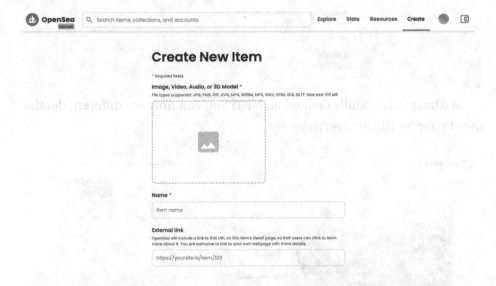

If you want, feel free to add additional details to your NFT. Once you are satisfied, scroll to the bottom of the page and click on the create button:

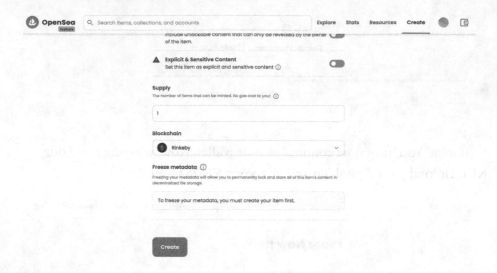

We have successfully created an NFT! You can now see different details about your NFT in an overview:

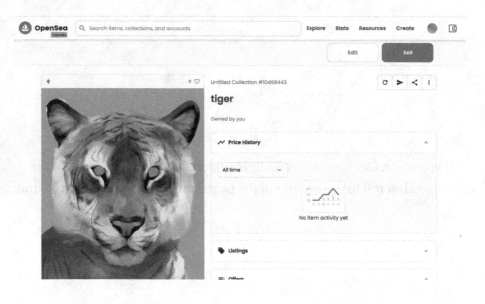

NFT Market Place

The worth of an NFT at any given time is determined by what people are willing to pay for it. In general, however, NFTs tend to go for high prices because they are scarce and limited. In 2018, the market cap was $41 million. Just 2 years later, the market cap rose to $338 million. In Q3 of 2021, the sales rose to $10.7 billion. Figure 6-1 shows the amount of collections that exist in each chain.

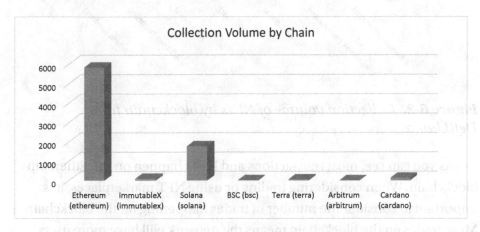

Figure 6-1. *Collection volume of NFTs by blockchain from DefiLlama*

To compare, we also have included a graph with the total amount of USD volume in each blockchain. Note that Ethereum is by far the most popular blockchain in collection volume and USD volume. According to this dataset by DefiLlama, Ethereum accounts for 98% of total USD volume in the NFT market.

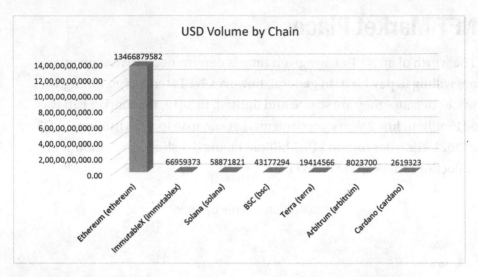

Figure 6-2. *Collection volume of NFTs by blockchain from DefiLlama*

As you can see, most transactions and NFTs happen on the Ethereum blockchain. When considering trading or using NFT marketplaces, it is important to consider the number of trades happening on the blockchain. More trades on the blockchain means the network will have more users and be more stable and decentralized. However, it is also important to know that tokens from an EVM-based network, such as Ethereum, BSC, and Arbitrum cannot be used on non-EVM–based blockchains, such as Solana, Cardano, and ImmutableX.

You can also see the success of NFTs just based on individual collections. We have taken the top 15 best-selling NFT collections from cryptoslam. io shown as in Figure 6-3. These are some of the most well-known and successful NFTs collections of all time, with sales from the top seven collections surpassing billions of USD in sale volume. All of the collections also have thousands of buyers and tens of thousands of transactions. The most impressive collection is the Axie Infinity collection with 1.7 million buyers, 17 million transactions, and 2.19 million owners. However, NBA Top Shot has an astonishing 21 million transactions on the network.

⚡ NFT Collection Rankings by Sales Volume (All-time) ❓ ⚒

	Collection		Sales		Buyers	Txns	Owners
1	⊠ Axie Infinity	🅱	$4,085,446,072	⬈	1,781,560	17,293,960	2,198,895
2	🖼 Bored Ape Yacht Club	♦	$2,403,080,869	⬈	11,936	32,328	
3	🏆 CryptoPunks	♦	$2,367,474,587	⬈	6,016	22,121	3,780
4	🖼 Mutant Ape Yacht Club	♦	$1,725,435,843	⬈	23,369	50,773	
5	⫰ Art Blocks	♦	$1,301,309,332	⬈	32,825	179,744	35,901
6	🖼 Otherdeed	♦	$1,036,283,166	⬈	25,364	56,820	
7	🏀 NBA Top Shot	F	$1,027,633,974	⬈	445,396	21,572,619	694,623
8	🖼 Azuki	♦	$792,895,262	⬈	14,557	32,307	
9	⌁ CloneX	♦	$723,035,800	⬈	10,757	20,878	
10	🖼 Moonbirds	♦	$586,400,207	⬈	13,077	18,605	
11	Vℱ VeeFriends	♦	$555,671,880	⬈	6,505	14,706	
12	🖼 Doodles	♦	$525,554,562	⬈	13,273	27,039	
13	🖼 Meebits	♦	$523,308,466	⬈	12,458	34,575	
14	⊛ Sorare	♦	$414,041,036	⬈	110,895	3,451,551	148,538
15	🆂 The Sandbox	♦	$371,371,615	⬈	26,379	59,446	19,033

Figure 6-3. *Top 15 NFT collections by sales volume from cryptoslam.io*

OpenSea.io

The most popular marketplace is OpenSea.io, which supports over 150 payment tokens and is easy to use. Signing up and viewing digital assets is free, and it also allows creators to easily mint NFTs:

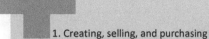

1. Creating, selling, and purchasing NFTs is simple	1. Only supports cryptocurrency
2. The most popular NFT marketplace, with over 80 million NFTs and 1.2 million users and $10 billion in sales	2. Is on the Ethereum blockchain which can have high gas prices per transaction
3. Minting NFTs is free of charge	
4. Listing NFTs for sale is a one-time gas fee	
5. Fee costs only 2.5% of sales	
6. Supports many types of crypto wallets	
7. Has many types of NFTs	

Rarible

Rarible is very similar to OpenSea—the platform allows users to buy, sell, and make art, videos, collectibles, and music. However, Rarible uses its own token (CRYPTO:RARI), which is also supported on OpenSea. Yum! Brands' (NYSE:YUM) Taco Bell has listed art on Rarible, and cloud software company Adobe (NASDAQ:ADBE) has partnered with Rarible:

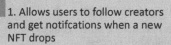

1. Allows users to follow creators and get notifcations when a new NFT drops	1. Only supports cryptocurrency
2. Creating, selling, and purchasing NFTs is simple	2. Is on the Ethereum blockchain which can have high gas prices per transaction
3. Community is very connected	3. Minting an NFT requires a gas fee
4. Multiple wallet types are supported	
5. Fee costs only 2.5% of sales	
6. Has many types of NFTs	

SuperRare

Another marketplace for digital creators, similar to OpenSea and Rarible, is SuperRare. The site includes art, videos, and 3D images that can be purchased using Ethereum, although many SuperRare NFTs cannot be purchased anywhere else. Every NFT is also a single edition. SuperRare announced its own token. SuperRare NFTs can be traded on OpenSea. SuperRare is also unique in the fact that it allows artists to upload NSFW, which stands for Not Safe for Work. NSFW is content that depicts sexual content, nudity, violence, and other potentially triggering topics for viewers:

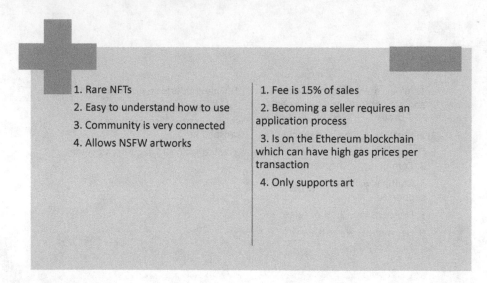

1. Rare NFTs

2. Easy to understand how to use

3. Community is very connected

4. Allows NSFW artworks

1. Fee is 15% of sales

2. Becoming a seller requires an application process

3. Is on the Ethereum blockchain which can have high gas prices per transaction

4. Only supports art

Foundation

Foundation.app is a place for auctioning and bidding on digital art using Ethereum. Over $100 million worth of NFTs have been sold on the platform. However, creating an account on the platform requires an invite from an existing Foundation community member:

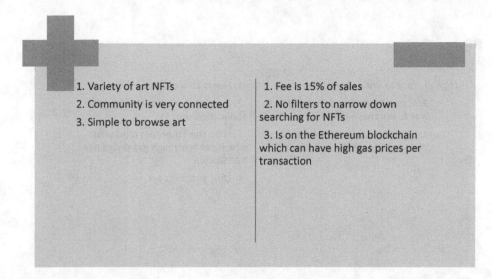

1. Variety of art NFTs	1. Fee is 15% of sales
2. Community is very connected	2. No filters to narrow down searching for NFTs
3. Simple to browse art	3. Is on the Ethereum blockchain which can have high gas prices per transaction

Nifty Gateway

Nifty Gateway has helped the sale of some of the most famous digital artists including Beeple and singer and songwriter Grimes. However, to get started, you must be an already established digital artist, celebrity, or brand and be approved to sell through an application process. The site is powered by the crypto exchange Gemini, and the NFTs, known as Nifties, are built on Ethereum. Nifty Gateway also hosts any NFTs purchased—meaning the NFTs aren't stored in your own wallet but are actually stored in Nifty Gateway:

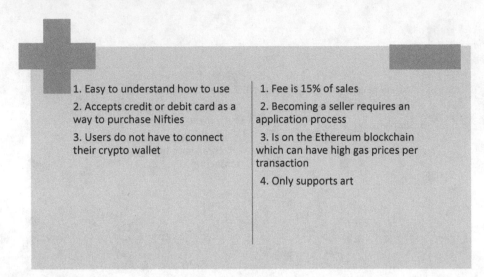

1. Easy to understand how to use	1. Fee is 15% of sales
2. Accepts credit or debit card as a way to purchase Nifties	2. Becoming a seller requires an application process
3. Users do not have to connect their crypto wallet	3. Is on the Ethereum blockchain which can have high gas prices per transaction
	4. Only supports art

Axie Marketplace

Axie Marketplace is actually a shop for a video game called Axie Infinity, where users can buy a creature called an Axie. Players can train their Axie and battle other Axies for rewards. Users can also buy lands and items as NFTs that can be used in-game. The Axie Marketplace uses a currency called Axie Shards. The token is on the Ethereum blockchain and can be used in other NFT marketplaces and Coinbase global:

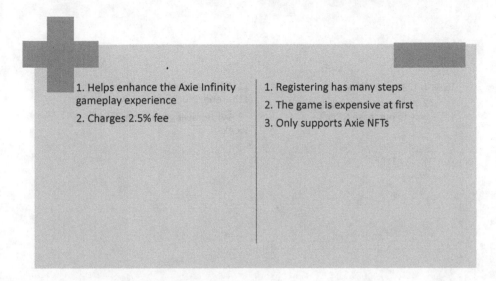

1. Helps enhance the Axie Infinity gameplay experience

2. Charges 2.5% fee

1. Registering has many steps

2. The game is expensive at first

3. Only supports Axie NFTs

NBA Top Shot Marketplace

NBA Top Shot is a marketplace created by the National Basketball Association. The marketplace is home to collectible videos and highlights of NBA plays that can only be acquired within the marketplace. In May 2022, the marketplace passed $1 billion in sales and is home to over 40,000 NFTs:

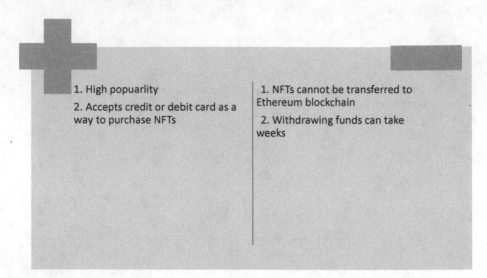

1. High popuarlity

2. Accepts credit or debit card as a way to purchase NFTs

1. NFTs cannot be transferred to Ethereum blockchain

2. Withdrawing funds can take weeks

Mintable

Mintable is similar to OpenSea—you can use Ethereum to buy and sell artwork. The platform also allows creators to mint their NFTs to sell their work as a digital asset:

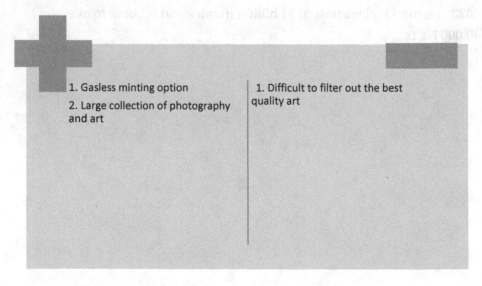

1. Gasless minting option

2. Large collection of photography and art

1. Difficult to filter out the best quality art

Larva Labs/CryptoPunks

Larva Labs has multiple digital art and Ethereum-based projects, but they are best known for their CryptoPunks NFT Project. CryptoPunks is astronomically successful—they have sold for millions of dollars. Currently, they are sold out and can only be brought from third-party marketplaces.

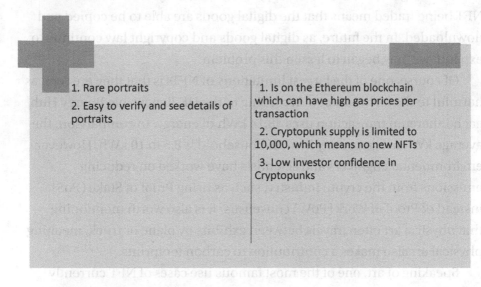

1. Rare portraits

2. Easy to verify and see details of portraits

1. Is on the Ethereum blockchain which can have high gas prices per transaction

2. Cryptopunk supply is limited to 10,000, which means no new NFTs

3. Low investor confidence in Cryptopunks

The Future of NFT

NFTs have a large amount of potential and interest in the field is rapidly growing. However, there are still many concerns about NFTs.

There is currently a debate over whether the NFT industry is a bubble waiting to be burst. As mentioned earlier, the value of NFTs is based on the market's demand for them. In these years, people are willing to pay thousands and even millions for NFTs because they believe the value of NFTs will increase in the future. But if interest in NFTs decreases in the future, then the investments of now may not come back in the future. If too many people pull out of the market at the same time, then the market may crash. However, the field of NFTs may end up similar to the dot.com phenomenon of the early 2000s—there may be an initial apprehensiveness and a large amount of speculation toward NFTs, but eventually they will be more integrated into society. NFTs have already proven their value with billions of USD in sales and millions of buyers.

Another issue is that NFTs also offer little protection against theft. While NFTs give proof of ownership, the fact that anyone can access the NFT being traded means that the digital goods are able to be copied and downloaded. In the future, as digital goods and copyright law continue to expand, we may began to lessen this problem.

Of course, one of the largest limitations of NFTs is that they are seen as harmful to the environment. According to the UK Renewable Energy Hub, each Ethereum transaction uses 48.14 kWh of energy. In comparison, the average kWh usage per day in a UK household is 8.5 to 10 kWh. However, environmental engineers and scientists have worked on reducing emissions from the crypto industry, such as using Proof of Stake (PoS) instead of Proof of Work (PoW) consensus. It is also worth mentioning that physical art often travels between exhibits by plane or truck, meaning physical art also makes a contribution to carbon footprints.

Speaking of art, one of the most famous use cases of NFT currently is in digital art. As NFTs continue to give artists an opportunity to share their work digitally, it creates more opportunities for artists of all different backgrounds and experience. Artists will no longer have to rely on corporations, brands, and collectors, and will thus be able to explore their creative vision more and find an audience that supports them. NFTs can also encourage creativity, as digital work can come in many forms, from VR to work that can be used every day.

In addition, NFTs can benefit the audience of an artist. NFTs increase accessibility of viewing art—viewers do not need to travel to the physical space the art is in, so people can explore galleries from anyplace, anytime. Patrons can also directly support artists and creators due to the direct nature of blockchain transactions.

Another possible use case could be selling concert and event tickets via NFTs. A paper ticket comes with the risk of being misplaced or copied, while the Ethereum blockchain can provide an indestructible and authentic record of ownership.

NFT and blockchain gaming may also see increasing popularity in the next couple of years. In-game items and currency being purchased and traded online is already common. NFTs can be the next step in securing the buyer's ownership of digital assets.

It is also worth mentioning that NFTs can also be used with the real estate market. An NFT could be issued as a proof of ownership of property. NFTs can also be used as a tool for verification—schools could give students NFTs as a proof of a degree completion.

Of course, there is another concept that is also rapidly gaining traction among the tech sector and general public: the Metaverse. NFTs are based on websites and typically used for digital goods, while the Metaverse is a digital space and VR-based. Although they may seem different at a first glance, many companies see potential and have found ways to combine the two topics.

Summary

In this chapter, we learned that NFTs are nonfungible tokens, or individual tokens that are unique. NFTs are most commonly exchanged on the Ethereum network; digital signatures that show proof of ownership make it easy to transfer and purchase files. The next chapter will cover the basics of the Metaverse, a 3D internet based on new immersive technologies.

CHAPTER 7

Metaverse: The World Reimagined

In 1974, philosopher Robert Nozick discussed an experience machine that would stimulate an individual's brain with happy experiences indistinguishable from experiences in the "real" world. Nozick asked a question: "If given a choice, would we choose the machine over reality?" In 1999, the sci-fi movie Matrix raised a similar question: red pill or blue pill? Pop the red pill and wake up in the real world where you see the world is just a simulation created by the Matrix, or swallow the blue pill and teleport to the virtual Matrix plot? The Metaverse concept is similar to the Matrix, where the real and virtual worlds merge in the "future version of the Internet."

Although the Metaverse is still in its early stages, it has rapidly gained mainstream consciousness in recent years. The Metaverse will be a 3D Internet in the future that is built based on a collection of new technologies that include virtual reality (VR), mixed reality (MR), augmented reality (AR), Blockchain, artificial intelligence (AI), and the Internet of Things (IoT).

This chapter will introduce the basics of the Metaverse. Then, we will discuss the concepts and technologies behind AR, VR, MR, and XR. By exploring the different layers of the Metaverse, we understand the structure of the Metaverse. Next, we discuss how NFT and crypto Games work in Metaverse. Then, with a detailed practical example, we understand

B. Wu and B. Wu, *Blockchain for Teens*, https://doi.org/10.1007/978-1-4842-8808-5_7

how we can buy our virtual real estate assets in the Metaverse world. At the end of the chapter, we will provide an overview of the future of the Metaverse.

In this chapter, we cover the following specific topics on blockchain:

- Introduction to Metaverse

- AR, VR, MR, and XR

- Understanding Metaverse layers

- Crypto games in the Metaverse

- Virtual real estate in the Metaverse

- The future of the Metaverse

Introduction to Metaverse

The Metaverse is a hot topic in various industries, especially when combined with other technologies, such as blockchain and AI, to build the future of the Internet.

What Is the Metaverse?

The Metaverse became one of the top technologies and trends in 2021 and continues to be as of date. The Metaverse is not here yet, but numerous big companies have already made large investments in the Metaverse development. Eventually, the Metaverse will be a 3D variation of the Internet and take the virtual reality experience to the next level. It will enable users to do almost everything—from work, leisure, socializing, education, shopping, and even purchasing land through digital avatars—in a purely virtual world.

The Brief History of Metaverse

"Metaverse" Term Created (June 1982)

The term Metaverse was initially coined by the American author Neal Stephenson in his science fiction novel Snow Crash in 1982. The story takes place in Los Angeles in the twenty-first century, numerous years after a global financial collapse. Snow Crash's main character, a katana-wielding hacker called Hiro Protagonist, jumps back and forth between Los Angeles and the virtual world called the Metaverse (a combination of "Meta," the Greek prefix for beyond, and "verse," means the universe).

In the book, the Metaverse is a three-dimensional environment that is populated by user-controlled avatars. It can be accessed using a specialized shiny goggle, like today's VR headsets. Dollars have no value within Stephenson's virtual world. Instead, money is replaced by alternate encrypted digital payments, such as Kongbucks, similar to our cryptocurrencies today.

Second Life—Step Moved Forward Metaverse (June 2003)

In 2003, almost two decades after the publication of Snow Crash, the online virtual world game Second Life, which was directly inspired by the Metaverse in Snow Collision, was released. Users could develop avatars, create homes, and communicate with others.

Roblox—An Online Multiplayer Gaming Platform (January 2006)

Roblox is a multiplayer online video game that enables players to program games and play the games produced by other individuals. As of September 2022, Roblox has more than 230 million registered players with 30 million players daily.

Decentraland—First Ethereum Blockchain-Based Virtual Reality Platform (June 2015)

Decentraland is an Ethereum-based decentralized 3D virtual reality platform created by Esteban Ordano and Ariel Meilich in 2015. In 2017, the Decentraland team issued an Initial Coin Offering (ICO), raising 86,206 ether funds. In Decentraland, users can create virtual objects like casinos, art galleries, laboratories, labs, farms, and theme parks, then open them to the public and charge other players to visit them. Decentraland has two types of tokens. The first token is LAND—a governance NFT token and the second is MANA, a Decentraland's native cryptocurrency token used to facilitate LAND purchases.

The LAND governs the procedures in Decentraland and represents the traversable virtual space and assets within Decentraland. Each nonfungible digital asset is divided into 16m x 16m parcels owned by the LAND token holder and contains the ownership of virtual goods and services in Decentraland.

Pokémon Go—First AR Mobile Game (September 2015)

Pokémon Go is the first augmented reality (AR) mobile game developed by Niantic Labs in partnership with Nintendo and The Pokémon Company. The Pokémon are pinpointed on a real-world phone map, and when players walk to the location, they use their camera to detect the Pokemon in the real and then capture them. The video game was launched in July 2016 and has taken the world by storm. Just seven days after launch, Pokemon Go had over 20 million active players in a single day.

Fortnite—The Multiple Player Game with Community (July 2017)

Fortnite is the first online multiplayer video game with game social networks. Fortnite is a survival battle game where up to 100 players battle against each other in the player vs. player (PvP) combat model until there is only one player standing. It enables players to connect with their partners, build a community, and extend their social network, which is among the strongest incentives for players to continue playing a game. Fortnite had over 10 million gamers only two weeks after its launch. In June 2022, there were still around 3 million players on Fortnite.

Movie—"Ready Player One" (March 2018)

Steven Spielberg's "Ready Player One" is based on Ernest Cline's book of the same name in 2011. The story is set in a dystopian future where the characters spend most of their lifetime in the OASIS Metaverse—including school, working, playing, and socializing in OASIS. OASIS uses digital currency for payment. The characters can teleport to multiple Metaverse worlds by simply entering portals. Most individuals are anonymous by hiding their real identities. "Ready Player One" is often an example of a future Metaverse.

Axie Infinity—NFT of Play-to-Earn Game Platform (March 2018)

Axie Infinity is an NFT-based online video game where players can buy NFTs of collectible electronic pets and match them against each other in battles. The Axie Infinity Metaverse enabled the video game with a "play-to-earn" design (likewise called the "pay-to-play-to-earn" version), where after players pay the starting expenses, they can earn Ethereum-based in-game tokens (SLP) by playing game. Players can cash out their tokens every fourteen days.

Microsoft Introduced Mesh (April 2021)

Microsoft Mesh is a fully virtual world. As a platform for Metaverse, customers can connect to Mesh on HoloLens 2, virtual reality headsets, mobile, tablets, or PCs—with any Mesh-enabled application.

Facebook Becomes Meta (Oct 2021)

On Oct 28, 2021, Facebook announced that it had changed its company name to Meta. The company has stepped into the new business, based on the sci-fi term Metaverse, and also attempted to embrace the Metaverse, a brand-new world built by virtual reality.

Figure 7-1 summarizes the brief history of Metaverse.

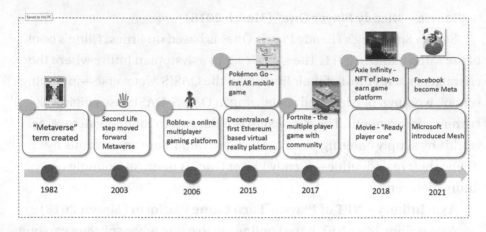

Figure 7-1. *The brief history of Metaverse*

Characteristics of the Metaverse

In the Metaverse, you can become who you want to be, create what
you prefer, where you want, how you want as long as we can imagine it.
This total freedom for the developer will bring some interesting special
experiences, but also for the open Metaverse to work. There are several
characteristics that creators should take into account when constructing
the Metaverse, shown in Figure 7-2.

- Interoperability
- Decentralization
- Immersive
- Boundless
- Virtual Economies
- Persistent
- Social Experience

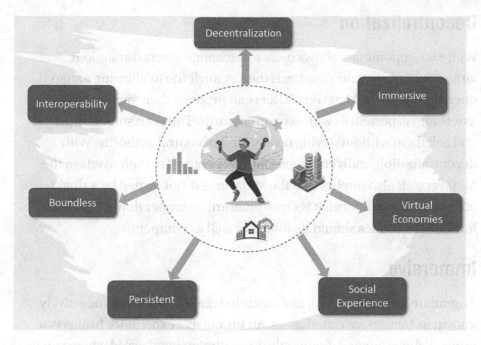

Figure 7-2. *Characteristics of the Metaverse*

Let's review them to understand how we can develop an open Metaverse offering distinct experiences.

Interoperability

Metaverse interoperability is individuals' capacity to communicate with various other users throughout different virtual worlds. Users can also transfer their data and digital assets from one virtual world to another and trade them to various other individuals at the market value established by the open market. Interoperability in the Metaverse functions similarly to interoperability in the blockchain. A user just needs one wallet to perform all transactions across different Metaverse virtual worlds.

Decentralization

While interoperability allows users to exchange assets throughout virtual worlds, decentralization is the key attribute in allowing a shared, open virtual world Metaverse. Users can produce their very own digital assets and experiences with economic worth. They can smoothly get and sell them without relying on any kind of central authority. With decentralization, individuals get complete control of their assets in the Metaverse. It also implies that the Metaverse is not owned by a single corporation or platform. It is cross-platform interoperability, and their interior economies should be robust as well as competitive.

Immersive

Augmented, virtual, mixed, and extended reality trends are collectively known as immersive experiences. An immersive experience brings you into a digitally created, frequently three-dimensional world where you can communicate with other visitors, virtual things, and your environment.

The Metaverse is one kind of immersive experience. It incorporates physical as well as virtual worlds experiences in a comprehensive, shared, interactive, always-on virtual world that consists of gaming, shopping, social, and working in the virtual economy. This is the level at which most users will certainly interact with the Metaverse.

Boundless

The Metaverse eliminates all kinds of barriers as an infinite, always-on virtual space. There are no limitations on the number of people who can use it simultaneously, the business that can utilize it, the types of activities that can happen, and so forth.

Virtual Economies

Metaverse individuals can take part in decentralized digital economic powered by cryptocurrency. It consists of digital assets marketplaces where individuals can invest, order, bid, and trade different goods and services like avatars, virtual clothing, house, NFTs, and event tickets.

Persistent

Metaverse is an infinite open world that can be accessed from across the globe at any time. Like the real world, a persistent Metaverse must remain, even if you leave. You can visit a virtual store whenever pinned at a specific location in the real world. You'll be able to speak with a real shop salesperson. You won't need to worry about these virtual shops' opportunities being gone—you will always see it the next time unless the creator erased it. Like in the real world, retail stores are always there and can just be removed with approval from the owner.

Social Experience

Metaverse is everything about the social experience. As a social platform, the Metaverse is a 3D virtual place where customers will simultaneously participate in a particular event/place/activity and meet each other. Every individual is represented by their favored digital characters. These customized avatars also open brand-new possibilities for gamification and strengthen the base of giving users a collaborative and immersive experience.

AR, VR, MR, and XR

One of the key characteristics of the Metaverse is immersive. Immersive technology produces special experiences by imitating the real world with simulated reality and making a surrounding sensory feeling, therefore creating a sense of immersion. For many years, immersive technology has come to be widely used in lots of industries, including video gaming, archeology, art, healthcare, ecommerce, industrial design, education, and entertainment, among others.

There are multiple ways to present virtual content to users from a first-person perspective through immersive media, including augmented reality (AR), virtual reality (VR), mixed reality (MR), and extended reality (XR).

Augmented Reality (AR)

In the summer of 2016, the release of Niantic's Pokémon GO took the world by storm. Gamers of all ages tried to catch Pikachu in the grocery store and Eevee in the home through their phone camera. That's AR, allowing virtual elements to be displayed in the physical environment. Since then, AR has become increasingly popular.

What Is Augmented Reality?

AR is defined as the technology and approaches that allow users to experience a real-world environment surrounding generated immersive and three-dimensional (3D) virtual digital content with an individual's perception by adding sounds, video, and various other details overlaid on top of it.

Types of AR

There are four types of AR: Markerless, Marker-based, Projection-based, and Superimposition-based AR, as shown in Figure 7-3.

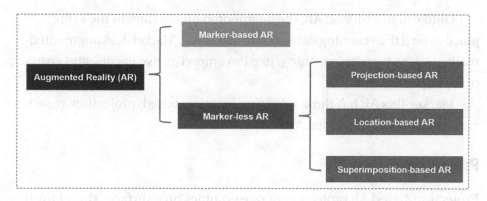

Figure 7-3. *Type of AR*

Marker-based AR

This kind of AR, also known as recognition-based AR or image recognition, depends on the identification of markers/user-defined images to work. Maker-based AR typically needs users to install a software application. Then users can use it to scan markers, which have distinct patterns that cameras can easily recognize and process. Next, the app will activate an augmentation experience (whether an image, text, video, or animation) to appear on the device.

Example: Augmented reality QR code is one of the marker-based AR examples.

Marker-less AR

Marker-less AR refers to AR without markers and does not require any specific image to display its virtual content. Marker-less AR software—Simultaneous Localization and Mapping technology (SLAM) —relies upon the device's hardware, including the video camera, GPS, and other sensing units like accelerometer and compass, to gather data and create proper virtual 3D objects.

277

Unlike marker-based AR, the augmented object stays in the same place even if the scanning device is turned away. Marker-less augmented reality is very popular in gaming, like Pokémon Go, live events, and virtual product placement.

Marker-less AR has three subtypes: location-based, projection-based, and superimposition-based AR.

Projection-Based AR

Projection-based AR projects generate graphics on a surface. Therefore, it does not require any smartphone or any screen. Instead, one or multiple projection devices projects light onto a surface to form a 3D model. The digital graphics can interact by touching the projected 3D object surface with a hand and creating inputs. After the projection-based AR receives the signal, it responds by updating the projected augmented object.

Example: Nike held a projection-based AR at its studio in London, allowing consumers interested to design their very own version of Nike shoes and project it in a full 3D spatial galley.

Location-Based AR

Location-based AR, also known as geo-based augmented reality, AR app reads the device's GPS location to analyze the user's location. When the site matches the predetermined location, it will trigger the generation of a virtual object to show at the spot.

Example: New York's Museum of Modern Art featured a unique experience based on location-based AR.

Superimposition-Based AR

This AR changes a partial or full view of the original object with upgraded, augmented 3D objects for the human eye. Object recognition plays a vital role, which indicates if an application cannot identify an object, then it can't enhance the item's appearance.

Example: Dulux Visualizer app is an example of superimposition-based AR. It allows users to select any color from a paint color visualizer, then upload a photo and "repaint" their room or house virtually to see the result before actually painting the wall.

How Augmented Reality Works

We just discussed Simultaneous Localization and Mapping technology (SLAM) plays a critical role in Marker-less AR. SLAM keeps track of a device's location by collecting data from the indoor or outdoor environment via the device's hardware, such as the video camera, GPS, and other sensors, and then creating proper virtual 3D objects.

SLAM technology is widely used in various industries, mainly autonomous vehicles, robots, and augmented virtual reality.

The architecture of a SLAM system includes two types of components used to complete SLAM. The first component is sensor signal processing, including front-end processing, primarily relying on the sensors used.

The second component is pose-graph optimization, including the sensor-agnostic back-end processing.

Two types of SLAMS can be used for front-end processing to collect data: SLAM Visual SLAM and LiDAR SLAM. Visual SLAM (vSLAM) uses cameras to capture or collect the surrounding imagery and track a set of points through successive camera frames, while LiDAR SLAM utilizes a laser sensor to read the data.

The front-end processing abstracts sensor data into models amenable for estimation, while the back end performs inference on the data produced by the front end. As a result, SLAM can estimate their 3D position to create the map. The SLAM process is shown in Figure 7-4.

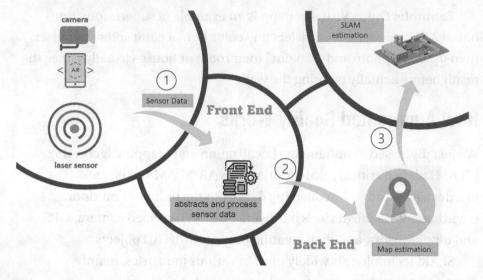

Figure 7-4. *Front end and back end in a Visual SLAM system*

Virtual Reality (VR)

The term "virtual reality" first appeared in the 1982 novel *The Judas Mandala* by Damien Broderick, a popular Australian science fiction author.

Widespread adaption of the term "virtual reality" as VR technology in the popular media is credited to VR developer Jaron Lanier, who designed the first business-grade virtual reality hardware, and the 1992 Lawnmower Man movie, which introduced the use of virtual reality systems to a wider audience.

What Is Virtual Reality?

Virtual reality is a computer-generated environment that makes users feel a rich, immersive experience in their surroundings. By wearing a Virtual Reality headset or related application, the VR produces computer

3D images and videos by adding depth. The system will also reconstruct the scale and distances between static 2D images to imitate real-life visual experiences. VR allows users to immerse themselves into unique simulations they can engage with and explore while believing that they are executing it in the real world.

Types of VR

VR systems are classified into three primary types: non-immersive VR, semi-immersive VR, and fully immersive VR, as shown in Figure 7-5.

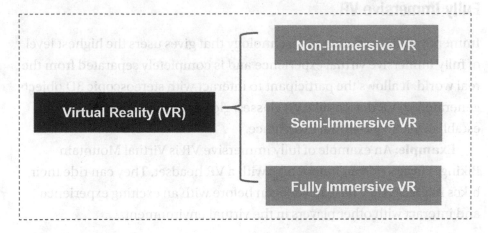

Figure 7-5. *Type of VR*

Non-immersive VR

Non-immersive virtual reality is a virtual reality that displays virtual content on screens via a computer or game console. It is the least immersive and least expensive of all VR types. Users interact with non-immersive VR using computer input devices like keyboards, mice, and controllers.

Example: A video game is a good example of a non-immersive VR experience.

Semi-immersive VR

Semi-immersive virtual experiences provide users with a partially virtual environment between non-immersive and fully immersive VR. Using a computer screen or VR device such as glasses tracking sensors and projector systems, the user can move around in a virtual environment but still see themself. The system is not considered a fully immersive simulator.

Example: A flight simulator for pilot trainees and a virtual tour are good examples of semi-immersive VR.

Fully Immersive VR

Immersive VR simulation is a technology that gives users the highest level of fully immersive virtual experience and is completely separated from the real world. It allows the participant to interact with stereoscopic 3D objects generated by VR devices like VR glasses, gloves, and body detectors and establish a realistic virtual experience.

Example: An example of fully immersive VR is Virtual Mountain Biking. Players ride an indoor bike with a VR headset. They can ride their bikes in places they have never been before with an exciting experience and interact with other players in the virtual environment.

How Virtual Reality Works

Truly immersive virtual reality can trick people's minds into believing it exists and take them somewhere virtually other than where they are. However, generating these experiences involves many complex technologies behind the scenes.

Field of View (FOV)

The approximate field of view (FOV) of an individual human eye is about 135 degrees horizontally and slightly more than 180 degrees vertically. A human typically can see a 200–220-degree arc around their head. The overlap of the same scene from a human's left and right eyes is around 114 degrees, which we can see in 3D. This FOV is necessary for a human brain to calculate depth perception. In the case of virtual reality, FOV means how much of the virtual world a participant can see around them simultaneously. The VR headsets camera simulates human eye positions and a defined FOV degree that people can expect. The headsets also have gyroscopic sensors to track how you're moving, adjust your view, and enable you to explore 360-degree scenes. All of these will greatly improve the fully immerses experience. Most VR headsets today generally support 114-degree 3d vision space to deliver virtual content.

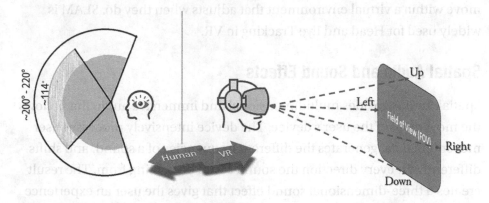

Figure 7-6. *Field of view (FOV)*

Frame Rate (FPS)

Frame rate/FPS (frames per second) defines the speed at which the Graphics Processing Unit (GPU) can process an image per second. Frame rate is related to resolution, which shows the amount of detail in the image over time. For example, with a frame rate of 50 FPS, you will see 50 samples in one second. In the next second, it will show another 50 samples. Suppose an object moves with your view. In that case, you will only see those 50 samples updated position per second. Other samples will be invisible to you between those snapshots. If you increase the frame rate to 500 FPS, you will get ten times more samples every second. The result will be much better imagery, smoother motion, and a more immersive experience. A lower frame rate will typically have worse effects. Studies have shown that anything less than 60 FPS causes feelings of disorientation, nausea, and other negative side effects in the user. VR developers typically aim for a minimum of 60 FPS–90 FPS.

Position and Head Tracking

In an immersive virtual environment, tracking the user's real-time headset position to determine position and orientation is important. Users can move within a virtual environment that adjusts when they do. SLAM is widely used for Head and Eye Tracking in VR.

Spatial Audio and Sound Effects

Spatial Audio provides multidimensional and immersive audio that follows the movement of the user's device. The device intensively processes user movement data, generates the different frequencies of a sound, and shifts differently for every direction the sound could be coming from. The result creates a three-dimensional sound effect that gives the user an experience that mimics how they hear sound in real life.

Mixed Reality (MR)

Mixed reality (MR) is an emergent technology that combines virtual reality (VR) and augmented reality (AR). MR merges the physical and virtual worlds to create new environments where physical and digital objects can interact in real-time.

Example: MR workstations will no longer be a single or dual physical monitor. The workstations will consist of multiple screens as desired in a 3D virtual space.

The user can define and create an infinite number of customized workstations and delete these virtual screens as needed. Such working environments will improve efficiency and create a more enjoyable, comfortable, and healthier workplace.

Extended Reality (XR)

Extended reality (XR) is an umbrella term that covers the full spectrum of real and virtual immersive technologies, including VR, AR, and MR.

To summarize what we have discussed so far for AR, MR, and MR, Table 7-1 displays the difference between these immersive technologies.

Table 7-1. *A comparison Between VR, AR, and MR*

Augmented reality (AR)	Virtual reality (VR)	Mixed reality (MR)
Virtual digital content overlaid on a real-world environment.	Computer-generated immersive virtual worlds completely independent of the real world.	The physical and virtual worlds merged.
Partial immersion in the virtual environment.	Complete immersion in the virtual environment.	Interaction with and manipulation of both physical and virtual world.
Proven and improved technology.	Realistic technical skill practice allows collecting key training metrics.	Real-time information and knowledge sharing with collaborators over long distances.
Special AR headsets can be used for displaying virtual content on a small display.	Special VR headsets and hand controllers can be used to enhance experience.	Special AR and VR devices can be used for creating mixed experiences.
Needs 3-7 years to adopt AR in different fields.	Needs 2-4 years to adopt VR in different fields.	MR is having a similar time as VR for adoption

Understanding Metaverse Layers

Imagine the Metaverse as a parallel 3D virtual world of existence that provides all kinds of products or services and will even come to integrate and interact with much of the physical world. As a simulated digital environment, Metaverse incorporates all digital technologies AR, VR, Internet of Things (IoT), 5G, big data, edge computing, artificial intelligence (AI), and blockchain to build virtual places for social communities that resemble the real world. Moreover, it has a self-contained virtual economy powered by digital currencies and nonfungible tokens (NFTs). Entrepreneur Jon Radoff, an author and a game designer, has divided the Metaverse world into seven layers: experiences, discovery, creator economy, spatial computing, decentralization, human interface, and infrastructure. These layers encompass the past, present, and future developments and forms of the different products or services in the Metaverse landscape. Figure 7-7 illustrates the layers in Metaverse.

Figure 7-7. *Layers in Metaverse*

Experience

Experience is the layer on which most Metaverse businesses, companies, and developers are now focused at the moment. A large feature of this layer will be community-driven events, social interactions, virtual services, and digital assets, such as games, NFTs, social, e-sports, meetings, theater, shopping, and events. Users can interact in virtual environments through its digital content. In this layer, the Metaverse will eventually create a brand-new dimension of virtual worlds by dematerializing physical space. As a result, the Metaverse will offer everyone a wide variety of experiences they have never seen before.

Gaming is perhaps the most commonly known platform to demonstrate many features of the Metaverse experience layer: virtual immersion experience, avatar identities, digital NFT marketplaces, 3D product presentations, and real-time social interactions. This layer also includes many other everyday experiences where the physical and digital worlds merge and blend: Zoom office VR meetings, HOLOFIT VR Fitness, or Netflix VR movie, TvoriVR UX and UI prototyping.

Here are several popular Metaverse platforms in this layer.

Examples: Decentraland, Fortnite, Roblox, Sandbox, Spatial, Rove, Activision Blizzard, Nintendo, and Xbox.

Discovery

The discovery layer is about the continuous pull and pulls of information that introduces people to learn about different new experiences. The pull represents an inbound system where the users actively seek information about a new experience. On the other hand, push means an outbound system where the Metaverse experiences await users and notify them.

Here are some examples in which inbound and outbound discoveries can take place.

Inbound:

- Search engines
- Real-time presence
- Community-driven content
- App stores
- A whitepaper
- A case studies
- Earned media

Outbound:

- Display advertising
- Notifications
- Emails and social media

Community-driven content can help spread knowledge about its concepts, supporting technologies, and experiences. NFTs are an example that has been one of the hottest topics since 2021. Many companies use NFT digital assets to brand their products or service as a marketing tool, such as Nike, Starbucks, Coca-Cola, McDonald's, and Louis Vuitton. It is a great way to grow community engagement and rise much more discovery in the Metaverse.

The real-time presence will also play a critical role in improving interactive user experiences. For example, video game services such as PlayStation and Xbox allow gamers to see what their friends do in real time. The most common approaches in outbound discovery are display advertising, notifications, emails, and social media.

Examples: Unity, Google store, Apple store, Steam, PlayStation, and Xbox.

Creator Economy

At the early stage of the Metaverse, producing digital resources, generating immersive experiences, and adding decentralized payment required a lot of professional skill and effort. This stage is similar to earlier versions of the Internet. It requires a lot of programming knowledge for creators to design and build apps. Nowadays, a tool like WordPress can allow content creators to easily build a website with payment options without code, with just a few clicks and drag-and-drop capabilities to achieve the creation process. With the growing Metaverse market, more and more commerce software tools will appear. As a result, the number of designers and creators on the Metaverse is increasing exponentially. For example, tokens like NFTs, build on a decentralized blockchain and have provable ownership for the digital asset with independent centralized platforms. This new model will give creators more influence than the traditional creator platform. Creators can build their Metaverse economies, sell more virtual NFT items to fans, and have opportunities to get more income.

Examples: Roblox, Unity, Adobe, Polystream, Shopify, Decentraland, and Microsoft.

Spatial Computing

Spatial computing refers to merging real and virtual worlds and reducing the boundaries between them. It is broadly synonymous with extended reality (XR):

- Various aspects of the technology solutions in this layer help us manipulate and enter into 3D Metaverse spaces. Here is a list of a few of them.

- 3D engines for displaying geometry and animation (Unity and Unreal Engine).

- Geospatial mapping and object recognition for mapping and interpreting the real and virtual worlds.

- VR, AR, MR, XR.

- Voice and gesture recognition.

- Internet of Things for data integration from devices.

- Human biometrics for identification purposes.

The UI will completely differ from spatial computing and can be built on physical space. The machines no longer need to be tied to a fixed location, and the hardware will be invisible. Cathay Pacific worked with ER ad platform OmniVirt to provide a visual tour for customers. The products enable marketers to give their target travelers, especially those who haven't yet experienced the airline, a "try before you buy" experience.

It allows consumers to virtually tour every aspect of the traveler's journey, from selecting a seat and check-in desk to the cabin—similar to how Google Street View works. By enabling 360° video units of airport lounges and flight experiences, consumers can click on certain hotspots in the view to get more information. They can also click to reserve their seat in immerses virtual environment. The result increased customer brand favorability by 25%.

Examples: Alphabet, Microsoft, Meta, Deere, Matterport, Unity, Unreal, Epic Games, and Nvidia.

Decentralization

One of the key features of the Metaverse is that it will be decentralized. There is no single central authority in Metaverse. The real-time generated 3D virtual worlds make up various Metaverses. Each Metaverse is governed by its own decentralized autonomous organization (DAO), a community-led organization with no central authority to govern them. Metaverse can operate autonomously, creating a new ecosystem built around blockchain.

In a truly decentralized Metaverse environment, creators have ownership and full control of their creative work and digital products in any virtual world. NFTs-enabled crypto assets will certainly play a critical role in ensuring no asset ownership has tampered within the Metaverse. Users can easily trade the product using cryptocurrency and transfer NFT ownership. Decentralized finance (DeFi) is a way to provide financial products into the Metaverse via a decentralized blockchain network. With DeFi, users can do most of the things centralized financial institutions offer—borrow, lend, exchange, buy insurance, trade derivatives, invest, and more.

One of the most well-known examples of the decentralized Metaverse is Decentraland, a decentralized 3D virtual world that runs on the Ethereum blockchain. Users may buy virtual plots of land on the platform as NFTs via cryptocurrency, and the game protocol is governed by a DAO, which the token holder votes.

Other popular decentralized Metaverse products are Axie Infinity, Sandbox, Bloktopia, Star Atlas, Polka City, Illuvium, and Sorare.

Examples: Ethereum, polygon, Cardano, Polkadot, Dapper, Ava Labs, OpenSea, SuperRare, and Rally.

Human Interface

People interact with the world in a variety of various ways. In the Metaverse, it's called a human interface. It consists of multiple approaches, such as gestures, vocal commands, and neural interfaces. Wearable devices like smart glasses, gloves, watch, and other garments are also included under the larger banner of human interfaces.

Those VR devices currently in use remain in a state of continuous development. At the same time, many new devices are also being invented and evaluated to access the Metaverse. These are cutting-edge solutions designed to make such improvements much easier to use. An example of such a tool is AR contact lenses, designed to allow the user to watch the digital world without putting on bulky glasses, earphones, or goggles. Clearly, this solution has yet to be widely publicly tested and approved, but it might indicate a breakthrough in this area in the short term.

Examples: Xbox, Samsung, Oculus, HoloLens, PlayStation, Alexa, Neural Link, and Magic leap.

Infrastructure

The seventh layer consists of technologies that make everything the other six layers mentioned become real.

Six technologies clusters the power of the Metaverse:

The computing power and network – It requires a 5G and 6G capable infrastructure to increase network bandwidth and decrease network congestion and latency. In addition, the devices also need components like GPU servers, semiconductors, microelectromechanical systems (MEMS), and tiny, long-lasting batteries

Artificial intelligence (AI) – AI has been widely applied in our daily lives over the last few years. Within the Metaverse, AI can be used to improve nonplayer characters (NPCs) in different situations. NPCs exist everywhere in virtually every game; they belong to the gaming setting created to react and react to gamers' activities. With AI's managing abilities, NPCs can be put across the 3D spaces to facilitate realistic conversations with users or perform other specific tasks.

Spatial computing, Digital Twin, and Internet of Things (IoT) – Spatial computing or 3D reconstruction is crucial to create realistic spaces in the Metaverse. It helps to maintain buildings, items, and physical locations in the Metaverse. Digital Twin is an essential building block of Metaverse. A Digital Twin is a computer program that uses real-world data to create a real-time virtual representation. It can simulate a real-world physical system or process (a physical twin) and predict how a product or process will perform. Digital Twin integrates AI, IoT, and data analytics tools to enhance the output. By deploying digital twins, Metaverse creators can build precise real-life spaces into the virtual mirror world.

IoT is a system that takes whatever is in our real world and connects them to the Internet via sensors and devices. One of the functions of IoT in the Metaverse is to collect and provide data from the physical world, improving the precision of digital objects. IoT devices can seamlessly connect the Metaverse to many real-life devices and enable the generation of real-time simulations in the Metaverse. To further optimize the Metaverse environment, IoT can integrate with AI to process the data it collects.

Video gaming technologies – This will include 3D game engines like Unreal Engine and Unity.

Display technologies – AR, VR, MR, and XR can give users an immersive and engaging 3D experience.

Blockchain technology – Blockchain innovation provides a decentralized and transparent feature for digital proof of ownership, NFT, DeFi, governance, DAO, anonymity, and interoperability. Furthermore, cryptocurrencies enable users to transfer value while they work and socialize in the 3D Metaverse.

Example: Azure, Aws, Google cloud, Qualcomm, Intel, Nvidia, Verizon, AT&T, T-Mobile.

While seven layers structure explanation helps a general understanding current Metaverse landscape, there is still a lot to learn. The Metaverse is still in a very early stage. Many new technologies will emerge in the future, and this layered structure will continue to evolve.

Crypto NFTs Games in the Metaverse

Video games have been around since the early 1950s, starting in the research labs of scientists. Today, video games are found in homes worldwide. The video game sector has been booming in the last several years due to the growing younger population, economic growth, increasing mobile users, and high-speed Internet. It is estimated that video game revenue will reach $208.60bn in 2022 and be worth $321 billion by 2026.

In Feb 2022, Microsoft CEO Satya Nadella was interviewed by Financial Times. He explained Metaverse—"What Is the Metaverse? Metaverse is essentially about creating games." As we discussed in the previous section, the Metaverse is all about virtual experience in a digital universe. However, the gaming industry has been using a similar virtual world concept for a long time. Players can have a close-to-reality experience while playing 3d games on the multiplayer gaming platform. Player game data are persistent in the game platform, and player sessions will resume after they log in. They will continue to play from their last session. That is closer to the persistent nature of the Metaverse.

Business Model in the Game Industry

A video game business model is a monetization strategy game creators use to gain revenue for their apps. Introducing new technologies, such as blockchain, artificial intelligence (AI), and virtual reality (VR), has become a major trend in evolving the game industry's business models.

Pay-to-Play

In 1972, the first consumer-facing video computer game, Pong, was available to the public. In 1978, the game Space Invaders declared the beginning of the golden age of the arcades. During the 1970s and 1980s, each video game was built in the form of Arcade machines which required a large physical space. Gamers need to insert coins in exchange for time or lives in the game. This is a "pay-to-play" business model.

Pay-to-play, sometimes called pay-for-play or P2P, refers to online games that the players must pay to play the game. P2P games are the standard business gaming mode and typically have more features, challenges, and modes than their free player. For example, most online gambling games are P2P models, which require online casino players' registration and real-money deposit before accessing them. P2P is also commonly used in classic MMORPGs (massively multiplayer online role-playing games) such as World of Warcraft and Everquest.

Pay-to-play requires the player to continue paying the game company a monthly or annual subscription fee to access various in-game items. If the fee is not paid, the player's account will be suspended, and they cannot access nor use the game. Also, the subscription is quite expensive. In many cases, free-to-play business models may be an option when players just want to play games occasionally.

Free-to-play

The first free-to-play video game was Nexon's QuizQuiz released in October 1999 and developed by Lee Seungchan. The free-to-play game business model was created by Nexon in South Korea.

Free-to-play, also known as free-to-start, F2P, or FtP, refers to online video games that give players access to the game to play and enjoy a major part of the content without paying. However, there are always additional game features, such as premium parts of the stories, unique abilities, special game items, and new characters. These features typically encourage players to pay microtransactions to get access.

The popular free-to-play games are Apex Legends, League of Legends, Hearthstone, Eve Online, and Fortnite Battle Royale.

Free-to-play has been a great commercial success and is very popular in current game design. Many online games follow this model.

Traditional video game companies build games on centralized servers in today's video game industry. They fully control player accounts and game data. Platform administrators can remove a player's game item or suspend players' accounts. So even if players play games and pay fees for years, they don't really own the value of items or in-game currency.

The above issues are being solved with the advent of blockchain technologies. Crypto games take advantage of the innovations in Web 3.0, which brings cryptocurrencies and NFTs into video games and creates a new business model—Play-to-Earn.

Play-to-Earn

The play-to-earn are decentralized games that allow players to farm or collect game and NFTs tokens. Then, the players can sell them on the market to earn rewards. By completing game tasks, combating other players, and playing the game regularly, players can earn more cryptocurrency to trade and transfer their assets in crypto exchange for fiat currency as income.

Play-to-earn games take advantage of the innovations in the blockchain, which brings cryptocurrencies and NFTs into the world of video games. In crypto games, there are three main ways to let players earn income through gameplay.

Earning or Trading In-game NFTs

In the game, NFTs represent a unique virtual collectible in-game asset. They can come in all sorts of different forms, such as weapons, characters, skins, pets, food, tools, and virtual land, to be used as part of the game. Once players have collected them, they can be exchanged for other assets within the game or sold for actual money on a real-world NFT marketplace. Players create value for the entire game system by participating in the in-game economy. For example, in one of the most popular blockchain games, Axie Infinity, there are creatures called Axis. Axis is a fictional, fierce creature that loves to battle, build, and hunt for treasure. The player can collect, trade, and raise Axis and use it to battle, other players and enemies. The Axie as a game asset is defined as ERC-721 NFT tokens. Players can buy and sell their Axie NFTs in the marketplace (https://app.axieinfinity.com/marketplace/).

Figure 7-8. *Axie Infinity marketplace*

Earning In-game Cryptocurrency

1. **Native Cryptocurrency**

    Most crypto games have native cryptocurrency in
    the form of game tokens created by smart contracts.
    For example, in Axie Infinity, there are two native
    cryptocurrencies—Smooth Love Potion (SLP) and
    Axie Infinity Shards (AXS).

    SLP

    SLP is an ERC-20 token used to breed Axie. Players
    can earn SLP in-game currency through the Arena
    Mode in Axie Infinity when they complete daily
    quests or battle monsters and other players.

    AXS

    AXS is an ERC-20 governance token for the Axie
    Infinity ecosystem. AXS token is intended to
    reward players for participating in the Axie Infinity
    Metaverse. The top-ranking players will be awarded
    after each season. SLPs and AXS can be converted
    to real-life currency. One SLP is 0.000277 AXS, or

$0.0034 and can be purchased and sold in many crypto exchanges (i.e., Uniswap). SLP has been well known as part of the play-to-earn trend, letting players earn relatively stable earnings just by playing Axie Infinity.

2. **Existing Cryptocurrency**

   Some crypto games use existing cryptocurrencies, such as Bitcoin, Ethereum, etc., as a reward to players. CryptoKitties is an example of using ether to buy and sell kitties in the CryptoKitties market.

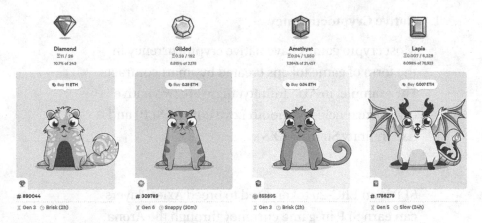

Figure 7-9. *CryptoKitties market*

It typically takes a while to accumulate a significant amount for existing cryptocurrencies like ether, but these others are real.

Staking

Many play-to-earn games allow players to lock up NFTs or cryptocurrency tokens in-game to earn rewards. For instance, Axie Infinity allows landowners to stake their land and earn the Axie token, AXS, as a reward. Players can stake 30 land plots in one transaction and get AXS rewards per day based on the rarity level of the staked land.

Figure 7-10 shows the game industry's evolution in the business model.

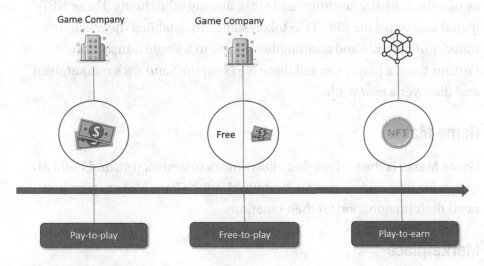

Figure 7-10. Game industry's evolution in the business model

Example of Play-to-Earn NFT Games
The Sandbox

The Sandbox is a community-driven Metaverse platform where creators can build, own, and monetize voxel assets as NFT. The gaming experience uses SAND Token on the Ethereum blockchain. The Sandbox project was initially developed by Pixowl (later, TSB Gaming) in 2012 on mobile platforms, with 40 million downloads across iOS and Android. The Sandbox has more than two million registered users and comprises three products: VoxEdit, Marketplace, and Game Maker.

VoxEdit

VoxEdit is a cloud-based NFT creation software. It allows users to create rig and animate 3D voxel-based NFTs products in the Metaverse, such as people, animals, furniture, and tools, among other items. These NFTs' digital assets use the ERC-1155 token standard, enabling the efficient transfer of fungible and nonfungible tokens in a single transaction. Furthermore, a player can sell these NFTs on the Sandbox's marketplace and discover a new world.

Game Maker

Game Maker is the toolbox that allows users to design, test, and build 3D games for free, and no coding is required. With Game Maker, users just need their imagination for their creations.

Marketplace

The Sandbox's NFT marketplace allows users to search and buy the creator's NFT assets made with VoxEdit. The creator can first upload the digital assets into an IPFS (The InterPlanetary File System) network, which is decentralized storage. Then associated assets with a smart contract and deployed onto the blockchain to prove ownership. Once this is accomplished, this NFT asset for creation can be found in the Sandbox marketplace.

To build an enclosed economic system among players, all players will depend on four user-specific tokens—SAND, ASSET, LAND, and GAME. Users will use these tokens to interact with the platform: players, creators, curators, and landowners. The remaining two tokens are GEMs and CATALYSTs, saved for use with VoxEdit when creating assets. Figure 7-11 shows these six tokens in the sandbox games.

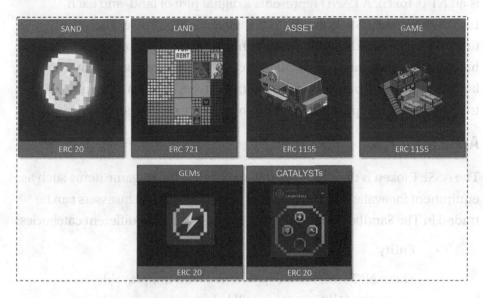

Figure 7-11. *Six tokens in the sandbox game*

SAND

SAND is an ERC-20 utility token built on the Ethereum blockchain and powers all of the Sandbox's transactions and interactions. SAND Token is Sandbox's native token.

Access the Sandbox platform – Players spend SAND in order to play games, buy equipment, or create their Avatar character.

Governance – SAND is a governance token that allows token holders to vote in Governance decisions on the platform using a DAO structure.

Staking – The Sandbox will allow landowners to stake SAND on their LANDs, and Staking will be returned to users along with yields paid out in SAND.

LAND

In the Sandbox Metaverse, a LAND token is the ERC-721 standard and is an NFTs token. A LAND represents a digital plot of land, and each LAND comprises 96 x 96 meters in the Sandbox Metaverse. There's a total of 166,464 Lands with different dimensions. LAND token holders have ownership rights to a specific space on the platform and allow the landowner to rent, buy, sell, stake, host, and form districts. With a LAND token, the user can participate in the governance of the ecosystem via DAO.

ASSET

The ASSET token is the ERC-1155 token representing in-game items such as equipment for avatars and creations to populate LAND. The assets can be traded in The Sandbox's marketplace. An asset has three different categories:

- **Entity**

  These NFTs refer to an experience with nonplayable characters (NPCs), which will bring a game or world to life, such as a farmer, tree, chicken, dragon, or treasure hunter.

- **Equipment**

  Equipment is an NFT that can be attached to the player's inventory and help the player to complete the game experience. For example, a sword, an epic Viking axe, a shield, a helmet, and so on.

- **Block**

  In addition to the existing basic blocks, such as water, mud, and sand, players can create new blocks. These blocks can bring unique experiences, for example, colorful water and cute sparkly lava.

GAME

A GAME token is ERC-1155 token, combining assets and game programming to create an interactive experience. The GAME token must be paired with a LAND token.

CATALYSTs

Catalysts are ERC-20 tokens. Catalysts have four empty sockets, which can be filled with Gems to make a player more powerful.

GEMs

GEMS are the ERC-20 that defines player asset attributes. Depending on play's need, every Gem has a different function that can be applied to an asset and increase the Sandbox's game experiences throughout the Metaverse.

Decentraland

Decentraland is a play-to-earn 3D virtual world Metaverse game running on the Ethereum network. Using the native MANA cryptocurrency, users can create avatars and purchase digital assets, such as parcels of virtual land, called "LAND." The user will receive the NFT LAND token after they buy these spaces. We will discuss more detail in the next section.

Virtual Real Estate in the Metaverse

In real life, a house is a place in which we live. When people buy a house, the seller will sign a deed, which is a legal document used to prove ownership of the land we own. The Metaverse is the future of the Internet and is about the immersive experience in the virtual reality world. In the Metaverse, we issue an NFT as representative of digital asset ownership and keep track of ownership records in the blockchain NFT, as proof of ownership is verifiable within Metaverse.

What Is Virtual Land?

Virtual lands are NFT-ownable digital spaces or land plots, similar to physical real estate. The virtual lands platform creates large maps of land that is divided into small parcels to sell on the market. Virtual plots of land are smart contract programmable spaces that allow people to buy, sell, rent, construct, and explore in a virtual world. Owning virtual land is similar to owning physical real estate, where the owner can either keep the NFT or sell it directly to a buyer at an agreed-upon price in marketplaces. Buyers can directly pay with cryptocurrency or use a mortgage to purchase land. The virtual landowner will keep the assets in their wallet and then either sell the property or design and build on the land. Popular NFT virtual land projects include Decentraland, the Sandbox, and Axie Infinity.

Decentraland (A Case Study)

Decentraland is a decentralized, virtual reality Metaverse platform powered by the Ethereum blockchain. The platform enables users to create, buy, and sell virtual content and digital real estate. Land parcels are NFTs based on digital assets. You can do whatever you like with your LAND once you've owned it. Each plot of land can only be 33 feet by 33 feet in size with unlimited height. This plot allows users to organize their LAND more efficiently by merging adjacent parcels.

Three Native Tokens in Decentraland

In Decentraland, there are three native tokens, two ERC-721 NFT tokens, and one ERC-20 token.

The parcels of digital land where a user interacts and creates are called LAND, an NFT token, Parcels are 1x1 land plots. There are a total of 90,601 parcels of land in Decentraland. The second NFT token is ESTATE, allowing the user to merge two or more adjacent parcels of LAND through the Marketplace. Estates are very useful for managing larger LAND holdings.

On the other hand, MANA is an ERC-20 token that is the official native cryptocurrency of Decentraland. One LAND can be purchased for 1,000 MANA. In Decentraland, users can use MANA to do the following:

To buy parcels, digital goods, and services in the virtual world

To burn in order to claim LAND parcels

The token holder has the right to vote on platform policies through the DAO

Decentraland Architecture

The Decentraland protocol is comprised of three layers:

Consensus Layer

Each parcel of LAND is an NFT token, defined by LANDregistry smart contract. The EstateRegistry contracts define ESTATE tokens. Smart contracts power the consensus layer and track the ownership of land parcels and their content. Users can buy new parcels of LAND with the MANA token. And the LANDregistry contract burns MANA whenever it creates a new LAND.

Land Content Layer

Land content stores the reference of a hash of the file's content. From this reference, the application can download digital content of parcel of digital land from BitTorrent or IPFS. The downloaded file contains a description of the image, textures, sounds, and other elements needed to render the scene.

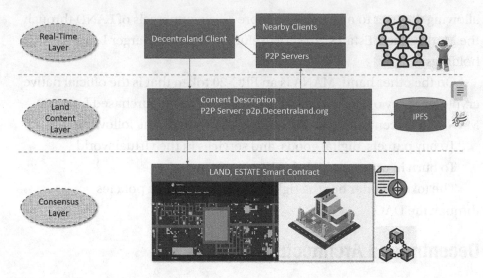

Figure 7-12. *Decentraland protocol layers*

Real-time Layer

The real-time layer enables peer-to-peer connection, or the ability for users to communicate with each other. These connections are necessary to build community social interaction. Decentraland also has an avatar messaging voice chat.

Figure 7-12 summarizes Decentraland protocol layers.

Buy Land in the Metaverse

Anyone can buy, sell, or rent land on the official Decentraland Marketplace or through an NFT marketplace like OpenSea. Decentraland also provides the mortgage option of obtaining land. However, before starting with the land purchase, make sure you go through the following steps:

Step 1 – Select a Metaverse Platform and Sign In

In our case, we will select Decentraland platform (https://market. decentraland.org/).

Directly use Metamask to connect or register an account at the Decentraland platform. Metamask is recommended to purchase and sell land:

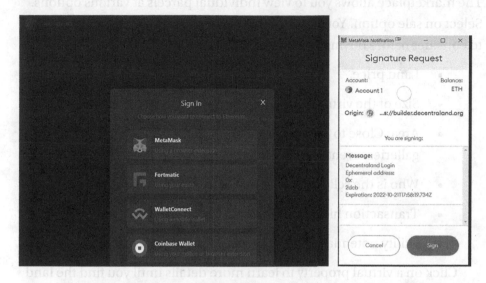

Once signed in, select the "Land" tab to be directed to the land parcels for sale (see the following image):

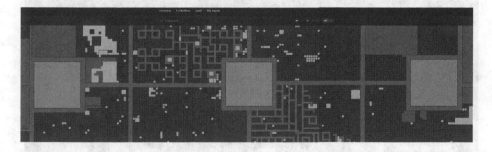

Step 2 – Buy Cryptocurrency

Most Metaverse platforms. and NFT marketplaces require you to have a native crypto token beforehand. You can purchase these currencies on crypto exchanges such as Coinbase and Binance and send these tokens to your wallet address, for example, Metamask or Coinbase Wallets.

Step 3 – Choose a Plot of LAND

The marketplace allows you to view individual parcels at various options. Select on sale option. You can examine nearby locations. The main things to consider before buying land in the Metaverse are:

- Land price.

- Size of the virtual land area.

- Area: Close to popular attractions (hubs, shops, galleries, event spaces, etc.).

- Who is the seller of the land.

- Transaction history.

- Utility potential (gallery, events space, shop, etc.).

Click on a virtual property to learn more details until you find the land you want to purchase. The land prices are listed in MANA with the owner's detail information:

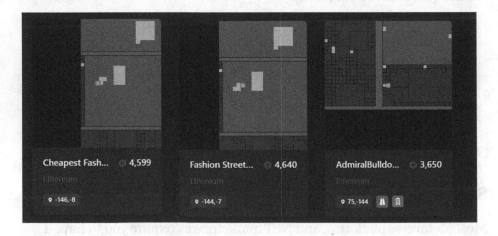

Step 4 – Purchase the Property

Once you have found and selected the property that you want to buy, the "buy," and "bid" buttons allow you to place an order and complete a purchasing transaction. You can use Ether or MANA to purchase.

Once you click the "buy" button, you will be asked to confirm your purchase. It will take a few seconds to a few minutes until the transaction is complete. Now you owned the virtual Metaverse land.

You can buy the land in Open Sea too. Click explore ➤ virtual land. You will see the Decentraland collections shows.

Click in Decentraland. It will show you available land for sale. Pick one of these lands you want to buy to complete your purchase:

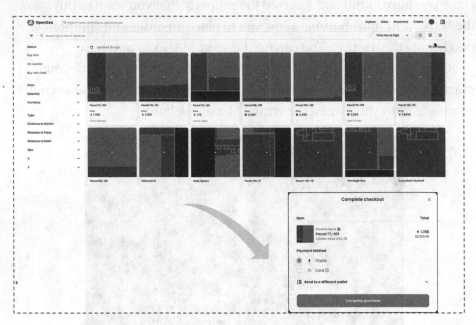

The Future of the Metaverse

When Neal Stephenson first described the Metaverse in his novel Snow Crash in 1992, the Metaverse was simply a concept from science fiction. However, since Facebook rebranded as Meta in October 2021, the nebulous idea that inspired the new name has been a hot topic of discussion, shown in the following diagram.

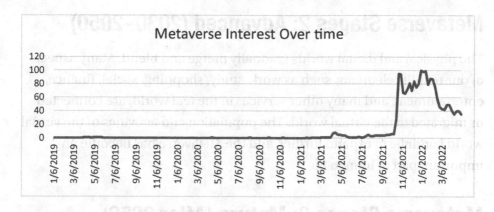

While it may seem that the Metaverse is everywhere and will happen in the near future, it may take several years before it is fully implemented. Mark Zuckerberg, the CEO of Meta, estimates it can take five to ten years before the key features of the Metaverse will become mainstream.

The future Metaverse would be similar to our real life in many aspects where people can do everything they do in real life: work, study, shop, play, social in the virtual world.

There are three stages of Metaverse evolution.

Metaverse Stages 1: Emerging (2021–2030)

In this stage, the Metaverse will continue to integrate various innovative technologies with existing systems to reconstruct its basis, from the experience layer to the infrastructure layer. With a relatively lower barrier for entry, the creator economy and discovery layer is likely to see the most activity. A virtual world consisting of a large-scale human society with a fully digital representation of the physical reality will appear. However, reality and virtuality stay as two parallel spaces.

Metaverse Stages 2: Advanced (2030–2050)

The physical and digital worlds gradually merge and blend. Many aspects of our real-life elements, such as work, study, shopping, social, finance, entertainment, and many other services in the real world, are connected or migrated to the virtual world. The population and activities of the virtual world continue to expand further, and the Metaverse has become an important part of human life.

Metaverse Stages 3: Mature (After 2050)

The Metaverse becomes a persistent and self-sustaining real-world reality, and achieves a virtual universe depicted at the "Oasis" level in the 2018 movie "Ready Player One." The concept "Full dive VR"—a term coined by the Japanese light novel Sword Art Online in 2009—describes a virtual reality experience where a person fully "dives in" to the virtual world and becomes disconnected from the actual physical reality; in a sense, it would almost be like teleportation.

At that time, the virtual and real worlds will be indistinguishable, and the population and usage of the virtual world will be numerous.

Summary

In this chapter, you were first introduced to concepts of the Metaverse, including its history and characteristics. Then, you explore various immersive technologies, including AR, VR, MR, and XR, and learned how these technologies work. Next, you learned Metaverse layers to understand different products or services in the Metaverse landscape. Also, we discussed how NFTs and crypto games function in the Metaverse. Finally, you entered a virtual blockchain world to buy virtual land to experience the current stage of virtual real estate in the Metaverse.

By the end of this chapter, we discussed the Future of the Metaverse.

In the next chapter, you'll explore decentralized finance, or DeFi, one of the most popular topics in the 2022 crypto space. We will give an overview of DeFi's core concepts and structure and deep dive into DeFi products, such as decentralized stablecoins, decentralized exchanges, and decentralized Lending and Borrowing. You'll also see a step-by-step guide to using DeFi products in practice. The chapter will be a good opportunity for you to understand DeFi protocol in general.

CHAPTER 8

Decentralized Finance (DeFi): Reinventing Financial Services

The global financial system consists of many institutions, such as banks, insurance companies, stock exchanges, and various governmental agencies that regulate these institutions. The traditional finance service is centralized. Central authorities issue the currency and control the supply and distribution of money that fuels the economy. Centralized financial institutions manage the assets and carry out transactions through the centralized system to reduce fraud. However, these processes also increase complexity within the system and lead to high intermediary costs as well as slow transaction times. In addition, these transactions are not fully transparent to all parties involved.

Cryptocurrency adoption has accelerated rapidly over recent years, and crypto markets that trade digital assets in decentralized networks require no third-party intermediary. As a result, the popularity of these markets is reshaping the global financial industry.

Decentralized finance (DeFi) represents an innovative way to rebuild traditional financial services. Financial products are built around public or consortium blockchain and smart contracts. Users control their assets and personal data when transacting in the DeFi system. As the crypto

B. Wu and B. Wu, *Blockchain for Teens*, https://doi.org/10.1007/978-1-4842-8808-5_8

industry matures, more investment will be going toward building DeFi solutions. Subsequently, the global decentralized finance market has experienced tremendous growth since 2020. It is expected to grow at a steady compound annual growth rate (CAGR) of 43.8% from 2022 to 2030.

The DeFi ecosystem comprises a wide range of products, including infrastructure, decentralized exchanges (DEXs), lending and borrowing, stablecoins, insurance, payments, Decentralized Autonomous Organizations (DAO), and custodial services.

The goal of this chapter is to introduce you to DeFi. We will provide an overview of DeFi's core concepts and structure, as well as an in-depth look at specific products in DeFi, such as decentralized stablecoins (e.g., MakerDAO's DAI), decentralized exchanges (e.g., Uniswap), and decentralized Lending and Borrowing (e.g., Aave). Finally, by providing a step-by-step guide to using DeFi products in practice, the chapter will help you gain the knowledge needed to make real-world DeFi investments and trades.

This chapter will help you to understand the following practical topics:

- What is decentralized finance (DeFi)?

- The structure of DeFi

- Decentralized stablecoin

- Decentralized exchanges (DEXs)

- Decentralized lending and borrowing

- Decentralized insurance

What Is Decentralized Finance (DeFi)?

Decentralized finance, also known as DeFi, uses cryptocurrency and blockchain technology to provide a full spectrum of financial products and services, from everyday payment, lending, and borrowing to complicated derivatives and margin trading.

Traditional, centralized financial systems control user transactions using their centralized services. The services charge a high transaction fee due to third parties involved transaction process for facilitating money movement between parties and compliance. In 2021, the banking industry earned an estimated $33.4 billion in overdraft revenues.

Users have to trust the centralized system to manage their funds. Finance services require the customer to provide personal information to verify their identity when doing business with banks and other financial institutions. The process is due to government regulations that require the bank to perform KYC (Know Your Customer) and AML (anti-money laundering) complex compliance. Financial institutions use AML to prevent money laundering.

However, increasing banking requirements are adding complexity to protecting customer data. As a result, the financial industry had to maintain and upgrade its system to make business services functional and ensure customer data is safe for implementing new technology.

Because financial institutions are involved in protecting customers' money and highly sensitive personally identifiable information (PII) information, they have very high protection standards to take security most seriously. Furthermore, cybercriminals typically pick their targets based on maximum impact and profit. The financial industry perfectly meets these conditions and has always been a favored target for incentivized attacks by cyber attackers.

Modern software systems are typically very complex and involve many computer infrastructures, software, and components, such as open source libraries, databases, cloud ecosystems, containers, networks, operating systems, etc. Hackers use vulnerability search engines, such as Nmap, Ransomware, Trojans, and Worms, to find vulnerable computer systems, software, servers, and much more. To keep the highest level of data security is often very expensive and challenging, and many financial institutions have to tighten their budgets on IT spending.

There are around 44,000 banks and credit unions around the world. Unfortunately, not every company can adequately take care of user data for their customers. Today, banking and finance data breaches often happen. Therefore, banking and finance data breaches often occur.

Cybersecurity risks to the financial system have increased in recent years. Figure 8-1 shows financial data breaches from January 2018 to June 2022.

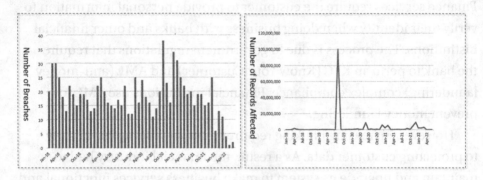

Figure 8-1. *Financial Data Breaches in January 2018–April 2022*

There were 982 financial data breaches from January 2018 to June 2022, and these breaches affected around 153 million individual records. Data breaches have increased by 13% from 2019 to 2020 and 11% from 2020 to 2021.

In March 2019, more than 100 million Capital One banking customers' credit card information, including *Social Security Numbers,* dates of birth, credit card numbers, credit scores, credit limits, and balances, suffered a data breach. As a result, the bank has to pay $190 million to settle a class-action lawsuit.

The financial protocols can be defined in smart contracts in DeFi. The financial services are running on the decentralized blockchain network, which is available to anyone with an Internet connection. There are no traditional centralized authorities, intermediaries, and trust mechanisms. Users can maintain full control of their assets in a secure digital wallet instead of managing them in a bank. On Nov. 11, 2022, FTX, "Futures Exchange," as the second-largest cryptocurrency exchange, filed for bankruptcy. The exchange was valued at more than US$30 billion in early November 2022. As a centralized exchange, FTX held users' wallets and private keys and managed user funds. However, the exchanger improperly loaned customer funds to Alameda Research which led to problems when FTX ran into its "liquidity crisis." FTX's collapse reminds investors of 'Not Your Keys, Not Your Coins' and has spurred a rising interest in decentralized finance platforms.

Due to the transparent nature of public blockchains, data privacy has become a rising concern regarding DeFi systems in the blockchain. There are already many privacy-focused solutions on the blockchain, including secure Multi-Party Computation (MPC), zero-knowledge proofs, federated machine learning, off-chain data storage, etc.

DeFi is booming. DeFi's total value locked or TVL has dramatically grown nearly 40,000% in the last two years from $601 million at the start of 2020 to $239 billion in 2022. The global financial services market is worth $23.32 trillion, and DeFi TVL is 240 billion as of 2021. DeFi is only 1% of the total global financial services market. It is still in the very early stages in this space, with plenty of room for innovation. DeFi TVL should continue to increase dramatically in the next few years.

The Structure of DeFi

DeFi services are built based on layered architecture, which comprises multiple layers and the logical separation of components. Each layer's components communicate with another layer's components to execute its function. Communication happens through predefined interfaces.

The DeFi ecosystem consists of five different layers, which encompass the followings: aggregation, application, protocol, asset, and settlement layers, as shown in Figure 8-2.

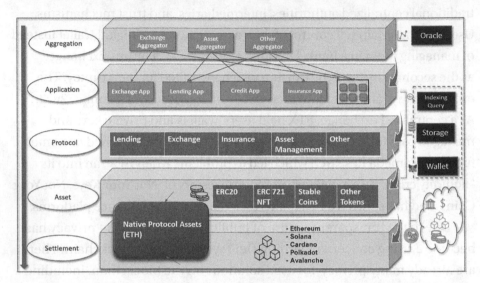

Figure 8-2. *The structure of DeFi—five layers*

Layer 1: The Settlement Layer

The settlement layer provides the foundation for all DeFi transactions—public blockchain and its native cryptocurrency form the settlement layer. One example of the settlement layer is Ethereum and its native token ether (ETH).

The blockchain transaction data are permanently stored in the network. Therefore, any asset ownership state changes will adhere to the network's consensus mechanisms, smart contract conditions, and other rules to ensure that transaction execution will only happen in line with established protocols.

Since this layer is principally composed of blockchain and distributed ledger technologies for trustless execution, it serves as a settlement layer.

At the time of writing, most DeFi applications are built on the Ethereum network, which holds over 25% of all decentralized finance protocols. Ethereum has 35.81 billion, which is 58% of the $62.32 billion entire DeFi TVL. All EVM-related Defi TVL is worth 50.85 billion, which is around 82% of the whole DeFi TVL. Figure 8-3 illustrates the blockchains' top DeFi protocols and TVL.

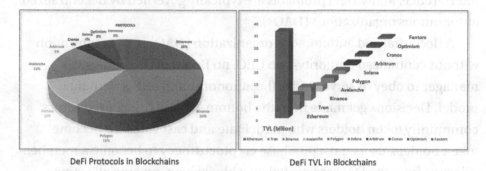

DeFi Protocols in Blockchains   DeFi TVL in Blockchains

Figure 8-3. *Blockchains' top DeFi protocols and TVL*

Layer 2: The Asset Layer

The asset layer sits on top of the settlement layer. This layer consists of all tokens, including native protocol token assets like Ether and any additional tokens such as ERC-20, NFT, etc., issued on the blockchain. In this layer, it is worth mentioning are stablecoins.

In Chapter 1, we learned that the cryptocurrency market's high volatility brings a risk for many financial products and general spending. Stablecoins provide investors with a safe harbor to minimize price volatility by providing stable value. Their value stays pegged to another less volatile asset, usually a popular currency like the US dollar or the British pound. Stablecoins act as the medium of exchange and are widely used as currency for daily transactions in DeFi. We will discuss more later in the decentralized stablecoin session. Here are some popular stablecoins in DeFi: Tether, USD Coin, Binance USD, TrueUSD, DAI, and Pax Dollar.

Layer 3: The Protocol Layer

The protocol layer provides a set of principles and rules in a given industry that participants have agreed to follow. The protocols are written in smart contracts to govern DeFi transactions and are self-executable in a predefined manner without a central authority or third party's interference. Many DeFi protocols are typically governed by decentralized autonomous organizations (DAOs).

A decentralized autonomous organization (DAO) is an organization without centralized authority—no CEO, no Board of Directors, no manager to obey or serve, and is the autonomy and self-governance model. Decisions get made from the bottom-up and distributed across community token holders who participate and cast votes. To become token holders, users must purchase cryptocurrency to become a member. All votes from the DAO are posted on a blockchain, making all actions auditable. Smart contracts establish the DAO's rules and will automatically execute when a set of criteria are met. The entire DAOs process is fully transparent and autonomous.

In 2020, a DeFi lending protocol Aave launched its own governance token toward autonomous and decentralized governance. DAO community votes will determine Aave Market Policies and Protocol Policies, formalized in Aave Improvement Proposals (AIPs). Other DeFi projects have since adapted the model and moving toward DAO. The Popular DeFi project use DAO like Uniswap, Maker DAO, BitDAO, Aragon, Decred, 0X, Dash, Compound, and Curve DAO.

All protocols defined at this layer are highly interoperable, which can be used by any Dapp built simultaneously and provide liquidity for the DeFi ecosystem. The main protocols in this layer are lending, exchange, insurance, asset management, and others. We will provide detailed DeFi use cases in the DeFi Products section.

Layer 4: The Application Layer

The application layer runs user-specific applications that connect to individual protocols. These applications serve as DeFi services which typically build Dapps to interact with a set of smart contracts functionality on the protocol layer, for example, asset management, loan, and insurance applications.

Level 5: The Aggregation Layer

As DeFi exponentially grows, the number of new platforms and protocols in the DeFi ecosystem appears quickly. Consequently, keeping an eye on all the upcoming DeFi products has become increasingly challenging.

The aggregation layer utilizes the application layer to aggregate various applications and protocols to provide a broader service and tools and allow users to efficiently perform complex tasks by connecting to several protocols and applications. DeFi aggregator platforms provide simply a one-stop solution that allows users to use a single aggregator dashboard to execute multiple types of DeFi transactions. Those aggregator platforms have become very popular among active DeFi users. Around 20% of decentralized trading volumes were through the DeFi aggregator in mid-2020.

One of the top DeFi aggregator examples is 1inch. It is designed as the price aggregator to provide tools that extract price data for various tokens traded on decentralized multiple exchanges (DEX). 1inch aggregator uses custom wrapper smart contracts that wrap/unwrap tokens at the current exchange rate. Traders can explore and trade cryptocurrencies across DEXes. Aggregators support cryptocurrency exchange at popular DEXes on Ethereum, Binance Smart Chain, Polygon, Optimistic Ethereum, Arbitrum, Avalanche, Gnosis Chain, and many others blockchains. Figure 8-4 shows a 1inch aggregator interface.

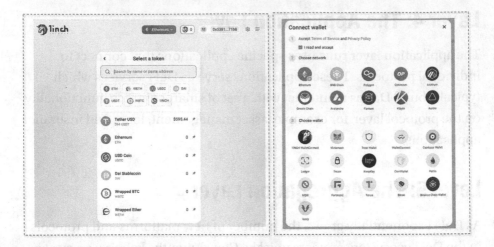

Figure 8-4. *1inch Aggregator Interface*

The DeFi product aims to reshape the traditional industry by providing various decentralized financial services such as lending, payment, insurance, trading, credit, risk, and many other financial products. The products eliminate the centralized third-party firms within a permissionless peer-to-peer network. Furthermore, DeFi products are designed modularly, enabling applications much freedom to integrate these open DeFi services into their products.

Decentralized Stablecoin

The crypto industry is still in its infancy stage. Compared to the traditional global finance market, the liquidity of digital assets is still relatively small. Moreover, volatility comes with any emerging market with low liquidity.

All of this led to the rise of stablecoins. A stablecoin is a crypto that aims to provide a safe digital asset to maintain stability in value. It is pegging the price to other types of money, such as a fiat currency, like the USD or commodity money like gold or oil. In the past few years, stablecoins have significantly gained popularity, and many stablecoin projects have been launched in the cryptocurrency market.

Stablecoin History

The first stablecoin, bitUSD, was issued back in July 2014. bitUSD is pegged to USD and can be traded freely on BitShares. Another stablecoin, Tether (USDT), was launched in October 2014, and Like bitUSD, the tether is also pegged to USD. Today, USDT is the stablecoin leading in the market cap.

Figure 8-5 shows a timeline of the launches of primary stablecoins in the last few years:

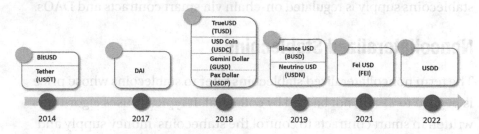

Figure 8-5. *Stablecoin Timeline*

Types of Stablecoins

Stablecoins are classified into several types.

Commodity-Collateralized Stablecoins

Commodity-backed stablecoins refer to stablecoins collateralized are backed using physical assets like gold, oil, and real estate. The most popular commodity collateralized stablecoins are Tether Gold (XAUT) and Paxos Gold (PAXG).

Fiat-Collateralized Stablecoins

Fiat-collateralized stablecoins are pegged to the value of fiat, such as USD, EUR, or GBP, which is real money issued by governments. Most often, fiat is USD. For example, tether (USDT) and USD Coin (USDC) are examples of fiat-collateralized stablecoin.

Crypto-Collateralized Stablecoins

Crypto-collateralized stablecoins refer to stablecoins that are backed by existing digital cryptocurrencies such as BTC or ETH. One example is MakerDAO's stablecoin, DAI. DAI is an ERC-20 token pegged to USD with a ratio of 1:1 achieved on-chain via smart contracts with incentives. The stablecoins supply is regulated on-chain via smart contracts and DAOs.

Noncollateralized Stablecoins

The term noncollateralized stablecoins refer to stablecoins whose price is pegged to $1 and not backed by collateral. It typically uses algorithms written in smart contracts to control the stabecoins' money supply and stabilize the price. There is no collateral needed to mint coins.

Neutrino USD and USDD are algorithmic crypto-collateralized stablecoins examples. All operations, including issuance, collateralization, staking, and reward payouts, are transparent and governed by smart contracts and a liquidity pool.

A Deep Dive into Stablecoins—Maker (DAI)

Let us look into a popular stablecoins example Maker (DAI), to understand more. MakerDAO, a decentralized autonomous organization (DAO), runs in the Ethereum blockchain. MakerDAO is the two-token model design— governance token and stablecoin. There are three coins in the Maker platform: Maker coin (MKR), Sai (SAI), and DAI (DAI).

The MKR is a governance token used for voting rights on the Maker platform from community participants. MKR is not a stablecoin. The second token is a stablecoin called DAI. DAI is multi-collateral DAI and is used for payment, collateral, exchange for the asset, integration with many protocols, and many others service in the DeFi ecosystem. DAI is currently backed by Ether (ETH) and Basic Attention Token (BAT). The third token is Sai, which is a single collateral type backing DAI. The collateral backed in Sai is ETH only.

How DAI Works

DAI currently has a market cap of $6.93 billion and a 6.9 billion DAI supply. There is no cap on the total supply of DAI, and supply is managed based on the Maker Vault. Before multi-collateral DAI (MCD) was released in November 2019, it was called Collateralized Debt Position (CDP).

The Maker Vault is a core smart contracts component in MakerDAO which will create DAI after holding the collateral (ether) for the Maker system. Once the borrowed DAI is returned, Maker Vault releases locked collateral and burn these DAI.

DAI is over-collateralized to account for, which needs to lock up 150% of the value of collateral to handle infamous volatility. For example, if you deposit $100 in Ethereum, you will receive $50 in DAI. Assume 1 Ethereum is 1439.685 DAI. 100 DAI is backed by 0.104 Ether (ETH).

Let us look at an analogy example to understand how Maker Vault manages the DAI peg to the dollar.

An investor who wants to borrow DAI creates a Maker Vault and sends ETH into the Maker Vault. Maker Vault generates the amount of DAI and locks up these ETH collaterals in the form of Pooled Ether (PETH). The amount of DAI created is based on how much ether the user has put into the Maker Vault. Generate DAI will deposit into the user's wallet with interest over time, called DAI Saving Rate (DSR). Users can freely get their escrowed collateral back at any time. They need to pay the DAI plus some of the stability fee (MKR) to the Maker Vault. After that, these DAI are burned, and Maker Vault is closed.

Figure 8-6 illustrates the entire Maker Vault flow.

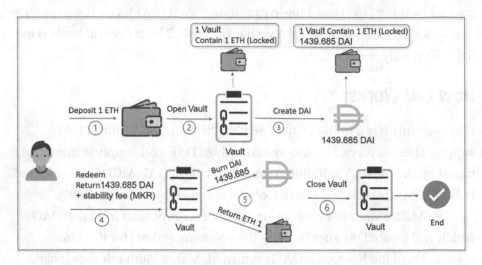

Figure 8-6. *Maker Vault Flow Manager DAI Creation and Burn*

When either goes down, or DAI goes up, it could cause the collateral ether value held in Maker Vault to be worth less than the amount of DAI's original backing. However, since DAI is created by over-collateralization, Maker protocol will ensure Maker Vault holds enough Eth to pay back DAI and liquidates Maker Vault when the account becomes too risky. For example, if the market ether price has dropped below a certain threshold, the Maker Vault will lock up collateral until the user pays back enough DAI or auction off ether to the highest bidder.

Maker (MKR) Coins Supply

MakerDAO initially launched with a supply of 1 million MKR tokens. As of September 2022, the circulating supply of Maker tokens is around 977,631, with a market cap of over 737 million USD. The total supply of MKR is a dynamic value depending on market price and the overall health of the Maker Protocol's system. Maker systems use complex mechanisms to govern DAI's stability by issuing and removing MKR.

DAI's value is secured by collateral like ETH, which is stored in Maker vaults. When the ETH market price is down, the value of ETH becomes insufficient to stay pegged at $1 with the corresponding amount of DAI. In that case, the Maker Protocol automatically triggers the liquidation of the vault.

The Maker Protocol will create new MKR tokens to increase the total supply. Then, those new MKR tokens will sell and cover the remaining value loss.

On the other hand, if the collateral price is up, to keep DAI in stable value, the Maker Protocol will buy back and burn MKR tokens. In this way, it will decrease MKR's total supply, resulting in excess DAI being auctioned.

The general flow is presented in Figure 8-7.

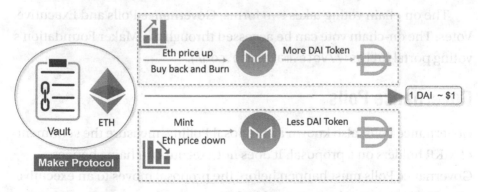

Figure 8-7. *Circulation of MKR Token*

MakerDAO's Governance

As we learned, MKR is the governing token of DAI. MKR token holders have voting power on any decision in the MakerDAO, including:

- Add a new collateral asset vault.

- Adjust risk parameters for existing vaults.

- Modify the DAI Savings Rate.

- Trigger Emergency Shutdown.

- Choose the stability fees.

- Choose the Debt Ceilings.

- Setup the set of Oracle Feeds.

- Upgrade the system.

Maker Protocol supports the rules for on-chain and off-chain governance.

Everyone, including non-MKR holders, can propose a new governance rule. First, the proposal can be discussed informally and voted on off-chain governance in the public MakerDAO forum (https://forum.makerdao.com). Then more formally, vote on the on-chain by MKR holders.

The on-chain voting takes two forms: Governance Polls and Executive Votes. The on-chain vote can be accessed through the Maker Foundation's voting portal (https://vote.makerdao.com/).

Governance Polls

Governance Polls, also known as Proposal Polling, measure the sentiment of MKR holders on a proposal. It does not execute on-chain changes. Governance Polls must happen before the proposal moves to an executive vote. Here are examples proposed in the past:

- Community Greenlight Poll—Cabot

- Collateral Onboarding Project-based Funding Request (PFR)

- Ratification Poll for Modify DAI Foundation Core Unit Budget

- Oh no, this should not be here

- PPG—Open Market Committee Proposal

POSTED AUG 15 2022 16:00 UTC | POLL ID 851

Community Greenlight Poll - Cabot (Cabot Renewable Energy Crypto Mining LLC) - August 15, 2022

Signal your support or opposition to prioritising onboarding Cabot (Cabot Renewable Energy Crypto Mining LLC).

Medium Impact   Greenlight

⏱ POLL ENDED   💬 4 COMMENTS

PLURALITY POLL ⑦

| View Details |

0%   11%   89%

WINNING OPTION: NO (DEFER) WITH 83,029 MKR SUPPORTING.

Executive Votes

Executive Votes execute technical changes to the Maker Protocol and changes to the state of the protocol or the DAO as a whole in the blockchain. Here are some examples of an executive Vote in the past:

- Onboarding real-world asset vaults

- Parameter changes

- Core unit budget distributions

- MKR vesting transfers

- Form consensus on important community goals and targets

- Collateral onboarding

Voting power is measured by the number of MKR tokens voters own and present.

For example, if 100 MKR holders with 100 MKR vote for Proposal A, while 50 holders with 1,000 MKR vote for Proposal B, Proposal B wins because of support from more MKR tokens.

Vote on a Proposal

Next, we will demonstrate how to vote on a proposal in Maker Foundation's voting portal.

Step 1: Get Your MKR Token

You can find an exchange to buy, sell and trade MKR, such as Coinbase, Binance, Kraken, crypto.com, and others.

Step 2: Connect to Ethereum Mainnet with Wallet

Click connect wallet button in Maker Foundation's voting portal and connect to Ethereum by selecting a wallet:

Step 3: Select an Active Vote

Find an active vote in the voting portal and choose vote options:

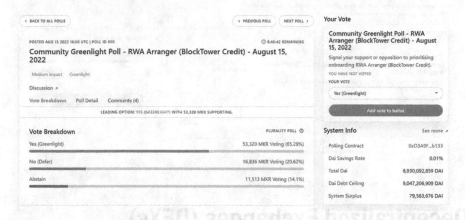

Step 4: Review and Submit Your Vote

Step 5: Vote Completed

You successfully voted on 1 poll
Share your votes to the Forum or Twitter below, or go back to the polls page to edit your votes
ⓘ Your vote and comment may take a few minutes to appear in the Voting Portal

‹ BACK TO ALL POLLS

POSTED AUG 15 2022 16:00 UTC | POLL ID 850

Community Greenlight Poll - RWA Arranger (BlockTower Credit) - August 15, 2022

YOUR VOTE

Yes (Greenlight)

Signal your support or opposition to prioritising onboarding RWA Arranger (BlockTower Credit).

Medium Impact   Greenlight

🕐 0:31:58 REMAINING   💬 4 COMMENTS

Share all your votes

You voted on 1 of 2 available polls

Voting weight ⓦ   0.04 MKR

Share all votes

PLURALITY POLL ⓦ
65%   14%   21%

LEADING OPTION: YES (GREENLIGHT) WITH 53,320 MKR SUPPORTING.

Decentralized Exchanges (DEXs)

Centralized exchanges (CEXs) work similarly to a bank. Both buyers and sellers trust these exchange platforms to trade their assets. Users can buy, sell, and trade digital assets such as Bitcoin, Ether, or other cryptocurrencies in the central wallet of the exchange by paying certain transaction fees, and exchanges will control those funds and execution of crypto trades through internal systems. Then sign the transaction in the blockchain on the user's behalf.

Liquidity means how quickly you can exchange an asset for cash without affecting its market price. Since centralized exchanges are highly regulated, they attract many active users. These users are creating more orders and lead to high trading volumes with a faster exchange rate, which means more liquidity.

To create a centralized exchange account, the user must provide a valid government-issued ID, banking details, and other personal information. The signup process is part of KYC (Know Your Customer) and AML (Anti Money Laundering) practices required by regulations. In addition, it helps exchanges determine a customer risk level and prevent criminal activity like money laundering and the financing of terrorism. Once a centralized exchange verifies and approves identity, the user can deposit funds onto the exchange account via wire transfer, ACH transfer, or by depositing cryptocurrencies such as Bitcoin or ether. Then, the user may begin trading.

Coinbase, Kraken, Crypto.com, and Binance are the popular centralized exchanges examples.

Although centralized exchanges (CEXs) currently *handle the majority* of cryptocurrency trading activity, decentralized exchanges (DEXs) are growing in popularity. DEXs are the direct opposite of centralized cryptocurrency exchanges, which manage token ownership of the exchange and hold user's private keys. Decentralized exchanges (DEXs) are peer-to-peer trading platforms that allow users to keep control of their funds and purchase or sell blockchain-based tokens and coin cryptocurrencies without an intermediary to control the transaction process. Instead, the user controls the wallet's private keys. DEXs use smart contracts, which define set conditions to execute and record every transaction on the blockchain with a low transaction fee. Since DEXs do not involve any centralized authority, meaning KYC/AM are not required. Anyone can open an account to attend the DeFi ecosystem to trade. The transaction is fully anonymous.

Table 8-1 compares the difference between centralized exchanges and decentralized centralized exchanges:

Table 8-1. *Comparing centralized and decentralized exchanges*

	CEXs	DEXs
Control	Exchange control funds	User control funds
Fee	Required. Higher transaction fees	Zero or very minimal fees
Liquidity	High liquidity	Low liquidity
Regulation	KYC/AML required	KYC/AML not required
User identity	Not anonymous	Anonymous
Usage	Easy to use (even for beginners)	Not user-friendly. Need profession knowledge
Security	Could be hacks and server downtime	No hacks and server downtime

Type of Decentralized Exchanges

DEXs are a foundation of decentralized finance (DeFi), which allow the trading of digital assets on automated smart contracts. There are three primary types of decentralized exchanges: Automated market makers, Order books DEXs, and DEX aggregators described in Figure 8-8.

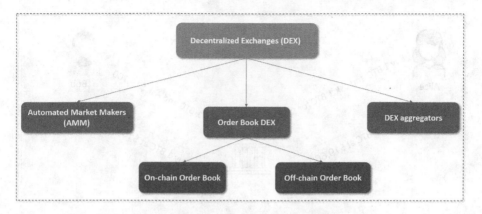

Figure 8-8. *Type of decentralized exchanges*

Automated Market Makers (AMMs)

On a traditional exchange platform, a market maker is typically a
brokerage house, large bank, or institution that will "create the market,"
as the name suggests. Market makers create liquidity for trading pairs in
the market by buying and selling securities for their own accounts. Buyers
and sellers offer different prices for an asset, and market makers always
quote two-sided markets for a particular asset. They compensate for the
difference in the bid-ask spread—the asking price exceeds the bid price
for an asset in the market by providing purchase and sale solutions for
investors.

Trader A, Alice, wants to buy 1 BTC at $19,600. The exchange needs
to find a Trader B, Bob, willing to sell 1 BTC at Alice's preferred exchange
range, such as $19,700. The centralized exchange will act as a middleman
between Alice and Bob. The exchange will offer $19,620 to Bob, assuming
Bob accepts the offer. The exchange will then sell Alice 1 BTC at $19,660.
The exchange will get a profit of about $40. The process is illustrated in
Figure 8-9.

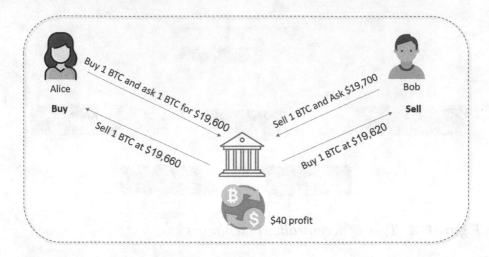

Figure 8-9. *Market maker activities*

In the case of an automated market maker (AMM), sometimes called proactive market maker, a market maker is replaced with autonomous protocols using smart contracts. The smart contracts in AMM always keep a quote between two (or more) assets and determine the price of digital assets and provide liquidity.

AMM Basic Concepts

Compared to CEXs, the number of buyers and sellers in DEXs are still small. Therefore, finding enough buyers and sellers to trade assets at matched prices will be hard. AMMs are creating liquidity pools to solve this problem. AMMs provide a practice called "yield farming" for liquidity providers (LP) to earn bonus yield by adding an appropriate balance of assets into a liquidity pool. LP will automatically obtain reward tokens, Ethereum-based ERC-20 tokens, known as liquidity provider (LP) tokens. These LP tokens represent LP ownership as a pool provider. When LPs withdraw deposited funds, LP tokens will return to the DeFi system. The pool will charge transaction fees when each trade occurs in the liquidity pool. LP token holders will be rewarded proportionately with the liquidity pool's growth, and LP can claim those rewards regularly. For example, if you contribute $100 worth of tokens to an AMM DEXs pool (such as Uniswap) with a total market value of $1000, you will receive 10% of that pool's LP tokens.

Asset funds in a liquidity pool are locked in a smart contract. With AMM, traders can seamlessly trade their assets in the platform using the liquidity pools without needing a centralized market maker. LPs will be rewarded a fraction of the fees and incentives on their investments.

There is no seller or buyer on the other side. Instead, an automated algorithm determines the price of the tokens in liquidity pools in the AMM smart contract. The smart contract algorithm in AMM will be automated and optimized, adjusting the price to react to market needs.

What Are the Existing AMM Models?

AMMs use a mathematical formula to adjust prices algorithmically based on supply in liquidity pools to maintain the balance of assets in the liquidity pool. Several constant function market makers (CFMMs) are utilized by popular AMM protocols such as Uniswap, Bancor, and Curve. The CFMMs include constant product market makers, constant sum market makers, and constant mean market makers.

Constant Product Market Maker (CPMM)

CPMM was popularized by the first AMM-based DEX, Uniswap, Bancor, and the most popular AMM in the market. CPMMs are based on the function x*y=k, where x is the amount of one token in the liquidity pool, and y is the amount of the other. The range of prices for two tokens depends on the available liquidity of each token. When the supply of token X increases, the token supply of Y must decrease in order to maintain the constant product K, and vice versa.

For example (Uniswap V2), a liquidity poll has 50% DAI and 50% Ether. Assume one Ether is $2000 and one DAI is $1. In the beginning, the liquidity pool has 9 Ether and 18,000 DAI. In this case, one Ether and 2,000 DAI pair have a total value of $4000, which can be calculated as 2000+ 1 * 2000 = 4,000.

A liquidity provider invests 10% of the pool assets—one Ether and 2,000 DAI in the pool. After the deposit, the pool has 20,000 DAI and 10 Ether, and each token has a 50% amount. The CPMM constant x*y=k is 20,000 * 10 = 200,000.

Now a liquidity buyer wants to purchase one Ether. The price for Ether is 2222 DAI based on the following formula:

$$(20,000 + x) * (10 - 1) = 200,000 \rightarrow x = 2,222$$

The buyer will need to pay 2222 DAI to get one Ether. In the end, the pool will have 9 Ether and 22,222 DAI.

The process is described in Figure 8-10.

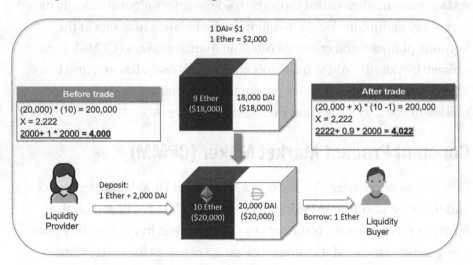

Figure 8-10. *AMM CPMM example*

An example of a DEX that uses CPMM is Uniswap V1 and V2 (Uniswap V3 uses a different function), Bancor (V1), Sushi Swap, Pancake swap, and other derivatives.

Constant Sum Market Maker (CSMM)

The second variation of constant products is the constant sum market maker (CSMM), which holds the sum of the X and Y assets by simply replacing the multiplication in Constant Product with addition $(x + y = k)$. The variables can change multiple times as long as the sum remains the same constant.

This design makes it easier to predict price, but when one of the token liquidity pools is drained, the remaining liquidity is just one asset with no more liquidity for traders. As a result, CSMM cannot provide infinite liquidity and is not profitable. Therefore, CSMM is seldom used by AMMs.

Constant Mean Market Maker (CMMM)

A constant mean market maker (CMMM) was first introduced by Balancer Protocol and allowed investors to work with more than two tokens and maintain an average weight outside of 50/50, satisfying the following equation:

$$\prod_{i=1}^{n} R_i^{w_i} = k,$$

where R_i are the reserves of each asset, W is each asset weight, and k is for a constant.

For the three locked assets example, CMMM utilizes the formula for a liquidity pool that would look as follows:

$$(x * y * z) \wedge (1/3) = c$$

where x, y, and z are chosen tokens, c is a constant product of them.

Hybrid Constant Function

If underlying trading pairs' prices are almost stable (e.g., two USD-denominated stablecoins trading pairs DAI–USDC into Uniswap liquidity pool), constant product function may not be the best solution because of the slippage and return is tiny. Therefore, curve finance uses the Stableswap Invariant formula, a hybrid of the constant product and constant sum formula, and the function is shown as follows:

$$An^n \sum x_i + D = ADn^n| + \frac{D^{n+1}}{n^n \prod x_i}.$$

where x is the reserves for each token, n is the number of stablecoins, D is an invariant representing the entire token value in the reserve, A is the amplification coefficient, which is a tunable constant that is directly proportional to asset's volatility and the DAO can adjust the value.

In the curve stableswap-paper, there is a comparison amount Stableswap invariant with Uniswap (constant-product) and constant price invariants, displayed in Figure 8-11.

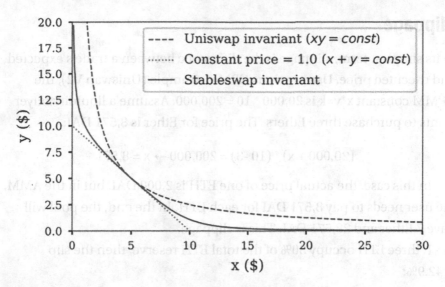

Figure 8-11. *Comparison of Stableswap invariant with constant product and constant sum(from Curve Stableswap-paper)*

The Stableswap invariant acts as a constant sum when the portfolio is balanced and provides a better tool for DeFi users to swap stablecoins.

The Limitations of AMM

As discussed in the previous section, DEXs often have low liquidity compared to CEXs. Therefore, DEXs must attract new users to contribute their assets and generate more liquidity. With LPs, the exchange cannot offer trading services. Since lower liquidity, AMM often has two main problems: slippage and Impermanent loss (IL).

Slippage

In its simplest term, slippage is the difference between a trade's expected and executed price. Use previous CPMM example (Uniswap V2), the CPMM constant x*y=k is 20,000 * 10 = 200,000. Assume a liquidity buyer wants to purchase three Ethers. The price for Ether is 8,571 DAI:

$$(20,000 + x) * (10 - 3) = 200,000 \rightarrow x = 8,571$$

In this case, the actual price of one ETH is 2,000 DAI, but in the AMM, the user needs to pay 8,571 DAI for each ETH. In the end, the pool will have 7 Ether and 28,571 DAI. This is slippage.

If three ETH occupy 30% of the total ETH reserve, then the slip is 42.9%:

$$(28,571 - 20,000/20,000) \rightarrow 42.9\%.$$

In this case, no one wants to pay 42.9% more DAI, and even actually, DAI keeps the same value as $1.

Impermanent Loss (IL)

When a user Alice acts as a liquidity provider, she will stake her assets in a liquidity pool (i.e., Uniswap V2). Impermanent loss usually happens when the market price of these crypto assets changes when Alice wants to withdraw the staking tokens from the pool. The liquidity pool automatically adjusts the token value based on the formula x*y=k. Therefore, the dollar value of the withdrawal could be lower than the dollar value of her deposit. No real losses will happen if Alice keeps her stake in the pool. That is why it is called "an impermanent loss." The loss could be reduced or disappear entirely, or even gain profit, depending on how the market moves. Let us look at an example as follows:

1. Alice stake 10 ETH and 20,000 DAI in Uniswap V2 liquidity pool when ETH price is $2,000. The constant product with addition is 200,000 (10 ETH * 20,000 DAI), and the total dollar value of tokens she is staking are:

    10 ETH * $2,000 + 20,000 DAI * $1 = $40,000

2. Now assume the ETH market price changes to 1 ETH = $2,500. The original tokens value will be:

    10 ETH* $2,500 + 20,000 DAI * $1 = $45,000

3. Alice wants to calculate the impermanent loss if she withdraws the funds. Assume the liquidity pool starts to adjust and rebalance token value. In this case, if the pool wants to keep 50% of ETH and 50% of DAI. DAI and ETH will have $22500 on each. The initial rebalance value will be:

    ($20000 + $25000)/2 = $22500

4. The number of ETH, in this case, will be 22500/2500 = 9 ETH. By applying x*y =9 ETH * 22500 DAI = 202,500. The number is different from the original constant of 200,000. So, the rebalance will continue.

The new distribution of each asset can then be calculated using the following formulas:

$$Xt = \sqrt{k/r_t} \qquad Yt = \sqrt{K * r_t}$$

Here r is the price between two token assets in the pool, t is the time in which r is calculated, and k is the CPMM constant (x*y).

Let us apply these formulae to our example to see how it works. Here r is 2000 before the ETH price changed and k is 200,000.

$$ETH - \quad X_{t1} = \sqrt{200{,}000/2{,}000} = 10$$

$$DAI - \quad Y_{t1} = \sqrt{200{,}000*2{,}000} = 20{,}000$$

We get the same original state of the token pair in the pool—10 ETH and 20,000 DAI. When the ETH price is changed to $2500 after a few days, the r is 2500. Let us reapply the same formula to do a calculation:

$$ETH - \quad X_{t2} = \sqrt{200{,}000/2{,}500} = 8.94$$

$$DAI - \quad Y_{t2} = \sqrt{200{,}000*2{,}500} = 22{,}360.68$$

The formula gave that the pool would contain about 8.94 ETH and about 22,360.68 DAI. Therefore, we can verify if it is a match to the constant 200,000:

$$8.94 * 22360.68 = 199{,}904 \approx 200{,}000$$

The new pair of token values are correct. If Alice continues to hold tokens in the pool, total DAIs will be $45,000:

$$10 * 2500 + 20000 = \$45{,}000$$

The return on the investment gain will be 12.5%:

$$45{,}000 - 40{,}000/40{,}000 = 12.5\%$$

We can simply earn 5,000 DAI (45,000 – 40,000).

Using those data, we can calculate the impermanent loss if Alice withdraws the tokens:

$$45,000 - (8.94 * 2,500 + 20,000) = \$289.32$$

$$289.32/45,000 = 0.64\%$$

Alice's impermanent loss is 0.64% and 289.32 DAI.

Figure 8-12 shows a diagram of impermanent loss estimation.

Impermanent loss from ETH price change starting from 100 USD per ETH

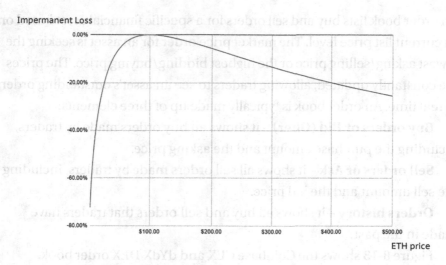

Figure 8-12. Impermanent loss estimation (from Bancor)

Here is a summary of losses compared to holding from the preceding graph:

- 1.25x price change = 0.6% loss

- 1.50x price change = 2.0% loss

- 1.75x price change = 3.8% loss

- 2x price change = 5.7% loss

- 3x price change = 13.4% loss

- 4x price change = 20.0% loss

- 5x price change = 25.5% loss

From our example, the losses are 0.64% when the price change from $2000 to $2500. There is a 125% change, matching the above graph estimation.

Several solutions to reduce the impact, including carrying out smaller transactions, increasing the price slippage tolerance, and greater liquidity.

Order Book Decentralized Exchanges

An order book lists buy and sell orders for a specific financial asset based on its current list price level. The market price order for an asset is seeking the lowest asking/selling price or the highest bidding/buying price. The prices are constantly updated, allowing traders to see an asset's outstanding orders in real time. An order book is typically made up of three elements:

Buy orders or Bid (Offer) – it shows all buy orders made by traders, including the purchase amount and the asking price.

Sell orders or Ask – it shows all sell orders made by traders, including the sell amount and the bid price.

Orders history – it shows all buy and sell orders that traders have made in the past.

Figure 8-13 shows the Coinbase CEX and dYdX DEX order book.

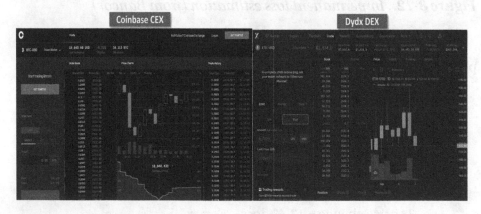

Figure 8-13. *Coinbase CEX and dYdX DEX order book*

Currently, there are two types of the order book at DEXs—on-chain and off-chain.

On-Chain Order Books

On-chain order books are hosted directly on the underlying blockchain, and every operation is done on-chain, including order submissions, updates, and cancellations. The blockchain records all order transactions, effectively removing the reliance on a centralized party. On the other side, every order is submitted to the blockchain, and the transactions will be broadcast to all blockchain validator/miner nodes to verify. It makes order book transactions slow and costly. When prices change dramatically, traders may need to update their on-chain orders. Because of the slow speed, the miner could inspect the order and then manipulate and execute their own orders before validating and confirming those transactions.

Here are some on-chain order books DEXs examples: ViteX, Demex, Bitshares, and Stellar decentralized exchanges. The typical on-chain order book process is illustrated in Figure 8-14.

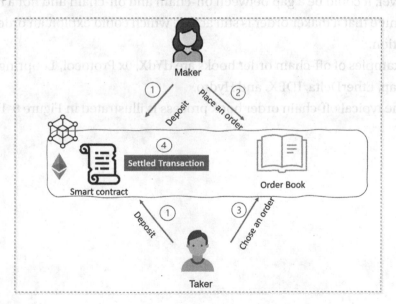

Figure 8-14. *On-chain order book*

The market maker is someone who offers an order to buy or sell, while the taker is someone who immediately buys or fills that order.

The on-chain process can be described in the following steps:

1. Market maker and taker deposit their funds in the smart contract

2. Maker placed an order in the order book

3. Taker then choose an order

4. Order is settled in the smart contract

Off-Chain Order Books

Off-chain order books are ordered book applications hosted and run outside of the blockchain. The order data are also stored in a central entity. Once a two-sided order is matched, the off-chain order platform will send a transaction to the blockchain smart contract to settle. The advantage of an off-chain order book is faster order management with low fees. However, it could be a gap between on-chain and off-chain and not a full guarantee that a maker order is still active, which could exploit an order execution.

Examples of off-chain order books are dYdX, 0x Protocol, Loopring, AirSwap, EtherDelta, IDEX, and Hydro.

The typical off-chain order book process is illustrated in Figure 8-15.

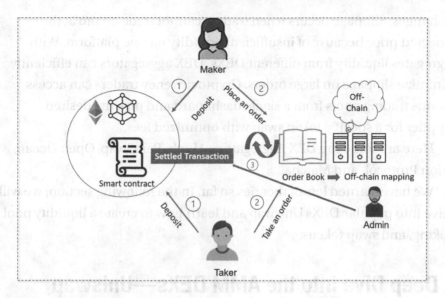

Figure 8-15. *Off-chain order book*

The off-chain process can be described in the following steps:

1. Market maker and Taker deposit their funds in the smart contract

2. The maker placed an order in the off-chain order book

3. Taker, then take an order

4. Off-chain service runs order matching

5. Admin sends the order to the on-chain smart contract and settled transaction

Decentralized Exchange Aggregators

DEX aggregators use several different protocols and methods to deal with issues associated with liquidity. The platforms have developed tools to aggregate liquidity across several centralized and decentralized crypto exchanges. Slippage occurs when traders cannot trade crypto at the expected price because of insufficient liquidity on one platform. With aggregates liquidity from different DEXs, DEX aggregators can efficiently minimize slippage on large orders. Cryptocurrency traders can access various trading pools from a single dashboard and pick the desired supplier for a specific token swap with optimized fees.

Here are some top DEX Aggregators: 1Inch, ParaSwap, Open Ocean, Orion Protocol, and Matcha.

We have learned lots of theories so far. In the following section, we will delve into popular DEXs Uniswap and learn how to create a liquidity pool, staking, and swap tokens.

A Deep Dive into the AMM DEXs—Uniswap

Uniswap is the most popular DEX and AMM. The platform was launched in Nov 2018. v2 was introduced in May 2020, and the current version is v3, launched in May 2021.

Users of the Uniswap platform can swap any two different ERC-20 tokens seamlessly without incurring too much slippage. In addition, the protocol runs on a series of smart contracts, making the platform permissionless and trustless. The native token of the Uniswap protocol is UNI, and it also acts as a governance token, giving the voting right to its token holder for changes to the protocol.

Currently, UNI is available in the following four liquidity mining pools:

- ETH/USDT

- ETH/USDC

- ETH/DAI

- ETH/WBTC

As of September 2022, there are over 50,000 trading token pairs with individual LP tokens for each pool in Uniswap. The Daily trading volume is $1.10b, and the Total Valued Locked (TVL) is $12.13b. Uniswap users can participate in the DEXs in several ways:

- **Create new pools** – Uniswap users can use smart contracts to create a pool for exchanging new pairs of tokens.

- **Swap assets via existing markets** – Token swaps in Uniswap allow traders directly swap from one ERC-20 token to another ERC-20 token.

- **Provide liquidity and earn rewards** – By staking the funds on the Uniswap platform, LP will reward with UNI.

- **Participate in Uniswap governance** – UNI token holders can govern and vote for the change for the Uniswap platform.

List Your Own Token on Uniswap DEX

With the knowledge of AMM we learned, let us convert theory into practice, create an ERC-20 token, and list it on Uniswap DEX.

Prerequisites

There are a few prerequisites that we must take care of:

1. Create an ERC-20 token.

2. Deploy it to the Ethereum network. We will use the Goerli test network.

3. Add deployed ERC token to your MetaMask wallet.

Create an ERC-20 Token

In Chapter 5, we have briefly discussed the ERC-20 token. There are many ways to create ERC-20 tokens. If you are an experienced smart contract developer, you can write your own ERC-20 token. To simplify, we will use a popular open source secure smart contract framework, OpenZeppelin, to create our ERC-20 token. It is really easy and just needs a few lines:

Step 1 – Open Remix IDE in your browser (`https://remix.ethereum.org`).

Step 2 – Create a smart contract named DeFiTeenToken.

Step 3 – We will import the ERC-20 token contract from OpenZeppelin. The ERC-20 token link from OpenZeppelin is here:

`https://github.com/OpenZeppelin/openzeppelincontracts/blob/master/contracts/token/ERC20/ERC20.sol`

Step 4 – In the contract, we define the initial supply for the DeFiTeenToken, when creating a token. The contract name is DeFiTeenToken and the symbol is DFTT. "msg.sender" is the person who is currently creating this contract. In our case, it will be a selected wallet account address to deploy the DeFiTeenToken contract.

Here is what our DeFiTeenToken smart contract looks like.

```
1  // SPDX-License-Identifier: MIT
2  pragma solidity ^0.8.0;
3  import "https://github.com/OpenZeppelin/openzeppelin-contracts/blob/v4.7.3/contracts/token/ERC20/ERC20.sol";
4
5  contract DeFiTeenToken is ERC20 {
6      constructor(uint256 initialSupply) ERC20("DeFiTeenToken", "DFTT") {
7          _mint(msg.sender, initialSupply);
8      }
9  }
```

You can also get this contract from the book's GitHub repository—Chapter 8:

`https://github.com/Apress/Blockchain-for-Teens.git`

Step 5 – Compile the DeFiTeenToken.sol smart contract.

Step 6 – Deploy the contract using Remix VM. We enter the initial supply as 100,000,000.

Step 7 – Conduct some quick tests under Remix "Deploy and run transactions" module.

By clicking name, symbol, and total supply, you should see the related value show up:

Step 8 – Test transfer function. Copy the second account from the Account drop-down list. Enter this account address in the transfer function to the input field and give the transfer DFTT amount of 1000. Once the transaction is completed, check the second account token by invoking the balanceOf function and entering the second account address. You should see the balance of the second account has 1000 DFTT tokens. The following screen shows the process to test the transfer function:

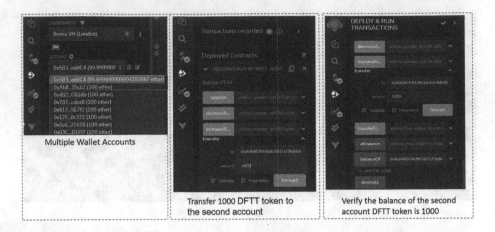

Multiple Wallet Accounts

Transfer 1000 DFTT token to
the second account

Verify the balance of the second
account DFTT token is 1000

Step 9 – Now let us deploy the DeFiTeenToken contract to the Goerli test network. This time, we enter 1000000000000000000000 (22-digit number) since the token unit is 18. Now it is time to deploy the contract. The Metamask will pop up for transaction confirmation. Click the confirm button.

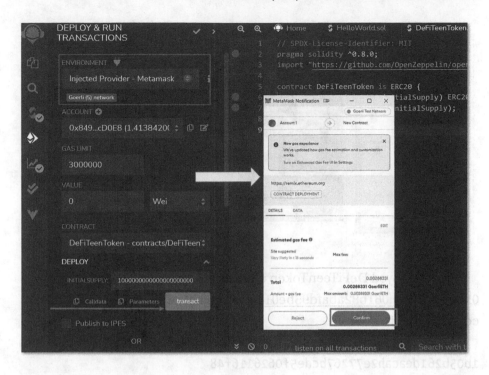

Note   To get the test ETH token using Goerli, you can go to the below addresses to request or mine a few tokens:

(1) https://goerlifaucet.com/; (2) https://goerli-faucet.pk910.de/; (3) https://goerlifaucet.com/

Step 10 – Once the contract is deployed, you can view the deployed contract from Etherscan via the link from MetaMask: activity ➤ contract deployment ➤ view on the block explorer. You can also verify the token name, symbol, and total supply in Remix IDE. You should see a similar result as follows:

Metamask   Verify in Remix   EtherScan for contract

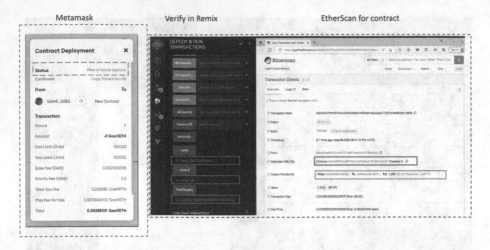

Our deployed DeFiTeenToken address is
0xbc438759cef061b82abafd95be018128cc4693f5, the ether scan for this
contract URL is

https://goerli.etherscan.io/tx/0x242401f79c53764342645058dfa
1b05b261deacab2e77267bcde5f0626116f48

Since the contract is deployed in a public test network, it is accessible
to everyone.

Step 11 – Import the DFTT token into your MetaMask wallet. Client
Asset tab in Metamask, select Import tokens. It will ask you to enter the
token address. You can get the contract address from Etherscan. With
entered contract address, you click the "Custom Token" button to import
the DFTT token.

After successfully deploying our DFTT token, it is now time to create a new pool in Uniswap DEXs.

Create a New Liquidity Pool in Uniswap

Step 1 – Go to Uniswap website: `https://app.uniswap.org/#/swap?chain=goerli`. The following screen will appear, and click connect wallet button. It will connect you to the Goerli test network.

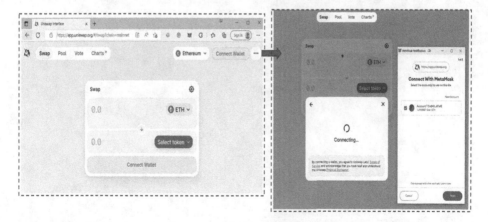

Step 2 – Once connected, Uniswap will pop up a screen and give you an address, showing all of your token transactions on the Uniswap platform.

Step 3 – Select "Create a pool."

Step 4 – Press the "Select a Token" option.

Step 5 – Enter your token's address in the "Search Name or Address" field and select your token from the dropdown.

Step 6 – Click on the "import" button.

Step 7 – An import token pop-up will show up. Ignore the warning. Click on the "Import" button.

You'll see a similar process (from step 3 to step 7) shown as follows:

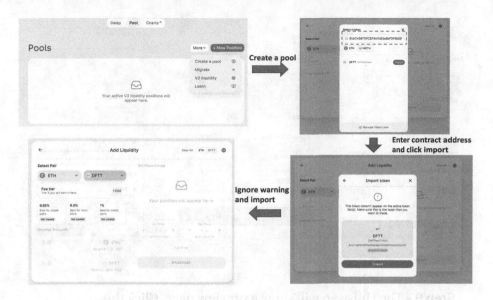

Step 8 – Enter the required information to create a new pool:

a. Select a fee from 0.05%, 0.3%, and 1%. Let us choose 0.05%.

b. Define DFTT token price compared to the current ETH price. Enter 0.001, for example.

c. Set a price range. Enter min price as 0.00001 ETH and Max price as 1 ETH.

d. Deposit Amount. We will deposit 0.01 ETH in this pool. The Uniswap application will automatically calculate the amount of DFTT, which is 0.000000978 DFTT.

With all information filled, click the "Approve DFTT" button. The Metamask will pop up and ask you to confirm the transaction. Click confirm button.

Step 9 – The Uniswap will show a preview page. Click the preview button.

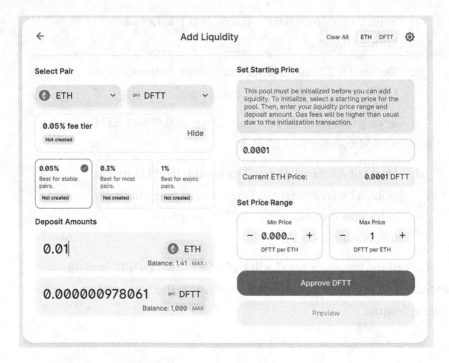

Step 10 – An "Add Liquidity" popup will show up. Click add button to add liquidity. Metamask will show confirm popup and click the "confirm" button.

Step 11 – Once the transaction is successfully mined in the blockchain, you should see your new liquidity pool in the Uniswap platform, shown as follows:

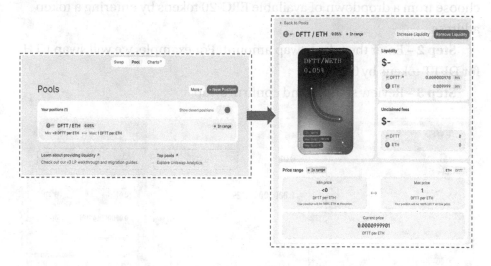

Add Liquidity in the Liquidity Pool

Adding liquidity is very similar to several steps for creating a liquidity pool. The entire process is illustrated as follows:

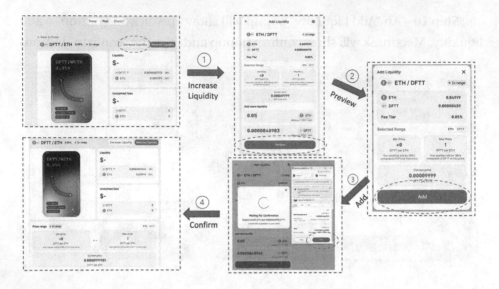

Swap Tokens in Uniswap

Step 1 – Select the Swap tab and choose the token pair. You can search and choose from a dropdown of available ERC-20 tokens by entering a token address.

Step 2 – Enter the token swap amount. For example, we will swap ETH for DFTT tokens by 0.01 ETH.

Step 3 – Review settings and confirm swap.

Step 4 – Confirm and Swap. You can see ETH total amount taken 0.01 from the wallet to create a swap.

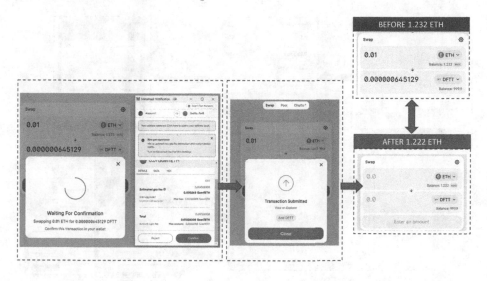

Note   You can see all recent transaction history from the wallet address. To set up the Swap transaction setting, such as Slippage tolerance, etc., you can click the top right corner setting icon.

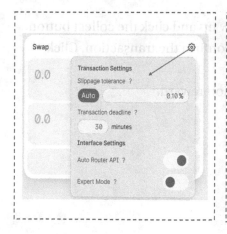

With similar steps, you can swap any token in the pool, including popular tokens like UNI. Here is an example:

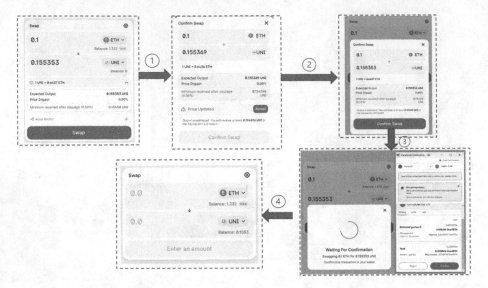

Claim the Reward from the Liquidity Pool

Finally, let us look at how to claim a review as an LP holder.

Step 1 – Click on the DEFT/ETH pool, and there is a collect fee button in the "Unclaimed fees" panel. We will select WETH as the return. Click the button.

Step 2 – A claim fees popup will show up and click the collect button.

Step 3 – Next, Metamask will ask to confirm the transaction. Click confirm button.

Step 4 – It will complete your collection reward.

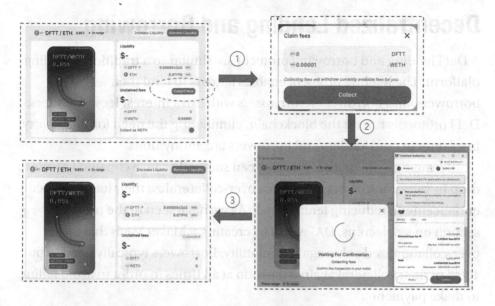

Step 5 – Import the WETH address to your Metamask. The WETH address in the Goerli network address is 0xB4FBF271143F4FBf7B91A5ded31805e42b2208d6. You can retrieve it from the Internet or Etherscan.

Step 6 – Now, you will see your claimed reward:

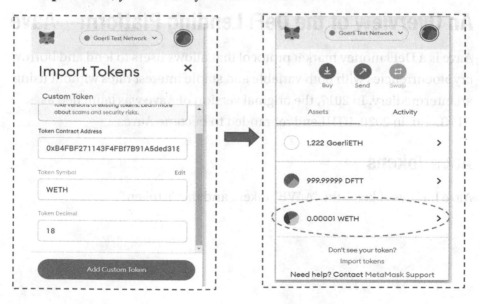

Decentralized Lending and Borrowing

A DeFi lending and borrowing protocol are similar to a traditional lending platform. The lending protocol enables lenders to lend their assets to borrowers, and borrowers return assets with extra interest fees to lenders. DeFi protocols run on the blockchain, eliminating the need for third-party involvement, and lenders and borrowers are anonymous.

Because crypto market volatility can suddenly cause collateral assets to drop in value, borrowers often must over-collateralize their loans for credit enhancement, reducing lenders' risk. As we have seen in the previous section on stablecoins, DAI works by creating a Maker Vault that locks over-collateralized value against volatility. Borrowers typically need to put 150% of their collateral against the ratio at all times in order to avoid failing to make payments.

Here is a list of a few most popular DeFi lending and borrowing platforms: Aave, Maker, and Compound.

We have discussed the Maker protocol in the stablecoin section. In this section, we will explore Aave lending and borrowing.

An Overview of the DeFi Lending Platform—Aave

Aave is a DeFi money market protocol that allows users to lend and borrow cryptocurrencies with both variable and stable interest rates without using an intermediary. In 2017, the original version of Aave was launched as ETHLend. In 2020, ETHLend rebranded to become Aave.

Aave Tokens

Aave has two tokens, the "AAVE" token, and the "aToken."

AAVE

The native token in the Aave lending protocol is AAVE, a governance token. Like Maker's governance token, AAVE allows holders to vote on proposals submitted by the Aave community.

aToken

The aToken represents the number of crypto assets supplied or borrowed with interest. The value of aToken is pegged to the value of the corresponding supplied asset at a 1:1 ratio.

As the Aave liquidity pool continues to grow, the accumulated interest of aTokens will increase. aToken holders can claim the staking reward directly to their same wallet address or redirect their interest payments to another Ethereum address.

For example, Alice provides one aETH token supply with 5% APY (annual percentage yield). Assume 1 ETH is $2000. The total asset is worth $2000. After Alice held her aETH token for a year, she redeems all of her aETH, assuming the 1 ETH is $3000. The value of aETH will be 1 + 1* 0.05 = 1.05 ETH, convert to dollar will be 1.05 * 3000 = $3150. The return on the investment gain will be 57.5%.

When a lender supplies crypto assets in the liquidity pool, Aave lending pool will mint aTokens to user accounts. When the lender decides to withdraw their assets, aToken contract will call redeem function with a calculated interest rate, return assets to the lender, and burn the related aTokens. The aToken contract redemption process is illustrated in Figure 8-16.

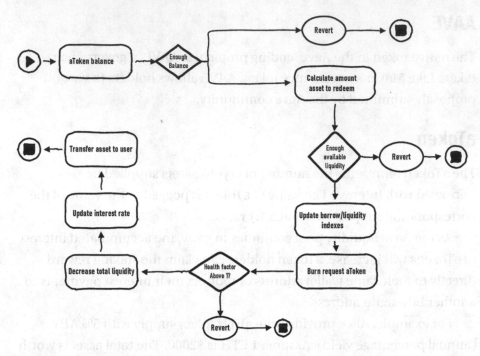

Figure 8-16. *Redeem an aTokens in AAVX Smart Contracts*

How to Deposit on Aave

Step 1 – Go to the Aave website: https://aave.com/. Click on the launch
app button. Then select and connect your wallet to the Aave platform.
In our following step-by-step guild, we will use the USDT token. You can
purchase USDT from popular crypto exchanges.

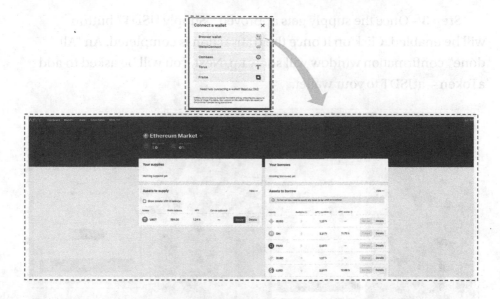

Step 2 – Click on the USDT Supply button in the "asset to supply" Panel. A popup will ask you to enter the amount to supply. In our example, we use 10 USDT. The Transaction overview section will give you Supply APY information, which is 1.24% for this supply example. Click "approve to continue" button. Confirm the Metamask transaction confirmation.

Step 3 – Once the supply gets approved, "Supply USDT" button will be enabled. Click on it once the transaction is completed. An "All done" confirmation window will show up. Next, you will be asked to add aToken—aUSDT to your wallet.

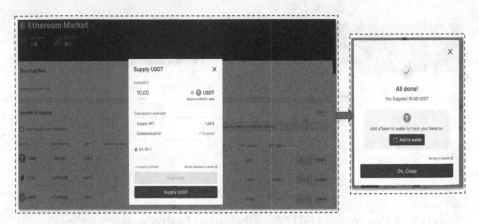

Step 4 – Add the aUSDT token to your wallet.

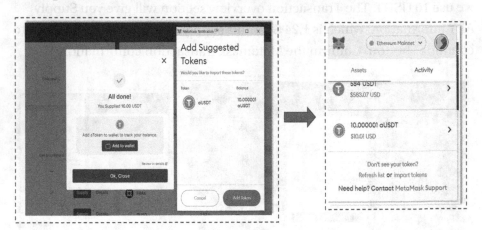

Step 5 – Close the "all done" window and return to the dashboard. The dashboard will show the supplied USDT information under the "your supplies" section. A withdraw button is enabled for supplied USDT assets:

How to Withdraw on Aave

Step 1 – Continue with the above process. Next, click on Withdraw button from supplied USDT asset. Withdraw window will pop up. Enter the amount you want to withdraw. Then click on "Withdraw USDT" button. Confirm the Metamask transaction.

Step 2 – Once the transaction has completed, close the "all done" window and return to the dashboard. The dashboard will show updated USDT information:

How to Swap on Aave

Due to its governance structure, the Aave platform treats the USDT, sUSD, and SNX tokens as a significant centralization risk. Their counterparty risk is too high both in terms of centralization and trust. So USDT as a collateral option is disabled in the platform:

In this case, we will convert centralized USDT stablecoin to Decentralized stablecoin DAI. We will use the swap function in Aave.

Step 1 – Click on the "swap" button from supplied USDT asset. A swap window will pop up. Enter the amount you want to Swap and select the target swap token. In this case, it will be DAI. The page will show the price impact in current market conditions and provide an option to select the Max slippage rate. Next, click on "approve to continue" button.

Step 2 – Once the swap gets approved, the "swap" button will be enabled. Click on it once the transaction is completed. An "all done" confirmation window will show up:

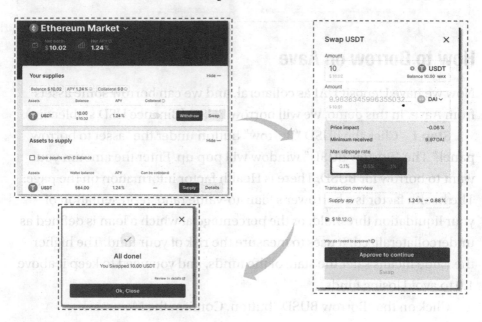

Step 3 – Close the "all done" window and return to the dashboard. The dashboard will show the swapped DAI token with collateral enabled under the "your supplies" section:

Your supplies   Hide —

Balance $10.03	APY 0.88 % ⓘ	Collateral $10.03 ⓘ

Assets	Balance	APY	Collateral ⓘ		
Ⓓ DAI	9.98 $10.03	0.88 %	◯⬤	Withdraw	Swap
Ⓣ USDT	0.0000030 < $0.01	1.24 %	⬤◯	Withdraw	Swap

How to Borrow on Aave

Now we have Deposit DAI as collateral, and we can borrow some assets from Aave. In this demo, we will borrow BUSD (Binance USD stablecoin):

Step 1 – Click the BUSD "Borrow" button under the "asset to borrow panel." The "Borrow BUSD" window will pop up. Enter the amount you want to borrow for BUSD. There is Health factor information on the page. The health factor is a borrower's loan-to-value ratio, representation of your liquidation threshold, or the percentage at which a loan is defined as undercollateralized. It uses to measure the risk of your fund. The higher the value means safer the state of the funds, and you need to keep it above 1.0 to avoid losing funds.

Click on the "Borrow BUSD" button. Confirm the Metamask transaction.

Step 2 – Once the borrow transaction is completed, an "all done" confirmation window will appear. Next, you will be asked to add the BUSD token to your wallet. Add the BUSD to your wallet.

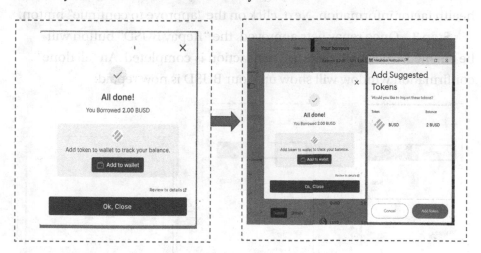

How to Repay on Aave

We just borrowed two BUSD from the Aave platform. In this section, we will demo how to pay back BUSD.

Step 1 – In order to pay back the loan, you simply go to the "Your borrowings" section of the dashboard and click on the "Repay" button for BUSD.

Step 2 – The "Repay BUSD" window will pop up. Enter the amount you want to borrow for BUSD. The page will show your remaining debt and health factor information. Next, click on the "approve to continue" button.

Step 3 – Once repay gets approved, the "Repay BUSD" button will be enabled. Click on it once the transaction is completed. An "all done" confirmation window will show up. Your BUSD is now repaid:

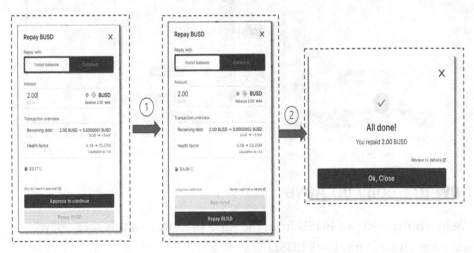

Decentralized Insurance

In the real world, insurance is one way to protect your health and prevent the loss of valuable assets. It reduces the risk of financial suffering when unexpected things happen, such as a car accident, prolonged illness, fire, unemployment, injury, or death. Most people that pay for insurance will not suffer a loss, and insurance companies bet that an accident happens with a low chance that most people who pay for insurance will not suffer a loss. So, the amount they collect from individuals will cover the losses of people that have an. Anything left over is profit for the insurance companies.

There are many different types of insurance available, such as financial insurance. It protects companies against various losses, including property damage, lawsuits, data breaches, massive drops in the values of stocks, or a business partner going bankrupt.

The exponential growth in DeFi in recent years has been remarkable. As a relatively new approach to blockchain-powered finance, DeFi bypasses traditional centralization intermediaries and inefficiency. Nevertheless, at the same time, these also come with risks. These risks include

Smart-contract risk – DeFi projects are open source and typically build on complex smart contracts. Any smart contracts logic errors or bugs may cause the software to malfunction. Once contracts are deployed to the public blockchain, it is almost impossible to fix errors. Although the governance protocols can upgrade the protocol change, it typically takes time to complete the voting process before making any changes.

DeFi technology is very new – DeFi protocol is quite complex, and fully understanding smart contract design is typically very challenging for investors. Therefore, the risk of DeFi products may not be understood until it happens.

Regulatory risk – DeFi protocols have thrived without KYC and AML regulation. However, this also means users miss protection when things go wrong, and there are no finance laws enforcing capital reserves for DeFi providers. Also, the government might implement regulations of DeFi protocols in the future, which will affect DeFi investments.

Private key requirements – In the blockchain, if you lose your wallet's private key, you lose the funds in it. Therefore, users must secure their wallets to protect their cryptocurrency assets.

Impermanent loss – we have discussed this in the DEXs section. It is caused by price volatility between tokens provided to the liquidity pool.

With the DeFi industry's fast growth and potential risk, they are needed for people who want to participate in DeFi while purchasing insurance against many of the potential risks they might encounter to protect their assets. Decentralized insurance acts as a safety net for the DeFi industry. This industry is still in the very early phase and is growing fast and improving its protocols. With decentralized insurance, users are not necessarily dealing with a centralized insurance company. Instead, a decentralized pool of coverage providers will provide policies by charging crypto service fees to protect against certain events. Some coverages are:

- Attacks on DeFi protocols

- Wallet protection

- Smart contract failures

- Crypto volatility and the flash crash

- DeFi deposit

Popular DeFi Insurance Platform

Nexus Mutual

Nexus Mutual is a decentralized insurance platform that creates a mutual risk-sharing pool on the Ethereum blockchain. NXM is the native Nexus Mutual token and acts as the governance token in Nexus Mutual protocol. The protocol is driven by its community of NXM token holders.

Every NXM token holder has membership rights. They have the right to do the following:

- Buy smart contract coverage.

- Deposit funds to the mutual and hold NXM tokens.

- Share risk with other members.

- Act as a Risk Assessor.

- Act as a Claims Assessor.

- Submit governance proposals.

- Vote on proposals.

The primary Nexus Mutual product is smart contract insurance. There are three ways Nexus can protect digital assets:

Yield Token Cover – This cover protects against token de-pegging. De-Peg refers to a stablecoin deviating from its intended peg, for example, a stablecoin pegged to USD as 1:1. When its value is lower than $1, the coin is said to be "de-pegged."

Protocol Cover – This cover protects against a protocol hack on a specific project.

Custody Cover – This cover protects halted withdrawals and cuts on an investor's funds stored on centralized exchanges.

InsurAce Protocol

InsurAce is a decentralized multichain protocol that provides insurance services for DeFi community members. The InsurAce protocol protects funds against various risks.

InsurAce has developed a wide range of cryptocurrency insurance products that cover many protocols running on the Ethereum, Binance Chain (BSC), Polygon, and Avalanche blockchains.

InsurAce protocol provides portfolio-based coverage with the following:

Smart contract vulnerability risk – Hackers are exploiting vulnerabilities in smart contracts to steal funds.

Custodian risk – Custodians lose at least 20% of their users' funds because of crime, fraud, or similar circumstances or if they freeze withdrawals for at least 120 days without providing advanced notice.

IDO event risk – Hackers steal funds from an IDO platform by exploiting vulnerabilities in its smart contract.

Stablecoin De-Peg risk – The price of a stablecoin is below its pegged value.

Etherisc

Etherisc is a blockchain-based platform for building decentralized insurance products. Common infrastructure, product templates, and insurance license-as-a-service make it possible for community users to create their own insurance products without having to invest the time and money necessary to create them from scratch. Products built by the Etherisc community include:

Crop Insurance

When government agencies report drought or flood events, smart contract protocol triggers automated payouts to farmers with crop insurance through the platform.

FlightDelay Insurance

FlightDelay is a decentralized application that runs on the Gnosis Chain Mainnet. Smart contracts in the FlightDelay application utilize Chainlink oracle data feeds to autonomously issue and payout insurance policies for travelers who experience flight delays or cancellations. As a result, automated flight insurance policies are now settling faster, provisioning at lower costs because of reduced human and technical overhead and are more transparent because of their running on the blockchain network.

Summary

This chapter is designed to acquaint you with the popular DeFi products in its ecosystem, which you should know when involved in DeFi projects or investments.

This chapter started with a discussion on concepts in decentralized finance. Then you were introduced to the five different layers of the DeFi services structure. Moreover, with a detailed introduction to the decentralized stablecoin, we took a deep dive into Maker stablecoin to understand how it works and demonstrates how to vote on a proposal in Maker Foundation's voting portal. Next, in the Decentralized exchanges (DEXs) section, we discussed the different types of DEXs, particularly for automated market makers (AMMs). We learned many popular concepts in the DeFi world, including yield-farming, slippage, impermanent loss, and liquidity pool. Later, we also explored the most popular DEX—Uniswap.

Finally, we provided a practical end-to-end guide to show you how to deploy your own ERC-20 token in the public blockchain, create a liquidity pool, add liquidity, swap your custom token, and get a staking reward in the Uniswap platform.

In the decentralized lending and borrowing section, we overviewed the most popular decentralized lending platform—Aave. Then we demonstrated how to lend, withdraw, swap, borrow, and repay crypto assets in the Aave platform.

The chapter also discussed decentralized insurance. The next chapter will be our last; we will discuss the future of blockchain.

CHAPTER 9

The Future of Blockchain

A blockchain is a global decentralized ledger technology consisting of a growing block list. These time-stamped, append-only blocks are linked together using cryptography. The data in the blocks are permanent, immutable, and impossible to tamper with. In the blockchain, anyone can carry out transactions directly and exchange any asset of value with another person without the need for middlemen. The blockchain establishes an alternative trust mechanism between two participants and enables a new era of Internet usage called the Internet of Value (IoV). In the IoV, digital assets can be exchanged with another person instantly in an automated, secure, and decentralized manner—from stocks to arts, medicine, intellectual property, and more. On today's Internet, we can freely share information. Tomorrow, we will freely share value in the blockchain. Blockchain as a revolutionary technology is a marching phenomenon that will gradually impact business and reshape the world economy. Every industry, including finance, healthcare, education, real estate, and supply chain, could potentially be revolutionized with the help of blockchain technology.

After completing the first eight chapters, you should have sufficient knowledge to think about how blockchain can resolve real-life problems. In this chapter, we are starting with an introduction to the evolution of the Internet from Web 1.0 to Web 3.0. Throughout this chapter, we will discuss

© Brian Wu and Bridget Wu 2023
B. Wu and B. Wu, *Blockchain for Teens*, https://doi.org/10.1007/978-1-4842-8808-5_9

how blockchain is changing traditional industries. We will start by covering the following core topics:

- The evolution of the Internet

- Blockchain in finance

- Blockchain in the supply chain

- Blockchain in healthcare

The Evolution of the Internet

The Internet is the world's most popular computer network, which connects billions of computers, and electronic devices. The Internet is being used by billions of people every day for sending emails, doing online shopping, connecting with friends on social media, or many other purposes. Life without Internet access seems quite hard to imagine.

In 1958, the Advanced Research Projects Agency (ARPA), now known as the Defense Advanced Research Projects Agency (DARPA), was founded, which aimed to create a way to direct communications and share information between computers.

In 1967, the ARPA created the first working model of computer network, ARPANET, which allowed numerous computers to communicate with each other on a single network.

In 1969, ARPANET transferred the first message from one computer to another. Thus, it became the forerunner of the Internet.

In 1983, ARPANET adopted open networking protocols called Transfer Control Protocol/Internetwork Protocol (TCP/IP), which later became today's core Internet protocol.

However, with more computers added to the network, network users needed to find an easier way to communicate with them. Thus, in the same year, Paul Mockapetris invented the Domain Name System (DNS), which provides an easier way to use computer names.

In 1985, symbolics.com became the first registered domain.

In 1989, the ARPANET was shut down. In the same year, Tim Berners-Lee invented the World Wide Web. Consequently, the world entered the Web 1.0 era.

Web 1.0 (1989–2004)—World Wide Web

The World Wide Web (W3 or WWW), commonly known as the Web, is a collection of websites or web pages hosted by web servers. Users can access and view digital content via web browsers from their computers. Web 1.0 refers to the early phases of the evolution of the World Wide Web. The period of Web 1.0 was roughly from 1989 to 2005.

In 1990, Tim Berners-Lee worked at the European Organization for Nuclear Research (CERN). There, he developed the first web client and server with three specified technologies: HyperText Markup Language (HTML), Uniform Resource Locators (URLs), and the Hypertext Transfer Protocol (HTTP).

In Web 1.0, a website comprised only static web pages, which would be filled with mostly text and image content and linked to other static web pages. Websites in Web 1.0 didn't allow users to engage with the site. That's why Web 1.0 is called the "read-only" web. The following screenshot shows a typical Web 1.0 page:

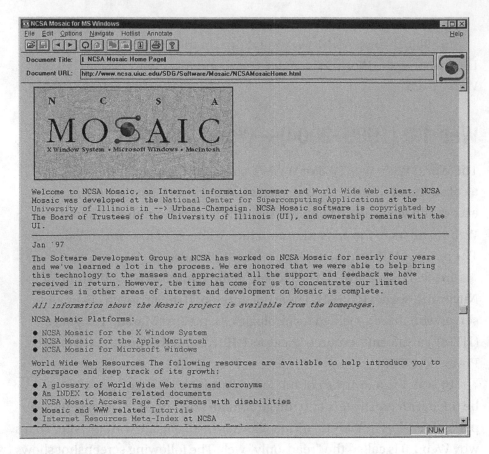

Figure 9-1. *Web 1.0 page*

A few of the characteristics that define Web 1.0 are as follows:

- The pages are static (page content is not dynamic).

- HTML forms are sent via email.

- Web content is loaded from the web server's file system.

- Web page layouts used frames and tables.

- GIF buttons and graphics could be used.

- The website was read only and used as an "information portal."

Web 2.0 (2004–Present)—Participative Social Web

Tim O'Reilly coined the term Web 2.0 in 2004 during a conference between O'Reilly and MediaLive International. It refers to the second phase of the transformation of the World Wide Web. Unlike the read-only Web 1.0, Web 2.0, also known as the participative social web, allows users to interact and collaborate through the website and social media platforms. Users can create profiles, connect with people, share their viewpoints, leave comments, and publish videos. Apps such as YouTube, Facebook, Instagram, TikTok, LinkedIn, Netflix, Twitter, and Amazon are popular Web 2.0 platforms and are visited by over 4 billion people worldwide.

These applications have been built based on many modern and powerful web technologies, greatly improving the end user's experience.

The emergence of cloud computing, big data, artificial intelligence (AI), the Internet of Things (IoT), mobile technologies, and front-end technologies have enabled the provision of a better user experience due to the ability of Web 2.0 platforms to connect users in real time. Mobile apps allow users to be online at all times. On the other hand, platform providers also collect and control users' data to analyze user activities for business purposes. As a result, web platforms have become more centralized.

Here's a list of Web 2.0's typical characteristics:

- Modern responsive web applications are accessible from anywhere.

- It provides a rich user experience and is very user friendly.

- It supports collaboration and information sharing among participants.

- Minimal programming knowledge is required to make platforms.

389

- It allows access via mobile and smart devices.

- The emphasis is on social networks and computing.

- It encourages the social network effect: the greater the contribution, the better the content and reward are.

Web 3.0—Decentralization

In Web 2.0, large companies constantly upgrade products on platforms and create new features to attract users to stay on their platforms. However, at the same time, these applications act as centralized guardians. Therefore, the user needs to follow their standards. Otherwise, their account can be banned from the platform.

Moreover, in Web 2.0, most popular applications can run on a mobile device, for which the user's phone will need to be always connected to the Internet. Although all these popular apps are free, they are designed in such a way that they target specific users and collect their data. From the moment the user downloads these apps, the apps begin to collect their personal data, including name, location, gender, and birthdate, as well as more abstract info such as social network connections, job and employment history, recent purchases, past vacation destinations, hobbies, and interests.

With a large amount of relevant personal data, companies use powerful big data analysis and machine learning (ML) technology to learn user data. They can not only discover more about their users' preferences but also predict users' thoughts, feelings, and actions in different situations. Farmed user data are hugely valuable to advertisers and marketers, who can use these data to efficiently target ads to relevant consumers. The users, in using those free centralized platforms, makes their personal data as the product. Unfortunately, there is no way by which users can own and control their personal data.

As time passed, the Internet started to enter Web 3.0. In this phase, instead of a centralized database, decentralized, nearly anonymous platforms are being built for applications and services. With blockchain's decentralized feature, every individual in the network is equal and can control their own data. Users can keep their data private or share and sell their profiles. Data become an asset for users.

Web 3.0 also leverages the latest technologies such as AI, ML, and the IoT to construct networks. This will make the network more intelligent and responsive to serve user needs, that is, more personalized.

In traditional corporate structures, C-suite executives typically have the power to make critical business decisions, often prioritizing shareholders and marketing demand. With the commencement of Web 3.0, decentralized autonomous organizations (DAOs) will invert centralized corporate governance processes and brings new insights for organizing communities. There will be no central authority in the organization, and its community members will make the decisions via proposals and voting. As a result, everyone can participate in decisions and have a voice in the DAO.

In Web 3.0, a three-dimensional (3D) design will be used widely on the Internet. The Metaverse has become vital to opening up a whole new world of economic prospects. In the Metaverse, all objects use 3D graphics. People have their own 3D avatars and can visit the shopping center, attend a conference, and play games. The Metaverse unlocks new ways of interacting, learning, playing, working, and living by allowing users to join in a 3D digital virtual world and experience it in reality. In this context, each digital asset in the blockchain is given a unique, verifiable identity; this record is called a nonfungible token (NFTs). NFTs represent 3D digital assets' ownership and can be traded in the Metaverse world.

Figure 9-2 shows the evolution of the Internet (from Web 1.0 to 3.0).

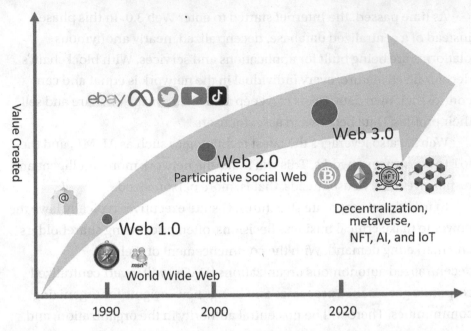

Figure 9-2. *The evolution of the Internet (Web 1.0, 2.0, and 3.0)*

Blockchain in Finance

Financial services refer to a variety of economic services discharged and products provided by the finance industry to manage money. They are one of the most important drivers of a nation's economy. Financial services cover a broad range of businesses, including the following major types of services:

1. **Banking** – The banking service is one of the most important services in the financial services industry. It offers various services, including personal or business banking (checking accounts, savings accounts, debit/credit cards, etc.) and the provision of loans (personal loans, business loans, home loans, car loans, etc.).

2. **Insurance** – Insurance services protect individuals against financial losses and help them recover from an accident. Most people have some sort of insurance, such as car insurance, house insurance, or life and health insurance. When an individual purchases insurance, they sign an insurance policy contract. Subsequently, when they encounter a loss covered by the policy and file a claim, the insurance company pays them based on the policy's terms.

3. **Wealth management** – Wealth management or wealth management advisory refers to investment management and the provision of high-level professional financial advice to address the needs of a wide array of clients ranging from affluent to high-net-worth and ultra-high-net-worth individuals and families.

4. **Mutual funds** – Mutual fund services allow individuals to pool their money with other investors to invest in a collection of securities such as stocks, bonds, money market instruments, and other assets. The price of the mutual fund, also known as its net asset value, is determined by the total value of the securities in the portfolio divided by the number of shares outstanding.

5. **Professional advisory** – A financial professional advisory service provides professional expertise to help individuals and firms to make financial decisions and achieve financial goals, including education saving planning, retirement planning, risk management, portfolio management, insurance, and tax strategies.

6. **Stock market** – Stock market services provide buyers and sellers a place for trading companies' shares and various other securities such as bonds, futures, and options.

7. **Debt instruments** – Debt instruments are tools utilized to obtain capital, including loans and bonds. Usually, repayment of debt involves a fixed payment to the lender or investor under the terms of a contract within the specified payment schedule. Companies use debt instruments to obtain funds for their growth, investments, and future planning.

8. **Tax/audit consulting** – Tax accounting services involve financial professionals providing services for preparing tax returns and payments. A financial audit, also referred to as a financial statement audit, provides reasonable assurance by evaluating whether an organization's accounting and financial statements comply with government laws and regulations.

9. **Portfolio management** – Portfolio management refers to managing an individual's investment, such as stocks, bonds, cash, shares, and exchange-traded funds. Typically, stocks, bonds, and cash comprise the core of a portfolio.

10. **Credit rating** – A credit rating evaluates a person or company's credit risk, predicting their ability to pay back the debt based on income and past repayment histories.

Scholars have estimated that the global financial services industry will be worth USD 25 trillion worldwide by 2022, expanding at an annual growth rate of around 6%. Trillions of dollars' worth of transactions occur every single day. Due to such a high volume of transactions, the financial industry has encountered many challenges, including excessive paperwork, data breaches, tedious processes and consequent high costs, consumers' lack of trust, and lack of transparency, which have persisted for a long time. Blockchain technology is decentralized, secure, transparent, and immutable. Its revolutionary design and properties have enabled it to become a possible solution for the challenges of the global financial system, and the banking and financial industry is accelerating its adoption of digital blockchain technology. The global blockchain in the financial market is estimated to grow from $1.89 billion in 2022 to $94.58 billion in 2030, at an annual rate of 63.1%. In the following section, we will discuss a few use cases of the adoption of blockchain technology in the financial industry, including trade finance.

Letters of Credit in Trade Finance

Trade finance is the financing of instruments or services that are used to facilitate international trade and commerce between an importer and an exporter. The global trade finance market reached $1.7 trillion in June 2022.

The types of trade finance include letters of credit (LC), purchase orders (POs), finance, stock finance, structured commodity finance, invoice finance (discounting and factoring), supply chain finance, and bonds and guarantees.

In trade finance, the importer's bank will provide an LC to the exporter. An LC is known as a draft, documentary credit, or banker's commercial credit. It is a letter from an importer's bank guaranteeing that an importer's payment to an exporter will be received with a specified amount in an agreed currency and provides the exporter with a contract with defined terms and conditions, to be met within a fixed time frame. LC are most often used in international trade, particularly, in importing and exporting.

Figure 9-3 shows an example of an LC process, although an actual transaction could be much more complex.

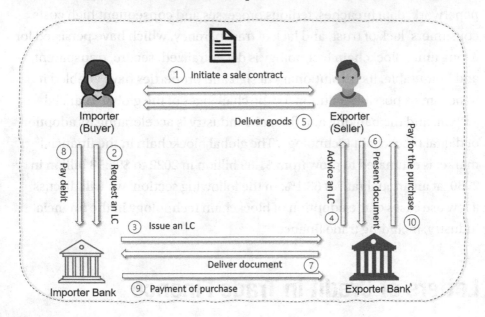

Figure 9-3. The LC process

1. **Importer and exporter initiate a sale contract.**

    The importer (buyer) and exporter (seller) initialize and agree on a sale contract. A sale contract is a legal agreement between the exporter and the importer, in which the exporter agrees to sell and an importer agrees to buy under certain terms and conditions. The contents of the contract should consist of information on the company of the seller and the buyer, the goods, the total amount and unit price of the goods, delivery date, penalties for a late shipment, and others.

2. **Importer applies for an LC with their bank.**

   The importer goes to their bank and applies for an LC for a certain amount with the exporter as the beneficiary. The LC is obtained either through a standard loan process or funded with authorization to debit the customer's account with an associated fee.

3. **The importer's bank issues the LC and sends it to the exporter's bank.**

   The importer's bank prepares the LC and then sends a copy of the LC to the exporter's bank. The importer's bank instructs the exporter's bank on whether to add its confirmation as per their customers' contract.

4. **The exporter's bank authenticates and advises on the LC.**

   The exporter bank forwards the LC to the beneficiary (exporter). The exporter should ensure that all terms and conditions in LC have been met in the sales contract.

5. **Goods are shipped to the importer.**

   The exporter starts to manufacture, assemble, and ship the goods.

6. **The exporter submits trade documents to the exporter's bank.**

    The exporter prepares an invoice of shipment and all other documents, including a description of goods and shipment date. All these documents are required according to the LC.

7. **The exporter's bank examines and delivers the document to the importer's bank.**

    The exporter's bank checks the trade documents presented by the exporter against the LC. Then, the exporter sends them to the importer's bank, claiming reimbursement and payment for the seller.

8. **The importer pays the importer's bank.**

    The importer's bank notifies the importer with the exporter's document, and the importer checks the document and pays the importer's bank.

9. **The importer's bank sends the payment to the exporter's bank.**

10. **The exporter's bank sends the payment to the exporter.**

An LC from a bank guarantees that exporters will receive payment as long as they meet all the terms and conditions, and importers can obtain exporters' trust via the use of an LC. Using an LC also reduces production risk. An LC also provides a way of payment when other payment options do not.

Despite all the advantages of the LC contract, the LC process still has many issues.

1. **High service fees need to be paid.**

   Exporters and importers must pay their bank high service fees when using the LC as a payment option.

2. **It is a time-consuming process.**

   Using an LC means that bank professionals will need to possess the LC using traditional banking methods. The process of issuing an LC is very slow, normally taking around 15 days to a few months for an international trade transaction. Many copies are shared with different parties by telecommunications such as airmail, fax, phone call, or scans. The trade transactions depend on paper-based documents, known as documentary credits. Banks need to manually check the papers to prevent fraud, authenticate transactions, and verify the balance of the buyer and the seller.

Many banks are starting to make use of blockchain technology to simplify the LC process and overcome its issues.

By defining LC as a smart contract between all parties, including the bank, the importer, and the exporter, all LC contractual agreements and conditions statements are programmed as smart contract functions, such as buyer and seller information, shipping time, description, and amount of goods shipped and documentary evidence, and LC status. Through smart contracts, each step of the LC process can be verified automatically. Furthermore, the secure blockchain network shares all transaction data via a smart contract.

Figure 9-4 shows how an LC contract is defined in a Hyperledger Fabric blockchain.

```
// ENUMS                                    //USER
enum LCStatus {                             participant User identified by userId {
  o CONTRACT                                  o String userId
  o REQUEST_LC                                o String name
  o ISSUE_LC                                  o String lastName optional
  o ADVICE_LC                                 o String companyName
  o DELIVER_PRODUCT                           o ParticipantType type
  o PRESENT_DOCUMENT                          --> Bank bank
  o DELIVERY_DOCUMENT                       }
  o BUYER_DEBIT_PAYMENT                      // CONCEPTS
  o BANKS_PAYMENT_TRANSFER                   concept ProductDetails {
  o SELL_RECEIVED_PAYMENT                      o String productType
  o CLOSED                                     o Integer quantity
}                                             o Double pricePerUnit
                                            }
enum ParticipantType {                      concept Rule {
  o BUYER                                     o String ruleId
  o SELLER                                    o String ruleText
  o ISSUING_BANK                            }
  o CONFIRMING_BANK
}                                           // TRANSACTIONS + EVENTS
// ASSETS                                   transaction InitialApplication {
asset LetterOfCredit identified by letterId { o String letterId
  o String letterId                           --> User buyer
  --> User buyer                              --> User seller
  --> User seller                             --> Bank issuingBank
  --> Bank issuingBank                        --> Bank confirmingBank
  --> Bank confirmingBank                     o Rule[] rules
  o Rule[] rules                              o ProductDetails productDetails
  o ProductDetails productDetails           }
  o String [] evidence
  o LCStatus status                         event InitialApplicationEvent {
  o Integer step                             --> LetterOfCredit lc
  o String closeReason optional             }
}
// PARTICIPANTS                             transaction BuyerRequestLC {
//BANK                                       --> LetterOfCredit lc
participant Bank identified by bankID {     }
  o String bankID
  o String name                             event BuyerRequestLCEvent {
  o ParticipantType type                     --> LetterOfCredit lc
}                                           }
//USER
```

Figure 9-4. *An example of an LC contract*

In 2018, a Spanish multinational financial institution Banco Bilbao Vizcaya Argentaria (BBVA) completed a blockchain-based LC transaction as a substitute for traditional trade documents. The project was involved to importing 25 tons of frozen tuna from Pinsa Congelados, a manufacturer located in Mexico, to Spain. BBVA issued the LC for this project. By carrying out the LC process in an Ethereum blockchain, BBVA reduced the time required to send, verify, and authorize an international trade transaction from around 7 to 10 days to just 2.5 hours.

In August 2019, the Hongkong and Shanghai Banking Corporation (HSBC), one of the world's largest banks, completed its first blockchain-based LC transaction. The LC smart contracts were run on the blockchain to execute and record the import of 20,000 tons of fuel oil from Singapore by United Mymensingh Power Ltd. to Hong Kong for a power station.

HSBC uses the Voltron platform, R3's Corda Enterprise blockchain platform. Voltron is an open industry platform to create, exchange, approve, and issue LC on Corda.

A review of a few real-world examples of blockchain-based LCs shows that blockchain provides an end-to-end digitalization life cycle from creating documents to making payments with increased security, transparency, and efficiency. As a result, blockchain technology can potentially redefine global trade processes and address the current trade finance bottlenecks.

Blockchain in a Supply Chain

A supply chain is a coordinated network comprising companies, facilities, and business activities that transform raw materials and components into a finished product and deliver it to the consumer. The entities involved in a supply chain include producers, vendors, wholesalers, transportation carriers, distribution centers, retailers, and customers.

A traditional supply chain flow follows a linear, step-by-step progression, including planning, designing, sourcing the raw materials, product development, marketing, operations, distribution, finance, and customer service. The current step typically depends on the input of the previous step. Effective supply chain management can reduce a company's overall costs and accelerate its production cycle. If any stage breaks, the entire linear chain will be disrupted, which can be costly. Currently, a supply chain oversees and integrates all the activities, including ordering, purchasing, manufacturing, transportation, and distribution, into a centralized platform.

Having a centralized platform has made the entire supply chain more efficient. Its advantages range from reducing operational costs to facilitating software upgrades, database data management, etc. However, many challenges still remain, such as if the server went down, information could be lost. These will be examined in more detail in the following sections.

Document Management

The supply chain consists of all stages and directly or indirectly involves multiple business units, ranging from the manufacturer, transporters, and warehouses to end users. The entire chain can be spread across multiple countries too. Throughout the process, many documents are generated and must be maintained as proof. These documents could include purchase orders, customs paperwork, inspection reports, dealer/distributor agreements, manufacturer and product information, and the location of all supply chain intermediaries between the manufacturer and the contractor.

The complexity of global industrial supply chains exponentially increases their risk of execution of entire chain. For example, automotive supply chains are one of the most complex in the world, with each vehicle requiring more than 30,000 parts originating from thousands of different suppliers. Each of those parts is either manufactured in house or sourced from a third-party provider. This complexity of the supply chain often means that it suffers from inconsistencies, disconnects in the processes, an increasing number of errors, and high costs.

Many transport and logistics organizations have already invested in digitizing and improving their documents with new technologies such as big data and the cloud computing. However, more than half of the companies worldwide are still experiencing issues with information verification and finding the data needed for customers due to a limited budget to upgrade new software systems. An efficient and lost-cost solution for connecting all components into a fully digital system has still not been found.

Integration of Various Centralized IT Software Systems

As a supply chain is complex, with many participants in the system, many suppliers have their own software systems for performing different processes under different standards. For example, some vendors allow process integration through an automated process via HTTPS and messaging technologies. Some vendors only support manual processes via email or paper invoices. Therefore, integrating and maintaining all disparate systems together will be complex, time-consuming, and costly.

Lack of Transparency Regarding Data

No easily accessible consolidated data source allows all suppliers to trace each step's information for the entire supply chain. Each supplier can only see their own and related suppliers' information. There is no natural and easy way to compile all this information and make it transparent. Integrating with other suppliers will be costly, with high maintenance effort on each side.

Therefore, the industry needs to reinvent the supply chain process from the ground up and move toward a high-speed, more efficient future. As a decentralized peer-to-peer digital ledger system, a blockchain can transform traditional supply chain business by optimizing processes, reducing costs and risks, and increasing supply chain transparency. Some key potential benefits of adopting blockchain technologies are as follows:

- **Increased supply chain transparency**

    High transparency in the supply chain network can help maintain the safety and quality of products and reduce costs. By generating a tamper-proof digital record in each step, blockchain enables traceability and trackability for supply chain procedures. The records in supply chain networks are transparent, and participants in the network obtain greater visibility across all supply chain activities. Consequently, when an incident occurs anywhere within the global supply chain, it will be considerably easier and less time-consuming to access and determine the root cause of the violation. As a result, all parties can spend more time delivering goods, improving quality, and reducing costs.

- **A resilient supply chain**

  Smart contracts with predefined business conditions can automatically trigger the supply chain process when certain criteria are met. Moreover, they can reduce risks and prevent many unexpected events.

- **Streamlined supplier onboarding**

  The supplier onboarding process, sometimes referred to as supplier onboarding, is time-consuming in many companies. For example, new supplier onboarding could take up to 30 days. Some processes need to be performed before onboarding a new supplier.

  1. The process starts after the requester's purchase order has been opened. First, the central system must identify the new supplier and counterparty. Then, the internal approval process typically takes place over email. Sometimes, other related business managers need to get involved for document verification and approval.

2. Once new suppliers get permission to enter the system, they need to complete a vendor onboarding form by providing relevant information, for example, financial information and the company's profile. Multiple stakeholders also need to get involved to verify that the new supplier company is qualified and does business with existing vendors legally and securely.

3. Once the new supplier submits the form, the finance team will check all the documents to ensure that the data provided are accurate and complete. Next, the finance team needs manually enter the form, which is typically more than 50 fields. It is a highly error-prone process and takes a long time. After this step, the new supplier can be onboarded.

There are many challenges in the supplier onboarding process:

1. The involved finance team do not have a history of suppliers information from the entire supply chain.

2. Only the persons of contact of a business have direct contact with the new supplier.

3. The supplier onboarding process lacks transparency.

A blockchain-enabled supply chain can dramatically streamline this process. It can reduce the duration from 30 days to 2–5 days. The operational cost of onboarding can be reduced by around 50%.

In traditional industries, supply chain models exist in several sectors: food supply chains, automobile sectors, manufacturing sectors, textile supply chains, energy, IT, electronics, and chemical. Next, we will discuss blockchain use cases in food supply chain industries.

Blockchain in the Food Supply Chain Industry

Consider how food can be delivered from the supplier to the customer through each step of the traditional supply chain.

The overall simplified process is shown in Figure 9-5.

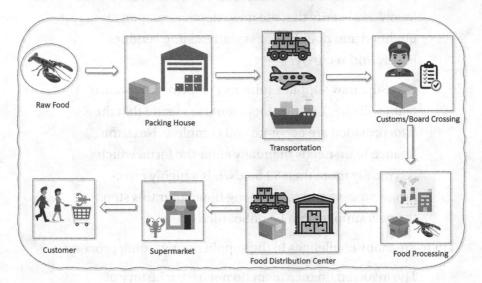

Figure 9-5. *A traditional supply chain in the food industry*

1. **Supply of Raw Materials**

   Raw materials could include seafood, meat, vegetables, fruits, and other dairy products such as coffee and tea.

2. **Food Packaging**

   Food packaging is required to provide basic information about the food such as the product's name, the quantity of content, nutrition details, and the details of the manufacturer or distributor.

3. **Food Transportation**

   Transportation needs to ensure food safety, minimal damage to goods, and timely deliveries.

4. **Customs or Board Crossing**

   Border crossing will examine shipment items to ensure goods meet entry requirements before crossing.

5. **Food Unpacking and Processing**

   Food items are unpacked, processed, and stored in a food storage center.

6. **Food Distribution (Wholesale and Retail)**

   The process of food distribution covers the transportation of the food item from the suppliers to the wholesalers, retailers, and customers.

7. **Food in Retail Stores or the Market**

   The food item is delivered to retail stores or supermarkets.

8. **Consumer's Purchase of the Food Item**

   The delivery of the food item marks the end of the food supply chain.

Bumble Bee Seafoods

In March 2019, Bumble Bee Seafoods, North America's premium seafood company, used System Applications and Products (SAP)'s Cloud Platform Blockchain service to track and trace tuna from the Indonesian ocean to local retailer stores and consumers' dinner tables. Recently, consumers have increasingly been demanding to know about the origins of their food and whether their food is safe. The supply chain will start when tuna is caught in the ocean by fish companies or fishers in the sea. Then, the company will provide related information on the tuna caught, including on the fish number, supplier, fisherman, weight, grade, date, and packs of Natural Blue® by Anova fair trade™ stamped with the blockchain-derived QR code.

From the fishermen who caught the fish from the sea to the packagers, transporters, distributors, and retailers, the blockchain will store information on each step of the process. All these blockchain data are visible to the fishermen and the buyers. The possibility of traceability increases the consumer's confidence. The consumer can scan the barcode or enter the code on the Bumble Bee website to check tuna information. The website will provide the supply chain information, including the date on which the fish was caught, fishery location, vessel information, and process information.

Figure 9-6. *Bumble Bee Seafoods blockchain information*

Keep Meat Cold: Golden State Foods

Each year, contaminated food causes an estimated 600 million foodborne diseases—almost one in ten people are affected worldwide, and 420,000 deaths are caused. Significant growth in the number of food safety incidents requires safe, healthy, and resilient food supply chains. As the food business has become more complicated over recent years, there is a need for improving tracking and detection for the entire supply chain. Moreover, over the years, supply chains have adopted IoT and blockchain technology to address their challenges.

As one of the largest produce suppliers to the food service and retail industries, Golden State Foods (GSF), a food service company located in Irvine, California, produces more than 160 million pounds of meat products and billions of hamburger patties every year. In 2019, GSF partnered with IBM (International Business Machines Corporation) on the IBM Food Trust platform to use radio-frequency identification to track fresh beef's movement automatically. Using an IoT sensor, devices monitor food temperature and log data automatically by sending them periodically (typically at 15-minute intervals) to the cloud, which is integrated with the Food Trust platform. On the IBM Food Trust platform, users can find out the food product or temperature data in near real time from anywhere in the world by entering the product's Global Trade Item Number (GTIN) or Global Location Number (GLN).

The IBM Food Trust is a modular solution built on the open standard Hyperledger Fabric blockchain. The platform integrates supply chain modules with blockchain core functions to securely connect suppliers, processors, distributors, retailers, and other ecosystem participants. The platform provides a provenance engine to verify vendor products through immediate access to end-to-end data.

Many other large companies, such as Walmart, Nestlé, Driscoll's, Kroger, Dole, and Tyson, have joined the IBM Food trust network as partners.

Other Sectors of Supply Chain Industries

The following are some other examples of the use of blockchain in other sectors of supply chain industries.

Brilliant Earth—Blockchain-Enabled Diamonds

In May 2019, Brilliant Earth, a global leader in ethically sourced fine jewelry, launched blockchain-enabled diamonds on its website. Customers can track thousands of blockchain-enabled diamonds along the transparent supply chain, including from their origins at the mining operator, through responsible manufacturing for cutting and polishing, all the way to the customer.

Brilliant Earth uses the Everledger platform based on the Hyperledger Fabric blockchain to build a transparent, traceable, and trustworthy supply chain platform. Companies on the network have the ability to apply smart contracts and share data securely with privacy protection.

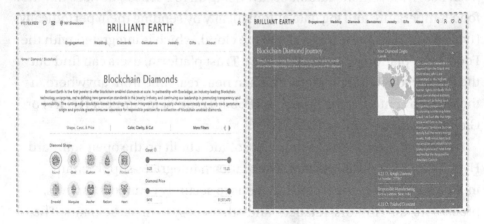

Figure 9-7. *Brilliant Earth—Blockchain-Enabled Diamonds*

Mercedes-Benz—Acentrik Blockchain Platform

In July 2022, Mercedes Benz launched a blockchain-based data sharing platform Acentrik. Acentrik is a decentralized data marketplace built for enterprise users. Acentrik has partnered with the Ocean Protocol since 2020, with a proof of concept analyzing decentralized data orchestration for Mercedes-Benz. The Ocean Protocol is an open source Web 3.0 platform for unlocking private data using data tokens—the OCEAN token. Users will get redeemed tokens from those who need access to the information. Acentrik uses an NFT to represent each dataset. Transactions are executed on the public Ethereum Layer-2 scalability platform— Polygon blockchains or the Ethereum Rinkeby test network, and enterprise users can pay for data using fiat-pegged stablecoins.

Blockchain in Healthcare

Blockchain is gaining massive attention in the healthcare industry. In 2021, blockchain in the healthcare market was valued at $1.5 billion and was projected to reach $5.61 billion by 2025. It could save up to $100–150 billion annually by 2025. Moreover, 40% of health executives see blockchain as a top-five priority.

Health Data Accuracy

One of the main challenges for the healthcare industry is proper health data management. In healthcare, computerization is required to process the massive volume of personal health data that medical professionals, clinics, and hospitals create and store for each patient.

Electronic health record (EHR) software and digital versions of paper patient cards have been adopted by about 72% of US hospitals. HER software is used to capture and manage patient health information, including medical histories, diagnoses, medications, billing data, lab and test results, etc. Another popular system, health information exchange (HIE), helps make sharing patient data among healthcare providers easier. Many other healthcare applications could contain health data sources, including wearables, fitness monitors, and on-body sensors. Many of the data gathered are inaccessible, nonstandardized across systems, and difficult to understand. Processing these unstructured data fragments is typically quite challenging and time-consuming and requires excessive resources.

Blockchain can help address the lack of a means of consolidating different system data by defining proper healthcare data structure in smart contracts. Healthcare providers and patients can use smart contracts to update data with the expected format and store it in the blockchain. Healthcare systems could create Dapps to view patients' historical data, which can improve the quality of treatments, ensure smooth communication, and enhance health outcomes.

Health Data Interoperability

Another challenge facing the healthcare industry is the lack of nationwide interoperability and secure access to electronic medical records.

With blockchain, healthcare systems could store critical medical records confidentially. Patients would allow providers access to their medical histories with their approval. Authorized healthcare professionals such as doctors would then be able to update patient data across multiple facilities and locations in real time and with security. Blockchain technology allows for an efficient collaborative execution environment where different providers can work together in real time to provide patients with the best service. Instant access to data via blockchain could reduce waiting times for patients and provide more accurate diagnosis data.

Following this discussion of the benefits of blockchain technology in healthcare, let's examine a few use cases of blockchain in healthcare and their real-world examples.

Insurance Claims

Traditional insurance claim management is an important part of a medical provider's routine.

A traditional insurance claim process is shown in Figure 9-8.

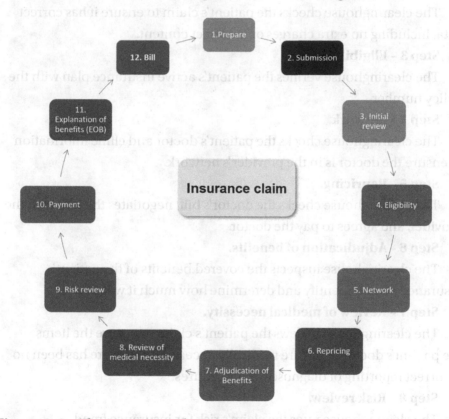

Figure 9-8. *The insurance claim process*

The process's steps are as follows:

Step 1 – Preparation.

The patient fills out paper forms and provides the doctor with details of their healthcare provider.

Step 2 – Submission.

The doctor's billing office mails an insurance claim to a clearing house. The claim request is electronically recorded in the claims system after a few weeks.

Step 3 – Initial review.

The clearinghouse checks the patient's claim to ensure it has correct data, including no extra charges or incorrect content.

Step 3 – Eligibility.

The clearinghouse verifies the patient's active insurance plan with the policy number.

Step 4 – Network.

The clearinghouse checks the patient's doctor and clinic information to ensure the doctor is in the provider's network.

Step 5 – Repricing.

The clearinghouse checks the doctor's bill, negotiates the fees with the provider, and agrees to pay the doctor.

Step 6 – Adjudication of benefits.

The clearinghouse inspects the covered benefits of the patient's insurance plan to identify and determine how much it will pay.

Step 7 – Review of medical necessity.

The clearinghouse reviews the patient's claim to ensure the items the patient's doctor billed are medically necessary and there has been no incorrect reporting of diagnoses or procedures.

Step 8 – Risk review.

The clearinghouse rates the claim's risk for insurance fraud.

Step 9 – Payment.

The provider sends a payment to the patient's doctor.

Step 10 – Explanation of benefits.

The provider creates an explanation of benefits (EOB) for the bill details and checks the EOB to ensure that all the information is correct.

Step 11 – Bill.

If a payment is due, the doctor's office will send the provider a bill matching the amount and services listed on his EOB.

When accidents happen, a patient can start the health insurance claim process, which is one way of communication. The process typically requires much paperwork from registration to claim approval. Several key challenges in the process are as follows:

- False claims

- Fraud detection

- Slow and long processing of complex claims

- Insufficient management information

- Human error

- Unpleasant customer experience

- High operational cost

- Inconsistent service delivery

Blockchain technologies provide an increasing number of solutions to address these issues and create new models for the industry in the real-life world.

Avaneer Network

Avaneer Network is a blockchain healthcare company backed by major healthcare leader companies, including Aetna, Cleveland Clinic, IBM, Anthem, and HCSC (Health Care Service Corporation). The blockchain network leverages Hyperledger Fabric-based blockchain technologies to remove administrative barriers, improve healthcare experience for people, provide faster and better claims processing, ensure secure healthcare data, and reduce costs.

ClaimShare

IntellectEU is a New York-based blockchain technology company. By leveraging R3's Corda blockchain, IntellectEU uses the ClaimShare platform to detect and prevent double-dipping insurance claim fraud when a user files a claim with multiple insurers for the same event. The ClaimShare uses Corda Conclave and Corda Enterprise blockchain to enable insurers to confidentially process and summarize data without revealing any sensitive personal data. Conclave is a confidential computing platform that uses Intel SGX® enclaves that increase data privacy and confidentiality by application isolation and encrypted region for code and data. ClaimShare can also enable the automation of the claims processing system efficiently.

Health Data Management

In the blockchain, each change made is recorded in the network, and the transactions are transparent and verified by all nodes. Thus, blockchain security allows users to control and own their data through private and public keys.

Patientory

Patientory is a blockchain-based health management company. The platform democratizes user ownership of health data in the PTOYMatrix blockchain network. It incentivizes users to take control of their health outcomes via the PTOY token. The Dapp gives users access to their health information in a secure and encrypted way.

Disease Prevention
GemOS

Gem is a California-based blockchain life science company that has teamed up with Philips Blockchain Lab, a European health service provider, to launch the platform GemOS. GemOS provides various tools for applications in the platform to connect large and disconnected health data on the platform. For example, the platform connects data to finished blood banks and DNA registers.

In September 2017, the US Center for Disease Control and Prevention (CDC) worked with Gem and used GemOS to process the spread of infectious disease data load onto a blockchain. These transaction records in the blockchain are publicly accessible by the node participants—local public health agencies, hospitals, and pharmacies—which greatly improves transparency, security, speed, and efficiency, thus saving lives.

Blockchain technology has far-reaching applications across many industries. Web3.0 continues to grow at a CAGR (Compound Annual Growth Rate) of 44.6% from 2023 to 2030. It is still in its starting phase, but without a doubt, the technology will continue to grow and use in all areas of our lives.

Summary

Blockchain technology is an enormous catalyst for changing existing business models, giving birth to new models, and becoming a new foundation for everyday tasks. This technology, which is without a centralized controlling entity, is built on trust, ensures transparency, increases productivity, improves security, and reduces costs. These advantages make it a game-changing technology across industries. Blockchains promise to shape the future, intertwining with our society just as the Internet, whether we choose to engage or not.

In this chapter, we first explore how the Internet evolved from Web 1.0 to Web 3.0. Then, we comprehensively examined popular blockchain use cases across industries, including the financial, healthcare, and supply chain industries. It is always fascinating to see how blockchain will integrate with other technologies such as Metaverse, AI, IoT, and other emerging technologies.

At this point, we have completed the final chapter in our journey of exploring the foundations of innovative blockchain technology.

Congratulations on reading the whole book! With that, we hope this book helped you with some insight into the future of the blockchain and cryptocurrency space.

Index

A

Aave, 384
  aToken, 369, 370
  borrow, 376
  definition, 368
  deposit, 371, 372
  repay, 378
  swap function, 374, 375
  tokens, 369
  withdrawal, 373
Aave Improvement
    Proposals (AIPs), 322
Advanced encryption
    standard (AES), 57, 68
Advanced Research Projects
    Agency (ARPA), 386
Anti-money laundering (AML),
    317, 334
Application Binary Interface (ABI),
    152, 197
Artificial intelligence (AI), 267, 268,
    286, 292–294, 381, 389, 391
The Aspirants Mystery Box, 240
ASSET token, 302
Asymmetric cryptography,
    51, 57, 63
Asymmetric key cryptography
  definition, 57

digital signatures, 62–65
hash algorithm, 65
public/private keys, 58–63
aToken, 368–371
Augmented reality (AR), 267, 284
  definition, 276
  types, 276–278
  works, 279
Automated market
    makers (AMMs), 383
  CMMM, 341
  CPMM, 339, 340
  CSMM, 341
  definition, 338
  hybrid constant function,
    342, 343
  IL, 344–348
  LP, 338, 339
  off-chain order books, 350, 351
  on-chain order books, 349
  order book, 348
  slippage, 344
Avaneer Network, 415
Axie Infinity, 240, 254, 260, 271,
    296–299, 304
Axie Infinity Shards (AXS),
    297, 299
Axie Shards, 260

Printed in the United States
by Baker & Taylor Publisher Services

Printed in the United States
by Baker & Taylor Publisher Services